MOZAMBIQUE
MYSTERIES

Lisa St Aubin de Terán

virago

VIRAGO

First published in Great Britain in 2007 by Virago Press
This paperback edition published in 2010 by Virago Press

Copyright © Lisa St Aubin de Terán 2007

The moral right of the author has been asserted.

A CIP catalogue record for this book
is available from the British Library.

ISBN 978-1-84408-299-5

Typeset in Janson by M Rules
Printed and bound in Great Britain by
Clays Ltd, St Ives plc

Papers used by Virago are natural, renewable and
recyclable products sourced from well-managed forests and certified
in accordance with the rules of the Forest Stewardship Council.

Mixed Sources
Product group from well-managed
forests and other controlled sources
www.fsc.org Cert no. SGS-COC-004081
© 1996 Forest Stewardship Council
FSC

Virago Press
An imprint of
Little, Brown Book Group
100 Victoria Embankment
London EC4Y 0DY

An Hachette UK Company
www.hachette.co.uk

www.virago.co.uk

For Mees

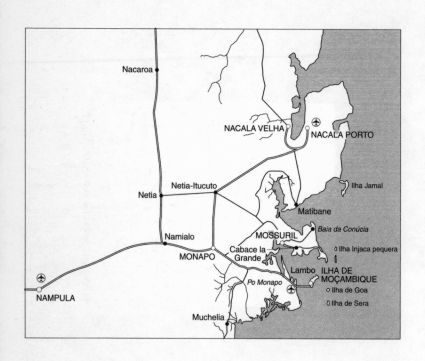

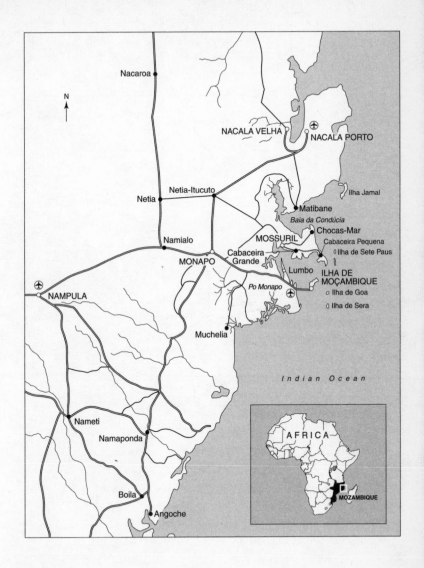

CONTENTS

PART FOUR

PART ONE

I

Squeezed Between the Bush and the Ocean

THE MANGROVES HERE IN northern Mozambique grow in
the sea or on beaches that the sea reclaims sporadically. The
sands they grow in are disinfected daily by the tide. The
vast expanses of watery forest are clean, fresh and beautiful.
Yet their name 'mangrove' has unfortunate connotations,
conjuring up images of the sweet-water mangroves of other
countries with their swamps, mud, mosquitoes and croco-
diles. Images of the likes of Dustin Hoffman struggling to
survive in their unhealthy vapours have helped give mangroves a bad name.

Generically, sea mangroves missed a press opportunity
and a world whitewashing when the tsunami devastated
Asian coasts. Many of the damaged areas had until recently,
been protected by mangroves. Had those mangroves still
been there to break the force of the tsunami, thousands of
lives and homes could have been saved. Alas, millions of
hectares of mangroves have been destroyed in the past forty
years and millions more are being wantonly cleared to make
way for prawn farms and holiday resorts. Mangroves are an
endangered species in need of protection. They are also
inspiring plants to be around: quite literally, they effervesce

the air and the water around them, thereby de-stressing every living creature near them. Their warm waters are a tactile lullaby.

Fish know that these Mozambican mangroves are a good place to be and a good place to breed. The safe pools between their roots are the nursery of the Indian Ocean: a breeding ground of multicoloured fish, prawns, lobsters, starfish, crabs and picture books full of sea creatures all coexisting in an orderly fashion within this seemingly endless sparkling tepid bath. By day, shoals of miniature silvery fish leap out in what look like choreographed flashes. By night, tiny electromagnetic sparks light up the warm natural champagne in the salt rivulets and lagoons. It is as though nature were giving a slide-show on the natural harmony of land and sea and all their plants and creatures. Every aspect of the landscape exudes peace.

When the local people disturb this harmony by taking life, they tend to pray for forgiveness. No crab, fish or chicken is killed without acknowledging the shame of disturbing the environment. Even nasty insects like the 15-centimetre-long centipede fatter than my thumb which dropped at my feet from an acacia tree one day are allowed to live. My first reaction was to kill it, my second was to imagine being sprayed by its juice if I did, and my third was to ask Adamji, a fearless guard, to kill it instead. But he picked it up with a stick and threw it far away muttering, 'Let it live.'

Adamji's beneficence doesn't extend to rats, which he chases and stabs with a sharpened bamboo cane without any qualms or regrets.

Not all animals, it would seem, are God's chosen creatures here. A few serve renegade masters, bad spirits – *aminepani* – and can be slaughtered without so much as a backward look. Some can be killed and the taking of their life absolved. Harming others, like the dolphin, the rare nashekura (a brown stork) and the common African crow, is strictly taboo. The same rules apply on land and sea and in the no-man's-land between them. There are no borders here between the one and the other, and yet there is no doubt that the sea is the ultimate ruler.

Very early on in my love affair with Mozambique, I learnt to respect both the mangrove and the tide. Instead of taking the long bush road to the Mossuril coast, I was coming in by sea with an itinerary I found so romantic that I got lost in the contemplation of it, to the exclusion of fore-sight.

Morripa had called my partner, Mees, and me several times during the day to stress at what time a local fishing boat would pick us up on Ilha de Moçambique, the island harbour a few kilometres off the coast. And he called us again on Ilha with strict instructions to be at the fortress beach no later than 2pm to catch the sailing dhow back to Varanda, where Mees had just become a project owner. This was the first and only time I have disregarded our local hero's advice.

We were at what was then the only restaurant on Ilha, Reliquias, a cavernous and curious converted warehouse decorated with maritime relics and photographs of old Ilha. Mozambican restaurants in general are very slow to serve. So slow, in fact, that our idea of starting a College of Tourism grew in great part from the hours and hours of waiting in bars and restaurants for a very simple meal. Reliquias was no exception. When I lived in Venezuela it took me years to get used to the Latino concept of 'mañana, mañana'. Here, with so many life-threatening obstacles between the waiter and any certainty of a tomorrow at all, slowness seems to spill over into the more secure realm of eternity.

The delicious lobster we ordered and eventually ate that day almost had time to complete its annual migration from the moment we chose it to the moment it arrived on our table. Two o'clock came and went before there was any hint of the lobster heading our way. Over a bottle of chilled Portuguese rosé, with the smell of grilled fish wafting out of the blackened kitchen, it was easy to gaze at the gentle sea from the comfort of our palm-leaf shade and see no real urgency to get a move on. Why abandon our lunch after such a long wait in favour of trudging down to the beach under a burning sun to sail back on an empty stomach when there were still over three hours of daylight left?

Morripa called yet again to remind us that the boat would be there from 2pm sharp. I thanked him and he thanked me: there are a lot of thank-yous traded in Portuguese. Then I reasoned that the dhow captain was getting paid for the day, so he would not mind whether he waited or sailed a few hours earlier or later. It wasn't until after 3pm that lunch finally arrived and it was nearly 4pm by the time we got through the bill-paying ceremony and down to the dock.

As planned, a small, chipped sailing dhow was waiting for us. The burly captain commented that the tide was not good now and the wind was frail and would slow down our crossing. We didn't mind. It was a beautiful view, and the rosé gave everything an extra glow.

Night fell while we were still at sea. The captain had somewhat understated the slowing down: we were becalmed for over an hour mid-channel. When a wind rose, it was a rough one and brought too many waves for us to be able to steer through the coral to Varanda. The captain explained he would have to take us to Cabaceira Pequena, from where we could walk through the mangrove back to our camp.

This was not ideal because we were arriving from Nampula, the provincial capital, and had a lot of luggage with us, including a laptop and heavy film equipment. Under the circumstances, there was nothing we could do. The dhow had no motor and its course was dictated by the wind and waves.

As we sailed towards the flickering pinpoints of oil lamps and the village, the boat leaked faster and faster. A boy in a ragged T-shirt and indecently wrecked shorts was bailing for all he was worth with a baobab seed scoop. We were the only sailing craft out on the sea. The captain kept calm and manoeuvred his home-made mast and sail and then punted us to the shore with the odd grumble about the perils of night sailing.

As we clambered out of the boat into thigh-high water and waded onto the beach, hundreds of children lined the shore and stared, cheering and laughing. Three of the workers from Mees's project at Varanda, who lived in the village of Cabaceira Pequena, were there to greet us, headed by Ibraimo, who took charge of most of the bags.

Walking through the village to Ibraimo's house brought several hundred more people onto the narrow street and a further swarm of half-naked children. We moved in a procession, dripping water from our disembarkation and hoping we would be able to head off quickly to camp. It had been a long day and the excitement had blended with the wine and the large lobster to induce a sudden need for sleep.

In the old days, when the Mossuril coast was fashionable, visitors could fly in via the tiny airport of Lumbo. Subsequently, this facility closed down. Needing to take aerial photographs of the area, we had hired a private jet and flown down in great style to this disused airport in the bush. Being the one who organizes things, I was concerned

beforehand how we would get from the airport to Ilha. We had
luggage and it was a twenty-two-kilometre walk, including the
four kilometres of road bridge. Mees assured me that local
people would see us fly over and land and we could pay a
local child to go and find us a lift into the island town. Having
never flown into the unknown before, I wasn't very happy
about this; but sure enough, on arrival, a dozen children ran
up to us and within half an hour, one of them had found a
truck willing to give us a lift.

With hindsight, knowing now how difficult transport is in
Mossuril District, that lift was little short of a miracle. It
would be quite possible to wait all day for a truck to pass
and another day to find one that would change course for
the airport to pick us up. But we had been lucky and our
trip was going according to plan – until we decided to
linger over lunch. Actually, we lingered over drinks before
lunch and ate at a gallop.

I asked Ibraimo if we could head on to Varanda soon but
he was adamant that the crossing on foot was impossible for
many hours. These were early days for me and Mees, and
what we wanted had not yet fitted itself to what could or
could not be. So we discussed our options and decided to
brave the sea and get to Varanda before the tide got any
higher. Ibraimo absolutely advised us not to do this. We
knew from Morripa that the local people see the mangrove
as taboo at night and are afraid of the restless spirits of their
ancestors there. So we mistook Ibraimo's reluctance for fear
of spirits rather than fear of drowning. Neither Mees nor I
had ever seen the mangrove in full flood from the village
side and had no idea that when a Cabaceirian says, 'Don't
go there,' he means it. In the light of Ibraimo's continued
warning, I tried to call Morripa in neighbouring Cabaceira
Grande to ask his advice, but the sing-song '*Liga mais tarde*'
(Call back later) showed that the phone network was down.

We checked the distance to our camp at Varanda: it was less than two kilometres. We had three guides with us to help carry the bags and each of them crossed the same mangrove at least twice a day. We were wet and tired and not much enjoying being the *Akunha* – the white person, or outsider – entertainment for a large crowd of gawping children and teenagers, so we told Ibraimo we had decided to go anyway, and five minutes later we set off following his reluctant footsteps. There were many stars and the night was balmy but almost pitch black. A screech owl followed us for the first part of our way. A dozen of the children who had stuck to us like limpets from the time we disembarked also followed us to the edge of the inland water, but where the sand started to be wet and a hem of salt foam gathered, they drew back as though stung and ran away, whooping and shouting.

We entered the mangrove at the end of the village beyond the ruined warehouses where a line of giant lilies grows between whitewashed stones to mark an ancient cemetery that is slowly being drawn back into the sea. The water was warm and gentle, but my Japanese thong slippers were not ideal water-walking shoes and the right one (which was looser) kept slipping off. Ibraimo offered to carry my laptop, but I decided that if anyone was going to drop it it had better be me.

For the first fifteen minutes, with the water still only knee deep, Mees and I wondered what all the fuss had been about. Then, almost without warning, the water was waist-high. Ibraimo said we could still turn back and he advised us to do so. It was nice in the water, soothing and peaceful, and we didn't want to turn back, so we overruled him and waded on.

Only now, after several years of working together, would Ibraimo or any of the other guards have the confidence to put their foot down and defy their boss for safety's sake. Back then, Mees was their new employer and no one dared countermand his will. Many Mozambicans lack self-confidence: their low self-esteem is borne of centuries of subjugation. No one talks much about the past brutality of the Portuguese, but the collective memory of it still weighs people down. In the Cabaceiras, to this day, not only will very few villagers contradict a 'boss', very few will stand up for themselves in the presence of any kind of authority.

On the night in question, Ibraimo knew we were walking into doom but he didn't dare insist that we stay back. He suggested it timidly several times, but he didn't say, 'If we go on we will all drown.'

And Morripa knew that we had to get the boat by 2pm. He knew the tide would be impassable after that. By calling me with gentle reminders he was actually trying to say the same thing: it is dangerous to sail back later, but he too was wary of sticking out his neck.

So we two stubborn *Akunha* were wading through the mangroves with the streaming tepid water up to our necks. I was balancing my laptop on my head while holding it steady with one hand. The moon was not up yet and it was dark. But for Ibraimo and the two guards ahead of us, I had no idea where I was heading. Mees had a torch which he used in a gentlemanly fashion to show me where to walk underwater. Ibraimo had said more than once that we were to place our feet exactly where he placed his. It is slow work wading through deep water, and what with my Japanese slippers and the laptop, I was slower than the others and kept lagging behind. Thankfully, Mees waited for me time and again until I caught up. One of my slippers finally got irretrievably lost, which meant I could keep up better but my bare right foot was prey to sharp coral rocks jutting out of the sandy bed.

Mees knew the area and he also knew the guides, but, like me, he didn't know where exactly we were and he didn't understand a word of the local language. The water was streaming faster now and it was quite an effort to stay upright in places. Wading the two kilometres was taking much longer than we had imagined and our insistence on crossing now was no longer looking like the good idea it had seemed back in the village.

Ibraimo and the guides were chattering as they walked. Some of the time it was clear that they were joking but their laughter sounded hollow in the night air.

After a while, I couldn't help asking myself what exactly I was doing there. My only answer was that, despite vowing not to, I had, unashamedly, come seeking adventure. It was exciting, because like Mary Kingsley in West Africa and Dr Livingstone in Malawi, I was aware of being somewhere where other travellers had not been. Unlike the intrepid European pioneer travellers from the past, we were not venturing into an unknown continent, nor would achieving our goals add anything significant to the world's existing stock of knowledge, but at a personal level on our mini-voyage of discovery, it was exhilarating.

Who can say to what degree life influences art or vice versa? Aged fifty, I certainly still don't know the answer. All that is clear is that for me the two forces are inextricably entwined and regardless of what initiatives I take to lead a more 'normal' existence, it seems that adventure and I will continue to walk hand in hand. Like a Vaudeville player who has retired from the stage, I am now making yet another 'last comeback'.

Quite suddenly, Ibraimo stopped and pointed to the other two guides, who were shorter than the rest of us. When he pointed out (in Macua and sign language) that the tide had risen over their chins and was still rising, the exhilaration turned to rank fear. We had been wading for well over an hour. We could not turn back and we could not go on. We clambered onto a sharp coral rock shaped like a field mushroom and crouched on its cap while the current swept in.

The water level rose swiftly and steadily. For the first fifteen minutes or so as we squatted on our rock, Ibraimo and the two guides seemed to find this hilarious. Their laughter and banter was reassuring. As time went by, the tide kept rising and more and more of our perch was submerged by fast swirling water, and the three Macua men grew increasingly sombre. At the point when they fell stoically silent I began to see that it was really in the lap of the gods whether we made it to dry land that night or whether we drowned. There is a Macua proverb that says, 'God is truly the judge of all things,' but if we drowned, *we* (the *akunha*) had dragged the guides with us, which was a sorry thought. Having just been sitting in Ibraimo's house with some of his eight children, the idea of turning them all into orphans on a whim made our night jaunt look like a terrible mistake. While I sat on that rock, I am glad that I didn't know then, as I do now, how many local people drown every year in the tide. Nor did I know that one false step can be deadly because it is riddled with whirlpools and sink holes.

Because the locals were afraid of their wilder ancestors and marauding foreigners whose malign ghosts supposedly lurked in the mangroves, I kept trying to persuade myself that our guides were really more afraid of spirits than the incoming tide. The minutes of waiting expanded into smothering tension too fraught to deal with. I opted out by imagining myself to be a mere observer of other people's plight.

As the Polish writer Ryszard Kapuściński observed, time moves very slowly in Africa, because it doesn't really exist in the same way as it does in the Western world. Days drift by in a continuum altered only by natural daylight and dark. Occasionally, something happens, and time clusters round that event. It becomes a momentary excitement, it gets inordinate attention, and then it slides into the collective memory as a landmark: a point in time.

In general terms, once you accept the concept that things are neither fast nor slow, that they just *are*, it is incredibly relaxing. It is as though a straitjacket has been removed and hitherto unknown dimensions reveal themselves. Alas, I had not yet slid into that rhythm; it was still only two days since I had taken the long-haul flight from Amsterdam to Johannesburg. The consumer bonanza of South Africa's number-one airport was still fresh in my mind and I was still fully into measuring time according to my Western medium. In the eerie moonlight, on our two square metres of coral island, it seemed clear that we would all be there for quite a while. So I used the interlude to observe and think.

For reasons I could not explain at the time, my thoughts were unusually clear and I felt exhilarated. This is a known effect of being in a mangrove. The plants have air roots which generate so much oxygen that it has the combined effect of making you high *and* intermittently knocking you out into the deepest and most peaceful of sleeps. As I had walked through the water, I had several times had to fight the urge to slip under and sleep, as one might in a warm bath. On the rock, I got the other side, the zinging, extra-alert effect.

Once my own fear factor subsided, I realized that I had sloughed off years of tiredness in less than an hour and I began to enjoy my predicament. My mood stopped on its road to euphoria every time I remembered that the villagers had watched us trudge past their mud and *macuti* (palm-thatch) huts that night with expressions which had struck me at the time as more like dread than 'Cheerio!' The ecstatic greeting we had received from several hundred jubilant villagers when our dhow was pulled to the shore had turned to something else entirely when we proposed wading through the mangrove. As we set off, my ability to partially read other people's thoughts either let me down, or the thoughts got lost in translation. I had thought: We are breaking a taboo and they are trying to scare me, rather than seeing that we were breaking a safety rule and the villagers were scared for our lives.

The memory of those looks, combined with the stoic but obviously growing gloom of our guides and my guilt towards them, began to unnerve me. When I mentioned this to Mees, he was very sanguine about it all, but he had spent thirty-one years as a news cameraman amid war, earthquakes, floods and riots. He suggested that, since we would probably have to stay on our safe haven for at least another hour, we crack open the box of patisserie I had bought that morning in Nampula. At which point, I remembered that I not only had my laptop and a box of cakes in the carpet bag I had been carrying on my head as we waded along the underwater path following the guides step by step like lobsters on a migratory path, I also had a thermos of coffee.

So we unpacked our little picnic and the five of us ate in the moonlight. Our guides had probably never seen a thermos, coffee, a confectionery box or a chocolate cream sponge before in their lives. I thought they were shy when they refused second helpings of both the cake and the pre-sweetened espresso. With hindsight, people who have lived almost exclusively on fish, corn and manioc must have found my delicacies quite disgusting. Had I looked more closely, I would probably have seen them discreetly dropping the slices of chocolate sponge into the raging sea.

Despite having travelled widely in search of a home, I have lived more as an experienced somnambulist than an active member of any society. Years of training have allowed me to get by while half my senses are asleep. That night, in a moment of truth, I found there was something so completely incongruous about drinking espresso while perched like a gannet mid-sea, in an environment in which I was to all intents and purposes nothing, that I woke up to life as though to a revelation. Far away somewhere, a screech owl staked its claim to the silent night and packaged the moment, so to speak. Above, the sky glittered with more stars than I had ever seen before.

The tide eventually turned and instead of surging on towards the village, it began to move decisively back towards the sea, summoning all its slipstreams and rivulets. As the Macua say, 'The sea has emptied again.' Everywhere, nature adapted to its rule. Millions of crabs scuttled across thousands of rocks. Perched on our jagged outcrop, we were like giant crabs: dependent on and irrelevant to the majestic tide. The sensation of physical harmony with the surrounding was like another kind of wave. When the water finally ebbed enough for us to go on our way, slipping back into the tepid water was a sensation I cannot describe without the inevitable Californian overtones, because it was like a rebirth, a new baptism. I was a minuscule and insignificant part, but every part of me recognized a visceral, cerebral and spiritual affinity with that watery domain. So I knew, even then, before I had seen the stillness and beauty of where I was to go, that this wild and wonderful place was the place for me.

Three hours later, standing on the edge of a lagoon cradled by white sand – with nothing but the murmuring ocean and whispering casuarina trees, swathed in warm air – I felt a huge relief knowing that all my days of running and seeking were over. This was what I had been looking for; and one day I would return to live and (hopefully) eventually to die there in that ancient, silent, magical place.

II

Dream Catching

I JOKE SOMETIMES THAT I don't drive a car because I am driven. In fact, I don't drive and I am an obsessive seeker of goals. I was always looking for something and I didn't know what that something was. I just knew, intuitively, that I'd recognize it when I found it. Find it I did in a place called the Quirinthe Peninsula just beyond Cabaceira Pequena on the northern coast of Mozambique. It is a place so remote that few have visited it since the time of Vasco da Gama.

Local legend has it (with some corroboration from history books and some embroidery, no doubt, by the local community) that Vasco da Gama stopped on Mozambique Island (Ilha) and asked for water from the massive Arabian reservoirs there. The islanders pretended that they had none to spare and sent the Portuguese captain to neighbouring Cabaceira Pequena. He sailed the four kilometres of the Mozambique Channel and demanded water from the thriving Afro-Arabian trading village on the coast. Supposedly, a fight broke out between two of his unruly sailors and the local Cabaceirians, who refused to give their precious water away without due payment.

So a thirsty Vasco da Gama sailed away again, to return

the following year for vengeance. Together with a small fleet, he bombarded the hapless Macua-Arabic village, razing its coral-stone warehouses and buildings to a pile of rubble. To this day, the bleached coral ruins remain.

Since then, few foreigners have been back. Across the mangrove, only three kilometres away, the Portuguese colonists built several palaces and both lived and traded in Cabaceira Grande for over two hundred years until their show town slipped back into the bush. At the turn of the twentieth century, having beaten the rebellious native population back into submission, they tightened the yoke and took up where they had left off, asset-stripping Mossuril for the greater glory of the King of Portugal. It was not until 1975 that Mozambique managed to free itself of the ensuing Portuguese colonial rule. After the colonists were uncere-moniously expelled once and for all, the people left the Portuguese legacy virtually untouched. The villas and palaces of the former masters stand abandoned, the soap and palm-oil factories are derelict, cashew plantations grow untended, and former farmland has reverted to bush.

However, in the first wave of colonization, back in 1569, the Portuguese built a stately church in Cabaceira Grande, which stands intact to this day, wedged between the seashore and a palm grove. This church of Nossa Senhora de Remedios has a garden of giant lilies beside it, around the tomb of an unknown conquistador. After the Portuguese left Mozambique over thirty years ago, the jungle crept qui-etly back over the village and pushed it back to a level of mere subsistence around the abandoned palaces and the church, which are the only testimonies on its mass of mud huts to it ever having been a town.

Meanwhile, its sister village, which had been the victim of Vasco da Gama's revenge, never recovered and sank fur-ther and further into obscurity. With its stocks and stores destroyed, it had nothing to sell. There was nothing to give and nothing to take.

Out to sea, the lighthouse of Ilha de Goa beams its intermittent guidance to passing ships. The lighthouse is zebra-striped. There are no real zebras left here in the hinterland. Along with all the other game, they were outrun by hungry villagers in the years of famine when the rest of the country was at war after independence. It looks as though what is left is a half-memory: the zebra stripes are maroon and white and the only hint of black is where the annual rains have mildewed lime. The lighthouse itself is a relic from the past. After dark, the four-kilometre-wide Mozambique Channel is the exclusive domain of submarine creatures. On this once famed trade route, ships used to find their way to Mozambique Island and then Zanzibar and Goa, guided by the Table Mountain visible on the horizon. By day, fishing dhows and hundreds of dugout canoes bob on the normally tranquil surface. Long ago, by night, the sole light of Ilha de Goa steered ships away from the perilous coral reef. Now the lighthouse continues its slow blink and the treacherous coral rocks are still underwater in the narrow Mozambique Channel, but no ships pass by day or night.

Around the full moon, a colour spectrum bleeds, seeping red, yellow and violet bands into the sky, tinting passing clouds a watery magenta. Around a full moon there is no need for a torch or lanterns, no need for candles or oil lamps because the moonlight is bright enough to read by. But for over a week around each new moon, no invisible hand throws the cloth of stars and it is so dark that on night walks one stumbles into trees and mud walls.

I am wandering in the dark, feeling my way, getting hopelessly lost until Morripa, my friend and guide, leads me back once again to mysterious tracks known only to him and a few hundred closely related and mostly forgotten Cabaceirians. Morripa is the most mysterious of all the inhabitants here. His call has anchored me among the mangroves. By association, he has washed a veneer of acceptance over my otherwise outlandish status of *Akunha*. His guidance steers me through all of this unknown territory. It is he who has assembled a team here and who finds most of its new members. From Adamji to guard, Fatima to cook the beans and Mestre Canira to make doors and windows, shelves and chairs, Morripa is the recruiter. Like a conjurer, he can find most things. Unlike a conjurer (and given the dire isolation of this spot), he needs a few days for each request. But with that time (and by paying up-front plus transport), and by using his enormous network gleaned in his other lives, he can come up with anything from a bull to a helicopter, a tractor, a rabbit, a dinner service, tarpaulin, computer cable or anything else one can think of.

Without knowing it when I first met him and pledged my support to his cause, Morripa is also a fellow dreamer and a fellow writer, workaholic, insomniac. While appearing to be the gentlest of men when, for instance, talking tête-à-tête with one of his twenty-seven children, there is also a fierce side to him which rarely shows. I know from his war record that he has been trained to strike deadly blows. I have seen his face set and his eyes narrow a few times and thereby seen why it is that no one messes with him. Mostly, though, in situations designed to provoke a saint, he stays incredibly calm and conceals all emotion, becoming as near invisible as flesh and blood can be. Lurking under the surface of all his diplomacy there is defensive violence, an iron will, a lot of poetry and a pureness of heart that often imbues mere proximity to him with spiritual feeling. If he were Jewish, he might be considered a Just Man, carrying the burden of other people's woes. But he is Macua through, and through, and he lives as a dream-catcher devising plans and schemes for himself and his people and making them happen.

Together, we are learning to pace ideas and actions. There are three of us, Mees (my partner), Morripa and me, sharing a vision too unlikely for many of our peers to see. By trial and error we take two steps forward and one step back in a dance whose steps we are partly copying and partly inventing. Sometimes Morripa or I shoot out in a false direction in what we call 'Bridge over the river Kwai syndrome'. Then a simple action mushrooms into a feat of engineering, labour and sacrificed energy only to collapse shortly afterwards. Mostly, though, we have found a good rhythm and a balance between talking about things, planning them and actually getting them done.

I am on the edge of the known world, surrounded by seawater yet not on an island. Twice a day the tide floods the mangroves enclosing villages. The Indian Ocean is so pristine here it is clear enough mid-channel to see thirty metres down to the seabed. Starfish, occasional sea urchins, corals, lobsters and sea creatures ranging from grey blobs to marlin, dolphins and whales inhabit the channel. To sail over them seems like watching an endless Discovery Channel documentary close up on a wide screen. Only at sea are we truly equal: if the leaking dhow capsizes, we will all drown. The sea is no respecter of persons. Although high winds bring the same gloomy fears to all the passengers, the crossings are usually relatively safe. So long as the bailer keeps bailing and the crew and passengers keep shifting their combined weight from side to side, laughter echoes across the waves from the various boats. Fair winds trigger hilarity and foment excited debates.

After my first dozen crossings, the women perched at one

end of the dhow ceased to stare at me with anxious wonder and their emaciated menfolk ceased to resent my presence on *their* boat. *Akunha* are supposed to charter their own vessels. The four battered local ferries are the domain of native Cabaceirians. A couple of times, in the early days, I was challenged by the captain of the early ferry as to why I was trespassing. When I explained that I had come to live among them and therefore was not, technically, an outsider, the captain pointed out that I could never be one of them because I was rich and they were poor. One early morning he told me, 'This ferry is for local people only. The price [ten MTS = forty USD cents*] is for us. You have more money so you should pay more.'

One of the other passengers, an old man from the village with bloodshot eyes and a scar on the side of his neck where something nasty had obviously been surgically removed, stood up for me. The captain listened to him attentively and even half-smiled at me to encourage my continued efforts on behalf of his village, but he stood firm on his first point: 'The *Akunha* can afford to pay more, so she should.'

Several other passengers agreed with this, while a few others joined my scarred and aged defender. In the typically democratic manner of village meetings, with a dhow acting as a forum, the captain then turned back to me and invited me to share my thoughts on the state of our relative wealth. By this time, we were quite far out to sea, so stepping out and running to Morripa for his usual protective mantle was not an option. He takes Draconian measures against anyone who attempts to rip off me or the college we are creating. I supposed I could stubborn it out and refuse to pay more money but a mixture of feelings surged

*In 2007 one USD = 25 Mozambican meticals

up and all of them pointed to the captain actually having a good point. Alone on that ferry, wedged between a flock of skinny people in rags, I could afford to pay more to sail to Ilha. The captain and crew worked hard for their pittance. Whenever a boat was becalmed, the crew would row, if need be, from shore to shore. And lastly, the charter fare for tourists sailing from Ilha was 400 meticals, which was forty times more than I was proffering and the wizened captain was rejecting. I capitulated and doubled my fare, thereby pleasing all but my champion who grumbled about my lack of spirit the rest of the way. However, the captain was delighted and took it upon himself to teach me Macua in return for my largesse. This he did, and still does, imparting words very slowly and with firm condescension as though my failure to speak his language is the proof of my mental inadequacy. He nods encouragement to me as to a dog with a stick.

'Ma – sca – mol – o. Say it, come on, bit by bit, ma–sca–mol–o.'

Failure to comply and repeat brings out the disciplinarian in him, expressed in stern disappointment and a refusal to acknowledge me for the remainder of the voyage. Repeating my word of the day breaks his tree-bark face into a wide smile and a doggie pat for me. When he is pleased with me as a pupil, he turns to praise my progress to his other passengers. I do not let on that I already understand a lot of what is said in Macua, so his invariable comment of, 'You see, she might be different but she isn't stupid,' is the nearest I come to a compliment in my new bush home far from the gallantries of Paris or Rome. Over the following year, this particular captain and I spent many hours conversing on many crossings to Ilha and back. We never made it on to name terms: he was always '*O Capitano*' and I was always '*A Akunha*,' but in our way we became friends. My name is less confusing than his. There are dozens of *capi-tanos* in the Cabaceiras but very few *Akunha*, of whom my daughter, Lolly, and I are the only ones to actually live here now. Telepathy and intuition play a great part in local conversation. Thus everyone else seems to know exactly which *capitano* is being referred to and which boy, which girl, which mother and which uncle, despite calling all boys *muido* (boy), and all girls *menina* (girl), all women *mae*, and all men *tio* (uncle), irrespective of any family tie. I was quite disconcerted when the first dozen students at the college here started calling me 'my mudder' until I realized that all women become 'mother' (*mae*), albeit in name only, once they cease to be a girl, and the name is a sign of affection and respect.

I rest my bare feet on sacks of manioc and baskets of live prawns with cloth bundles wedged behind and beside me as we loll across the sea. Far out, there are pools of startling turquoise in the mostly still water. Along the shoreline, a ribbon of pale beaches stretches north and south for hundreds of kilometres. For miles out along the coast there are strands of shallows in which flamingos and fishermen wade, gathering edible treasures from the rich seabed. Between them and the shore there are thickets, woods and forests of red and white mangroves. These marine trees have barnacles encrusted on their trunks and branches up to the high-tide mark. Their lush green tops are the nesting places of egrets and pelicans, gulls, storks and thousands of other birds that rise in startled flocks each time a sailing dhow punts by or a dugout canoe scarcely bigger than the muscular fisherman inside it paddles past the red lattice of hanging roots. The red mangroves have arched stilts. Their branches are beloved of egrets, which rise and flee as we glide by. Seabirds fly in circles, and then return to their perches to guard their watery realm. The air roots from the seedlings, saplings and large trees thrust up through the sand in knobbly spikes. These roots form palisades through which the fishermen have worn down a maze of narrow, almost invisible paths. Only the fishermen and the ferrymen know which paths are safe to follow and when it is safe to follow them as the tide comes rolling in.

III

Parallel Lives

BEFORE I LEFT ITALY – my adoptive country for twenty years – I pulled the pragmatic side of my character to the fore and planned my immediate future (for a seven-year stretch) like a military campaign. Then in the winter of 2000, in a reasonably orderly fashion, I moved to Paris and then to the Netherlands with my youngest daughter, Lolly (who was nine at the time).

Chastened and galled by having lost numerous court battles, the roof over my head, and the sleeves, at least, of my shirt, I was hell-bent on avoiding further escapades. I chose rather to immure myself in the business world under the tutelage of solid business people. I chose to do this in Amsterdam, a solid northern European business city.

In some ways, it would be hard to find a more down-to-earth approach to life than that of the Dutch. I had no idea that by choosing to make this exotic downshift I was actually launching myself into the biggest and most exotic challenge I have ever met: Mozambique. And yet, by a series of coincidences, I was launched into and have subsequently embraced life on the edge on a stretch of coast along the Indian Ocean.

There was a Dutch-African overlap during which I lived a double life: quite simply, day by day, I was a writer who lived in the heart of Amsterdam in the beautiful Villa Einstein overlooking a canal. And by night I was the person who ran a community college on the edge of the Indian Ocean, arranging for sacks of rice to be transported from Nampula to the college kitchens and for tree trunks to be shipped in from Nacala. A construction team of local builders were (and still are) working their way through the derelict rooms of what used to be a Portuguese naval academy, restoring them into classrooms and kitchens, dormitories and offices. The minutiae of one life and the other have made kaleidoscopic patterns in my mind.

Now, as I wait for sporadic gusts of breeze to waft through the doors to my ballroom office, with so little contact with the outside world, it seems hard to believe that for two years, every Wednesday, I flew from Schipol to London and was a film producer, Monday to Friday, from nine to five. I was a businesswoman stealing time from board meetings and banks to be a writer again. By night, though, and every time I could get away – even for a few days – I did what I have always wanted to do. I lived my fantasies to the full.

That may sound like sheer selfishness. And yet on the other hand I know that if I describe the work I do in Mozambique, the schools Teran Foundation is setting up, the farms we are planning, the water projects and my consultancy for the railroads and tourist projects there, then it might look as though, on the contrary, I were a selfless person. The truth is neither one nor the other. It lies in the balance of give and take. I give everything I have and am and can do. I take the most wondrous times and happiness as I have never known it before.

Every time I look out across the palm groves that flank

the college on two sides, I am reminded that nothing about my life up until 2002 has been as surreal or as magical as what I am doing now. Be it the beauty, the spirituality, the harmony, the friendship or just the warm weather and warm water and great beaches here: a combination of all has captivated me and it holds me in a grip no other place has exercised before to this degree. As a farmer, my work lies in coaxing new (to Mossuril) crops to grow in this salty sandy soil. And as a writer, my work lies in sifting through and selecting nuggets from an endless seam.

I have always come to know other villages from the edge in, unfolding their secrets with less clinical eyes than I have cast over the Cabaceiras. But then I have always passed through other villages, pausing for however long as a mere visitor and not with the intention of helping them out. This time, I had to establish what was missing so as to be able to help fill the gaps. The Cabaceiras have been both blessed and cursed by their isolation. They were blessed by being outside of the seventeen years of war after independence, by having had (to date in 2007) less than a dozen known cases of HIV/Aids, by being shielded from most of the ills of the West; but they are cursed by missing out on nutrition, transport, education, healthcare, jobs, basic technology and most basic consumer goods. Any form of communication beyond the village is a challenge.

An incongruous factor of such isolation is that the area has mobile phone coverage. Landline telecommunication might not have reached this particular bit of the East African coast, but the mobile phone has. Mozambique has a national network called M-cell which reaches right into the mangroves, even mid-channel when sailing to Ilha. Possession of a mobile is not only an enormous status symbol, but a unique and essential link to the outside world. Where mobile phones in the West are used more as business appendages and/or as the conveyors of continuously updated tittle-tattle to the exclusion of normal one-on-one conversation, a mobile in the bush is a life-saving device. However, there is a wide gap between its potential and reality.

Like Italian teenagers who dangle car keys to non-existent cars to show off their macho prowess, many local mobile phones are unavailable for use in critical moments due to lack of credit. The phones are topped up with two- or three-dollar cards, the purchase of which exceeds most family budgets. Those who can afford them tend to abuse their phones as rampantly as any Western teenager. Yet because most people cannot afford them and are therefore not used to phoning out, the use of the treasured mobile remains mysterious. When a new top-up credit has been installed, the ensuing glee is immediately shared. Any Mozambican with a mobile phone will use it to exchange inanities without any mobile etiquette at all. And no matter how inopportune a phone call might be, the idea of switching off a phone that works is inconceivable, as is the possibility that one might not answer a call.

When the tsunami devastated so much of the Asian coast, the local people here knew something strange was happening because the tide streamed in and out of the mangroves in rapid succession. Such a thing had never happened before. It didn't cause any damage though. It was a talking point: a moment of wonder. I was in Holland at the time and my first thought was of the Cabaceirians. I was able to call Morripa and ask if everyone was safe; he described the double tide to me.

So if the village were less poor, and if top-up phone credits were available more locally, and if phone parts such as batteries and chargers could be supplied there, and if there was electricity to recharge the batteries or solar energy to replace that, then in theory all the villagers could be linked by mobile phone to the rest of the world.

Morripa and about a dozen of his fellow village leaders have mobiles. There is no clearer sign that a person is upwardly mobile than such a possession. A man with a 'rooky tooky' (a bicycle) is a man to be reckoned with, but a man or woman with a mobile is in a higher class of achievement altogether. Horrendous ringtones are part and parcel of this elevated status. Deep in the bush, a carpenter or one of the Varanda workers will let their 'Peer Gynt', 'Auld Lang Syne' or 'La Cucaracha' ring repeatedly rather than rush to answer the offending mobile, just to enjoy the moment and share their good fortune with their friends and family. Every time I take my own phone out of my pocket and fiddle with my text messages, I see admiring eyes appraise my little silver Samsung. Because Lolly and I each have a mobile, and Mees has a stunning three of them, we are people who have made it.

Being a writer doesn't bring much credit in an area where there are no books to speak of. Not only are there no books, there are no bookshops or libraries, and, worse still, there are hardly any schools. A Cabaceirian can study to fourth-year primary; then the education system stops. Elsewhere in Mozambique this is not the case, but here behind God's back there is nowhere to go to get an education. Newspapers don't reach here and the internet has yet to arrive (waiting, no doubt, for electricity and telephone lines to precede it).

There is much talk in town of a new system called 'bla-bla', a wireless radio phone which is to come our way any day. So far, I have bought two bla-bla phone faxes and both were dead on arrival with irreversible faults that did not allow them to work either in town or out of it. However, with patience, this seems to be the way of the future, and in some kind of African timescale which will not be tomorrow, and which cannot name the day in the future when the miracle will occur, I believe that a new link to the great beyond is about to form.

Because the whole concept of telephones is new, many people with a limited circle of friends with phones have little idea how to use the magical object. Advice is freely given about how one should be held, used, kept and cosseted. Most of this advice comes from hearsay. Many people believe that this miraculous 'talkie talkie' must be moved continuously from ear to mouth. Others swear by holding it like a microphone. And when one breaks down (often), there is always someone ready to take it apart with a home-made penknife while a chorus of friends stand by to bewail the almost inevitable demise of that particular piece of technology.

Every day, someone will call me and launch into a conversation that makes no sense to me and has no context without the caller identifying his or herself. When I ask, 'Who am I talking to?', the answer is simply, 'Me.'

'Yes, but who is me?'

'*I* am.'

'But who are *you*?'

'I am me.'

'But what is your name?'

'What are you saying? This is me! I am talking to you.'

And so it goes on, consuming the little yellow top-up cards from M-cell and quickly bringing whoever that 'me' was to the end of their credit. Thus everyday phone calls are imbued with life's mysteries. The age-old search for identity is there, the philosopher's riddle permeates. Existence attempts to base itself on audio reflection: you must know who I am because you can hear me; I exist because you can hear me. Thus the sheer joy of talking into a phone overrules the need for the speaker to identify him- or herself or to stand by the idea that speech per se is not communication and only becomes that when someone else understands what has been said.

I hear the drums beat and relay their sound, slow and steady, filtering through the groves of palms and mango trees. The rhythm quickens, joined by new beats as more dried gazelle skins are pounded and more villagers gather round in ways that are known to them all, and which have been handed down religiously through the centuries by spoken words and gestures. While much of the rest of African culture was observed and anthropologically dissected, analysed, recorded and transported as a curio to the West, this Macua culture has survived unspoilt, unknown to us and untouched. As it unravels (and unravel it does) to reveal so many of its secrets, I feel so excited about sharing them that I am calling out of the bush as an anonymous caller. In this tale filtered through an 'I' and a 'me', I have so far assumed that you must know who I am because you can hear me.

Pre-empting the 'Yes, but who *are* you?' question, let me say that I am a writer who was once a farmer and has become a farmer again, and who has always been a rootless person in search of a place to call home. I was born and brought up in London, but my absent father is South American and can claim kinship across half the world. I started writing as a child and have been writing ever since (mostly novels, but also short stories, autobiography and travel writing). I was brought up in London in the 1950s by a mother who longed to be somewhere else.

From within a paradoxically close yet dysfunctional family (made up almost exclusively of females), I developed an intense clan spirit combined with an obsessive obligation to follow unorthodox paths. By proxy, my duty was to live life to the hilt, to make a mark and to do all the things my mother had been thwarted from doing. Apart from skipping school and indulging in minor childhood delinquency, for years I fulfilled this mission in an almost constant daydream. My expectation of how life should be was so rarefied that I managed to squeeze a few lives into the 1970s without really noticing them pass by. During that decade, I was benignly stalked by, and cradle-snatched by, a Venezuelan revolutionary and taken to his inherited lands in the Andes, and I became a farmer and a mother, a writer and then a refugee without realizing that *that* was my life, rather than the other more elusive dreams I was endlessly chasing.

While I lived in the Venezuelan Andes, I spent many hours crying, secretly bewailing the fact that life had passed me by. When I returned to England and found literary success, it took me as many years again to come to terms with other people's fascination with what had been, for me, a deep emotional trauma and eventual awakening, and over two thousand days of drudgery interspersed with an occasional highlight.

Then, by drifting from one country to another and one adventure to another with three children in tow, I lived for twenty years basking in the complacency of minor success. A few of my books made it on to bestseller lists but none rushed to top those charts. More critics were kind than brutal, and although my fame was more for the strange life I led than for the books I wrote, it was fame enough to keep me endlessly afloat. However, when I reached the age of fifty and took stock of myself, I was disconcerted to see how ill my dreams matched my achievement.

My life has been cocooned by unusual good luck and dogged by misfortune (sometimes simultaneously). The intensity of each frame of each scene has often excluded my seeing the bigger picture. Swathed in good intentions, I bumbled along in what often appeared from the outside to be a streamline, but which was actually a survival tactic. I could have continued bumbling to the end of my days and few would have been the wiser, but I was born greedy for experience, and when I scratch the surface of my own skin, I remember that I have always wanted more. The knocks I have received should have probably woken me up before, but, somewhat shamefully, they didn't. I had to pinch myself awake.

Successful writers receive a lot of praise and (despite some ups and downs in the reception of my sixteen books) so too have I. The modern cult of the writer makes praise for work written spill over into something much more personal. Fans of a book often become fans of the author, creating a halo-cum-swaddling band round the writer in praise of his or her life's achievement. Although I did not set out to be an 'autobiographical writer', explaining how I got into some of the places where I have been often seemed like the only way of introducing a reader into that world. Several of my books have revealed a great deal of personal detail, thereby inviting friend and foe alike to know me at a remove. Although the goodwill of strangers has been a sustaining factor I have often felt grateful for, it has also made me feel uncomfortable. Other than make a bit of an effort here and there, apart from writing and bringing up three children (all of which I enjoyed immensely), I haven't really *done* anything.

I was present when others were doing. I worked hard on the Venezuelan hacienda but I would have had to have a heart of stone not to. After leaving the Andes, the effort and organization I put into my domestic life were almost sufficient to run, if not a small country, at least a small town. It wasn't that I wanted to go into politics or run for mayor anywhere, but I felt my efforts could be better used else-where.

Long ago in Venezuela, I had made a foray into community service and worked closely with a group of isolated villagers. But far from being a success story, it was a failure for which I have felt consumed by guilt. In a world of give and take, I got far more than I gave. My engagement with life began there and although I retained elements of somnambulism after I left, *before* my seven years of hard labour in the Andes I was like someone from another planet. And no matter what good deeds I did while I was there as the teenage mistress of my mostly absentee husband's hacienda, I championed a cause and then abandoned it. I didn't stay there: I ran away. After seven years in an increasingly violent marriage, I saved myself, my sanity and my daughter. With hindsight, I still don't see what else I could have done (although, of course, I could have not married a complete stranger and not gone to South America in the first place).

After I make all my own excuses, there is still the moral issue of what I was doing in a place of such abject poverty: the Andean hacienda was firmly rooted in Andean snobbery in which I was the lady of the manor and the people I worked with were hardly better off than serfs. The only lasting mark I made there was in the hearts of a handful of people. I know that most of the socio-economic changes I made came undone and unravelled like a half-finished jumper caught on a fence within months of my leaving.

Then, three decades later, in Holland, while it seemed strange to live two such different but parallel lives, the strangest thing was that all the apparently disparate things I had done so far (from restoring palaces to farming avocados) served as ideal training for my new life. After nearly thirty years of searching, I have finally found the place I was look-ing for, and in so doing I seem to have found myself. This

is the second chance that so rarely comes around and which
I am determined not to blow. Long ago, I had a place, the
hacienda, and it made sense to me. Now, once again, I have
the chance to make a mark in the hearts of some fine
people. And once again, I have the chance to be their cata-
lyst for change. Given this new opportunity to stand by
them, in so doing I can lay my own ghosts to rest in their
heavily haunted mangrove.

IV

If Not Now, When?

BACK IN 1998 AND 1999, while living in Italy embroiled in
court cases, I sat by my telephone in Umbria, waiting for
one or other of my numerous lawyers to ring, and I had
hundreds of hours in which to plan a new life. It didn't take
me much reflection to realize that the two areas in which I
felt I had truly failed were in my search for an 'ideal' partner and in getting into any active philanthropy. On the
former count, after three marriages and various affairs, it
had become blatantly obvious, to me at least, that I was
hopeless at choosing anyone with whom I could delight in
sharing either my life or dreams.

I always used to be attracted to people who lived on
the edge. Whether that edge was approached by their passion for art or their proximity to mental instability was
not something I had weighed in the balance. More importantly, nor had I weighed the fact that even when that
edge was given exclusively by a passion for art, as was the
case with my last husband, the painter Robbie Duff-Scott,
such a drive leaves little over, in real terms, for someone
like me who is seeking a great deal of emotional and
moral support. One of my millennium New Year

resolutions was to stop seeking what I so obviously could not find.

Another resolution was to stop being passive and take action. I took steps to change my life in such a way that I could repair my fortunes and set off to sub-Saharan Africa to fulfil another dream. Because no matter which way my thoughts turned, one remained as a steady backdrop to all the others: come what may, I was determined to set up a chain of African schools and libraries. This particular goal had been in the back of my mind for over twenty years. It started long before I had ever been to Africa. It had been further shaped during ten years of travelling in West Africa; and had grown from a whim to an obsession. A lack of funds, know-how or help did nothing to deter it. It was a stubborn plan and it wouldn't go away. It really did not fit with my then predicament in Italy; but I knew all about stubbornness, and rather than try to quash it, I decided to shape my life around it instead.

Last but not least, as the millennium dawned, I promised myself to actually carry out my New Year resolutions, instead of just thinking them and then letting them get shoved aside by other things.

To which end, I went from one extreme to another: from searching for love to absolutely closing down my personal body shop and refusing to even contemplate a date, let alone a new partner. Soul searching, I had discovered that I seemed to consistently confuse a need to help and a plea-sure in so doing with my relationships. The solution to both seemed to lie in the same direction: I should actively work in charity and stop mistaking marriage as a way-station for the International Red Cross.

Resigned to being single and celibate, I indulged my capacity for long hours and hard work and turned my atten-tion to the movie business. It was during that phase of personal austerity and abstention that I met Mees. Although he is now my partner, getting there was a very gradual process: first we shared a love of the Cabaceiras, and only later did we share our lives.

When I moved to Holland, financially I was still reeling from a disastrous sale of the villa in Italy which had been my 'let's put all our eggs in one basket' asset. This sale had not only left me without a nest egg, it had also failed to cover all of my outstanding debts. I reckoned it would take me three years in business to break even and between five to six years to add enough zeros to my bank balance to be able to set up my own charitable foundation. By dabbling in the charity world I knew that I would need a duly registered vehicle through which to carry out my school and library plan. I had heard that trying to get money from bigger aid organizations was like trying to get blood from a stone, and the only way to get round that was to be disgustingly rich.

I knew that smart business people could make their first million in a year, but I also knew that I was no maverick in the business world. In fact, my track record to date was a disaster. I would have to go back to the beginning and learn. Whatever money I made would be through a combination of lateral thinking and a lot of hard work. I spent 2001 planning my next five to six years. I devised a film development plan and then persuaded people to believe in it. Somewhat to my surprise, a lot of people did almost as quickly as I had, and I went to work with a will and discovered, among other things, that I didn't know the meaning of drudgery until I set up an office. I take my hat off to all those who work in one for surviving a state so obviously at odds with human nature.

But even when things were going well in my glorified Dutch office, I couldn't see the point of most of what I was doing. I felt more like a character in a very dull movie than the person who puts movie packages together. I was cramming my brain with media tax laws and international treaties, finance, investment and regulatory laws and the like, and yet I couldn't – in the tapestry of life – see why.

Other, buried skills seemed much more real. I had learned a great many things as a young woman in Venezuela and I learnt most of them the hard way by trial and sometimes fatal error. They were useful, practical things like how to lower fevers and heal wounds, how to market-garden and keep sheep, how to build and mend fences and make walls, how to stock-take and cook for hundreds of people, how to grow sugar, and avocado pears, and oranges. I also learnt how to communicate with isolated, semi-literate people in a time warp, and to bridge some of the gaps between their reality and mine. Most of these skills were never called upon again except for the odd juggling act, and most are completely redundant in the modern Western world. So I put them on hold and lived an episodic life without them, struggling to stay in tune with a rhythm that wasn't mine. Yet not using the many skills I had amassed seemed like a waste and without them the pattern of my life felt incomplete. I wanted there to be a point, despite so palpably not being able to see one.

Although much has happened since I left Venezuela and the hacienda I lived and worked on, a part of me missed the life I led when I was girl with a mission farming crops and dreams. Despite the long hours of dull work inherent in any kind of farming, I had felt more alive on the hacienda and more in tandem with life than anywhere else before or after it. In other roles, I felt as though I was acting a part: pretending to be a chatelaine, a businesswoman or a member of the literary establishment. I didn't belong in these places under any guise; and was there, it seemed to me, under false pretences.

With more energy than I had work to do, I invented

ways to fill my time. In Italy, I had spent most of my days gardening and was happiest when so doing. The nights were restless times, probably because when others sleep, I roam about, thinking. I am not much of a sleeper and never have been. In Venezuela, this enabled me to farm by day and write at night. During the twenty years that I lived in Italy, I wrote in the very early mornings before anyone else at home was awake. Then when each day ended and everyone else went to sleep, I had time on my hands. When every day is twenty hours long, there is always time for reflection.

In Italy, although I enjoyed the ways I found to fill my nights, reading, watching movies, bottling fruits, and embroidering butterflies, with so many nights to think through, I couldn't help thinking: If not now, when? What exactly was I waiting for?

The room I use now as an office, study and bedroom is ten metres high and has a barrel-vaulted ceiling made up of hundreds of strips of wood. This ceiling is painted pale blue. There are three large windows on one wall and a fourth high over the double entrance door. It is a grand room by any standards but seems even more so to me because I moved into it in mid-2006 having spent the previous year squatting in a dark airless room at the end of a dark corridor. In that one, bats flew in and out of a hole in the false ceiling, frequently disproving the theory that bats have perfect radar and never knock into things. All the windows in my new office are too high to see out of except to look up to the palm tops and the sky. It is surprising how many variations one can spot in a palm frond if one looks at it for long enough. When sorting out the administration (a task I find supremely boring), I sometimes spend hours on end trying to find names for all the shades of green and words to describe the various sounds the wind makes as it rustles and creeps, rattles and shivers, shakes and judders, whispers and creaks through the ragged windmills of the surrounding coconut palms.

In 2003, talks with the Mossuril District Administrator revealed that this derelict mansion could be the government's contribution to a community college. My room was the ballroom in the nineteenth-century days when this was a naval academy. It had probably been built in the late eighteenth century as a convent. When we took over the derelict building, this huge room was the most ruined of all the rooms, and because a ficus tree had caused structural damage to an entire side of it, we left it till last. There was no time in the first rush of restoration to tackle such a big job. Numerous birds, mammals and insects had made their homes in it and when I and then Mees moved in, they did not take kindly to us. The screech owls who nested here gave up their tenancy with the least resistance, but several of the rats, bushbabies, striped squirrels, termites, tunnel beetles, ants, lizards, geckos, centipedes and scorpions that lived here undisturbed until we came have stubbornly refused to give up.

When I went to Malawi for a week in June 2006, the rats had a ball in the former ballroom. I arrived back exhausted from twenty-seven hours on the back of a truck and fifteen hours on a slow train to find that rats had eaten my clothes, shoes, books, papers, pencils, key ribbons, bed linen, towels, hats, baskets, the mosquito net, two pillows, six cushions, and tunnelled their way into our mattress. Good rat poison is one of the many things that cannot be bought locally but I was already prepared for battle with the rats and had scoured Limbe for the best Malawian poison. I brought back a jar of lurid pink pellets that were so cruelly effective it took a week to clear all the corpses. I located them with Adamji by their foul smell. I asked him to find them with me because I am very squeamish about dead rats and could not bear to touch them, whereas he seemed to quite enjoy the hunt. He told me that our kapok cushions were to blame for the invasion.

'*Epa!* Kapok is like piri-piri [chilli] to rats. They love the seeds that get stuck in the kapok fluff.'

And he was right. The kapok cones we had gathered from the skeletal tree outside the college entrance had lured them in. Every room that had been decked out with new fresh kapok-filled cushions had suffered a lesser but similar invasion.

I hope (in vain, I know) that I never see a rat again, dead or alive. The local squirrels, on the other hand, are another matter because they are sweet and furry and have striped bushy tails. The first time I saw one, it was scampering over the wall of the governor's palace. Mees and I followed it and took a photo, thinking it was both rare and wonderful. Now, upwards of a hundred live with us in the college, dislodging tiles and stealing peanuts from the outdoor kitchen, raiding the rice as it is picked over by students, dangling off the passionfruit vines and, when they can get away with it, darting into my room to share whatever biscuit or breadcrumbs they can find. Now, if I didn't shoo the squirrels away when I see them, my room would be overrun by them.

I have become so used to shooing squirrels, bushbabies, mongooses, genets, lizards, eagles, falcons, tarantulas and bats away, just as the local people do, that I have ceased to see them as exotic creatures. Occasionally, though, after chasing one or more of them from our domain, I still pause to wonder at the loveliness of the bird or beast were it to be in another context (i.e. not attempting to steal or destroy college property).

And sometimes I pause to wonder at the strangeness of my being here and the leap from Amsterdam to the Cabaceiras. But, in general terms, since I wanted to work in Africa, being here and being steered into helping develop

Mossuril District was actually a logical step on a path I had already chosen.

Step one had been to fantasize endlessly about starting a chain of libraries, selecting books and shipping firms and working out filing systems in my head. Step two had been a clumsy attempt to try and organize something in Mali. Then step three, after visiting the Cabaceiras, was to write over a thousand letters to over a thousand aid organizations. The next step grew out of their rejection: no one, it seemed, cared enough about the Cabaceirians to do anything to help them. So when Morripa asked, 'Can't we just do it ourselves?', I thought: Why not?

I had wanted to start my own charity for years but I had imagined that to do so would be slow and difficult. Yet when it came to actually doing it, the act was surprisingly swift. It didn't require millions of dollars: anyone can do it with just six hundred euros. Perhaps one of the reasons why there are so many charities is that one can be born with almost indecent haste. One day I made the first formal enquiries in Holland about opening a foundation, and the next day, the Amsterdam Chamber of Commerce was asking what name to register the new charity in. As with some premature babies, I didn't have a name ready. A family brainstorm didn't produce one, and if I wanted to go ahead and register it while the wheels were in motion, I had to come up with one fast. My then business manager suggested using my name, but my very cumbersome name is not one readily pronounceable worldwide. As closing time at the Chamber of Commerce approached, in homage to my eldest daughter and her family of unsung achievers in the Venezuelan Andes, I opted for 'Teran Foundation'.

There was a scurry of paperwork and then the forgotten villages of Mossuril District had a registered charity at their disposal as a vehicle to help them on their way. The Teran

Foundation came into being in April 2004 and work began in the Cabaceiras soon after. All the walls of the former naval academy are half a metre thick and built from coral rock which had absorbed decades of damp, which damp re-emerged as a thick layer of green slime that had to be laboriously scraped off. The first group of thirty workers made this their first job.

Meanwhile, with a few notable hitches, the Dutch-based movie development was all going well until the autumn of 2004, when it began to fall apart with substantial help from a saboteur on my own team. On the brink of going into production with our first movie and recouping our invest-ment, our development budget was stopped with no notice. Most companies close when they are doing badly: ours closed when it was riding high. It was a powerful lesson in pointlessness. Nearly three years chained seven days a week to a desk and computer had just been flushed down the drain. More than anything, this act confirmed my desire to put my work into something that actually mattered within the big picture of life.

The difficulties in the movie company dovetailed with the birth of the College of Tourism and Agriculture. Both started at the end of September 2004. I had been secretly longing to get out of my office and set off to Africa with a mission ever since I had fallen in love with Mees and through him found an enormous energy untapped since the days of my youth. The end of my film venture left me with a financial headache, but this was outweighed by giving me back the freedom to live wherever I chose and to spend my time however I chose. After a three-year detour, I could get back onto that precarious road which is the pursuit of truths. As a writer and a free spirit, who can rarely say 'no' to someone in need, I was not meant for the business world. I would never choose to enter it full time again or to live in a gilded cage again or to sit in an office trapped in the micro-drama of office politics.

Perhaps I have entered this new world with such gratitude and energy because I was catapulted into its reality and its pure dreams directly from a world full of greedy schemes. Such is its spell that I, the perpetual traveller, have stopped travelling by will and now only travel through need. If I need to renew my visa, I leave the area. I go reluctantly and can't wait to get back. By so doing, I hardly know myself: I have been a compulsive traveller since the age of eight when I started travelling to the seaside five days a week instead of going to my London school. That urge to be on the move had never stopped until I came to Mossuril.

Life in the bush for someone like me who chooses to come here is relatively easy. Even in Nampula, the provincial capital some 230 kilometres away, friends imagine my days as being filled with unspeakable hardship and want. Some are appalled by the mere idea of our not having electricity or running water. Living without modern conveniences is a challenge and can sometimes be a problem, but mostly (with ingenious and time-honoured substitutes) daily life is reasonably comfortable and the conditions improve month by month.

Now things are happening here that are a force for good; being around them is exciting. While I am growing I am helping to make some of those things happen. And my greatest luxury is that all my masks are set aside. The lack of domestic luxury is more than compensated for by spending part of every week at a beach which is a terrestrial paradise. Being here is a privilege; the hardship and want is the exclusive domain of the local people.

This is easily said because I did not live through the first months of trial and error when the systems that substitute lanterns and oil lamps for electricity began or when the

various water needs were established. I was in Holland
when the interim chaos was tamed. The really hard slog at
the start-up was not achieved by me at all. I was just an occasional fly-on-the-wall in the ongoing soap opera of life in a
palace in the middle of nowhere with a team of local villagers
and a team of international volunteers. The latter was led by
my niece, Ellie, who left her job as a personnel manager at a
youth programme under the British Home Office to go out
and administer the College for Tourism and Agriculture in
the languorous backwater of Cabaceira Grande.

With her boyfriend Ramon, Morripa, and the first
twenty-one students,* it was Ramon and Ellie who fought
the daily battles and breathed life into the college. They and
Morripa discovered the tenuous supply lines that enable it
to survive. Two sacks of charcoal are now brought in every
Thursday, wobbling on the back of the charcoal burner's
bike from 35 kilometres away on a bumpy dirt road. Now it
is the coalman who arrives hot and exhausted from ped-
alling in through the heat, but in the early days it was
Ramon who staggered into the courtyard after marathon
charcoal runs. The mysteries of where to buy washing-up
liquid (Ilha), loo paper (Nampula), salt (at the salt pans), a
bicycle (Monapo), string (from the two old sisters who live
by the mosque in the village), bleach (Nampula), peanuts
(Nacavallo), a torch (Nampula), petrol (Naguema) and cold
drinks (Chocas) are easy patterns to follow. Yet each pattern
had to be discovered. There was no point asking any of the
villagers where one could buy washing-up liquid or sham-
poo or any of the other things because decades of isolation

---

*Abdala Morripa (director and student), Amina Abdala, Amina Sadique, Ancha
Abacar, Anifa Serra, Anifa Sualehe, Assina Atija Amade, Selemane, Cabo
Canira, Fatima Alberto, Fifinha Ibraimo, Ibraimo Essaica, Jaleca Abudo, Juma
Roche, Manema Abili, Marufo Ussene, Momade Ussene, Sergio Abdul,
Sumaila Ali, Victorino Alberto, Vulai Ussene,

and poverty had turned all but a handful of basic goods into unheard-of luxuries. Neither the needed items nor their names were known.

With a lone motorbike as the sole means of transport, Ramon and Ellie battled to keep the college supplied. Every day, over fifty people needed feeding in a place almost devoid of food or shops, and without a gas station. There was land, seeds and willing hands but not one gardener in the first group of volunteers. Six months went by before so much as a lettuce leaf or a blade of spinach, a tomato or sprig of parsley was sown. The students knew how to cook manioc porridge and cornmeal porridge, rice and beans. And they could grill fish. None of the early helpers were cooks, so none could show the students any new recipes. Only salt and chilli are available locally by way of herbs or spices. Only later did the few women in the village who know how to cook other things (like cakes baked in saucepans with hot stones on their lids, and duck stew, chicken in coconut, and a variety of dishes with pounded manioc leaves, peanuts and garlic) come forward to share their knowledge. Even the fishermen stayed away in the first months, unaware that a cash-paying client had finally arrived on their doorstep.

In the early days, a regimen of rice and beans was begun and for four months it was adhered to like a religious ceremony: twice a day, mountains of rice and beans were ladled out of cooking pots the size of baby baths. When Sofia, a professional cook from Maputo, arrived in January 2005 to take charge of the kitchen, she was welcomed like a returning hero. In the same village that had seemed completely devoid of ingredients, she rustled up shellfish, crabs, prawns and many types of fish. And refusing to be deterred by local lack, she located enough foodstuffs in the neighbouring towns to transform everyone's diet. Not surprisingly, she was an instant hit.

V

Meaning and Distance

THE PEOPLE HERE ARE MACUA: Mozambique's largest ethnic group. The name 'Macua' (also written as 'Makua') was externally applied and does not take into account many distinct subgroups. Their ancestors migrated from West Africa via the Congo basin and began reaching the southern continent soon after the first century BC. Even apparently separate ethnic groups such as the Lómuès and Chirimas are actually subgroups of Macua. Theirs is a melting pot whose past is a blur wrapped in myth. Theirs is a matrilineal society influenced by centuries of Arab occupation. Theirs is a language full of questions, emphasis, excitement and laughter.

At first, not a hint of meaning reached me from their rapidly repeated syllables. Then, gradually, words jumped out and lit the way through otherwise dark and unintelligible dialogues full of elongated 'eeeees' and resigned 'ayos' and a lot of 'nya, ya nyas'. Spoken Macua is a branch of Kiswahili, so it is peppered with Portuguese and Arabic words. Before I came I tried to find a Macua dictionary but was told many times that it is an oral and not a written language. Despite this, I see it written down on signs and notebooks, lists and memos. It is full of 'Ns' and 'Ks'. It took me some years to discover that it isn't true about it being unwritten, it is just that most people, including hosts of its natural speakers, can't read or write it, and it has no written literature. Rather like Old English, the spelling is still unstable: if I ask five people to spell any given word for me, they will tend to spell it (if at all) in five different ways.

One or two words can convey very specific ideas that it would take at least five times as many words to communicate in another language. For example, there is a star that comes out in the early hours of the morning, between 2 and 3am. It is called *Nttharara*, which means 'star that gives to souls the perception that they must retreat to their hiding places because dawn is approaching'. Then there is a tree with a white shiny trunk called a *Muthrenha-kholé*, which means 'tree that does not permit monkeys to climb its branches because its trunk is slippery'. One of my favourite words is *okhwahurya*: to defoliate a palm tree by removing the leaves one by one. In a village where every mud hat has a palm-thatch (*macuti*) roof, *okhwahurya* is in everyday use.

The first words of Macua I learnt to use were '*vakháni vakháni*' (slowly slowly, or 'bit by bit'). My saying it makes the local people laugh, it breaks the ice, it allows for a giant learning curve. And, *vakháni vakháni*, it helps move things forward. These two words helped to shoehorn me into the heart of this Macua homeland.

Much as I would love to become fluent in this poetic language one day, I despair of ever being so. The above is more than 50 per cent of the sum total of my written Macua. I hope that a better and younger linguist than me will come and broaden the existing lexicons and thereby help increase the written potential of Macua.

*

Through a mixture of observation and initiation, I am learning the things the local people know. It is a slow process full of mysteries. Initiation into this watery place is more by osmosis than anything else. Knowledge seeps in, soaks in and is absorbed as by the local limestone. Then it dries out slowly and some remains. By nightfall each day, I know a little more, but I cannot isolate what I have learned: it is just there, wedging me a little further into this seemingly simple but incredibly complex culture.

Information seems to be coded. This is not done in an overtly secret way or even with covert concealment. There are numerous clues and hints, mysteries and riddles; to learn more is to follow each and every one along dead-end tracks until the Right Path is found. This Right Path is an important concept grasped by great and small. Life is about aspiring to find it, fulfilment is in the finding. There is not one Right Path for everyone, there are many and each must find the one best suited to him or her. The easiest way is rarely the right one but neither is the hardest one necessarily the way to enlightenment. In the soft-spoken way of Mozambique, in which almost every conversation is reduced to whispers, I probe local knowledge for extra clues to add to my existing hoard. Attempted shortcuts tend to result in new waves of confusion. The necessary shortcut is the one that goes from learning to feeling. Knowledge without understanding is as friable as the sea urchins' shells that wash up on the beach.

I watch a white flurry of egrets circling the college, swooping and rising with the currents of hot air. And I watch the lone fish eagle gliding above the palm trees in search of prey in the limpid shallows, and I watch the pair of kingfishers on their daily visit to the arthritic branches of an old frangipani tree. Every bird and beast seems to know where it is going. Every man and child moves with a slow and measured determination as though edging towards a communal goal. I envy their sense of direction, both topographically and spiritually. They all seem to move without questioning their movement while my own feet are fettered by the need to know not only where I am going but why I am trying to get there. I have yet to learn to take African steps and walk by instinct.

It is an old cliché to comment on the natural rhythm of Africans and to marvel at their ability to dance. But the rhythm of life is less obvious yet equally present in their every movement, of which walking is one of the best examples of the inherent harmony between man and nature. Following in local footsteps brings home the extraordinary precision, the subconscious mathematics of movement. With tree trunks or baskets, sacks of manioc roots or sacks of coral rocks balanced on their heads, pedestrians move with unstinted grace.

As far as possible, I have stopped asking questions. I learn more by waiting and watching. Most of the villagers do not know why things are, just that they are. Asking questions disturbs the serenity of such things. Elsewhere, waiting in friendly silence has triggered verbal confidence more quickly than here. Silence is a comforting *capulana* (wrap) known to everyone. Although the villagers often break into chatter and laughter, none is unnerved by silence. So it has taken many months of quiet companionship to break through its barrier. People communicate on different levels and speech is only one of many. Despite my (admittedly rather scant) Western education, it is sometimes unnerving and often humbling to be surrounded by people who all know so much more than I do about the essentials of nature, life and survival. The irony of having been appointed as the helmsman to so many thousands of souls is not lost on me. Luckily, as I struggle to guide them to a place of safety from marauding poverty, none of them know that I have so little sense of direction I can get lost in my own house. If our economic odyssey were to require even the shortest of actual journeys, ours would be a lost cause were I to lead them. As it is, my guidance is merely the application of common sense and the benefit of hindsight.

The Italian comic actors Massimo Troisi and Roberto Benigni made a film together (*Non Ci Resta Che Piangere*) in which they play two latter-day losers who get hurtled back to the Renaissance. When they meet Leonardo da Vinci, they are able to astonish him with their ideas. And day by day they impress their fifteenth-century neighbours with their erudition, as much to their own surprise as anyone else's. In many ways, this is the story of my life here, because most of what I can add are the things that most of us take for granted. It is easy to shine with a bag of gadgets, a digital camera, a laptop and access to the internet. When someone has never seen the modern world in action, either in real life or on TV, some of the credit for the invention of every labour-saving device tends to rub off on the person who first shows each ingenious miracle. To date, the most popular import has been a tin-opener. Some of the students bring family members to see it in action, and the admiring 'Oohs!' and 'Aiis!' must bring pleasure to whoever actually invented it, lying in his or her grave.

Only a few of the local people can read or write and only a few can speak Portuguese, the official language. Macua is spoken at home and Portuguese is learned at school. There are only two primary schools here for this population of approximately seven thousand souls. Primary school is supposed to go to grade seven, but in the Cabaceiras it stops at grade four. This elementary education is taught to classes with over a hundred children in each, with virtually no books or teaching materials beyond a blackboard and (sometimes) a piece of chalk, no furniture and no proper school building. At the end of 2006, there were over eight hundred children sharing five heroic teachers.

After four years of primary school, there is nowhere to go. There is no local school to carry children on through later grades. There is no secondary school and nor are there any jobs. Hundreds of Cabaceirian children do not attend school at all. Thanks to the unity of this forgotten society and its own internal efforts, instead of creating a cultural desert, the extreme isolation of the Cabaceiras has magnified Macua culture. Despite the almost universal lack of formal education, everyone is steeped in the oral culture of the area.

Their ancestors, known as *Makholo* (big people from long ago), settled here over a thousand years ago. The spirits of their ancestors live with them, guiding the people via the *mukhulukana* (*curandeiros* or healers/witchdoctors), *malio* (*al'mos* or benign magicians), and *namirrette* (*feticeiros* or shamans), *recule* or *mwene* (*regulos* or chiefs) and imams, the religious leaders.

The ancestors are revered, recalled, consulted and sometimes feared. Every time someone dies, they join the army of older spirits to watch over and assist, punish and advise the survivors in their community. There are good and bad spirits, just as there are good and bad people; at night, uneasy spirits roam the mangroves and catch stragglers unawares.

The sun rolls into the horizon here rather than gradually setting as it does in other places. Its disappearance is almost as fast as a fireball. Night descends so suddenly it feels as though someone had switched off the light. Miniature oil lamps are lit in bright sunlight in readiness for the daily blackout, which invariably occurs at 5.50pm.

Every day, year round, it is hot, and body movement is hampered by this heat. People pace themselves to balance what the body can bear without dehydrating. The long evenings are also hot by European standards, but the edge is off the melting sensation and an almost constant breeze rolls in from the sea. Out of direct sunlight, the villages come alive. Night markets gather round myriad flickering oil lamps in home-made tins. It is in the evenings that the bakers bring out their best bread from their clay ovens and the day's catch is sold, bartered, shared and fried.

In the cities, people say that in rural Africa people go to bed at sundown and rise at dawn. That is a mere myth here: they do rise at dawn, but night-time is for drumming and traditional ceremonies, for gossip and courting, night markets, dancing and visiting. When eventually the chatter dies down, the drumming keeps going, with dozens of different beats and tempos. Some are accompanied by singing and chanting, while others are sombre or frenzied percussion solos.

The Macua language has dozens of words for drums. Four years after my first visit to Mossuril, I am still very much a novice in the field of identifying them. *Nlapa* is the generic term for a drum, but it can also be a small drum covered in lizardskin to be played by hand and never with a stick. Having taken my first step into drum identification, the rest became, and remains, endlessly confusing. So far, I have sifted out the following. A *soro* is a little drum. An *ettahura* is the biggest of all: it stands chest-high and has a diameter of approximately seventy centimetres. A *shapumpa* is a drum in a band. An *ekushasha* is one I have heard of but have yet to track down. A *kokhorona* is a big drum. An *ekhavette* is a big drum kept at the traditional leader's house and used only for boys' initiation ceremonies and the investiture of village leaders. A *mkwelo* is a bigger drum than an *ekhavette* but smaller than an *ettahura*.

What the rhythms and use of most of them are is still a mystery to me. The *khupura*, on the other hand, is barrel-shaped and covered with antelope-skin (*ntthapwe*) at either end and it is used for Tufu dancing all along the northern coast. The *mukhunha* has to be beaten by hand on one side and with a stick on the other. The *evijiya* is both a drum and a dance for wedding ceremonies. The *mirusi* is a drum and a dance. During the *mirusi*, the dancers become frenetic and shriek like banshees. The funereal *marilo* is more sedate. The *erika* is both a big drum beaten by women and a dance. It is used at girls' initiation ceremonies. Like the reverberating drum beats themselves, the list goes on and on and it will take me many more years to decipher. Their rhythms underline almost every moment of every day, and although each beat conveys meaning and triggers emotion, it does so in a language impenetrable to outsiders.

The village elders and drummers here know of all these drums, but Cabaceirians are too poor to own them. Mestre Canira is both village carpenter and the drum-maker. Bit by bit, the right woods and skins are gathered and tucked away, and one by one, as though by magic, new drums emerge to replace the simple wood frames covered with goatskin with which the village used to make do. With or without the right drums, the rhythms get played and handed down. In the absence of a big *khupura*, drummers beat crates, pots, jerry cans and old oil drums.

In May 2006, when a theatre group from distant Pemba came to play in our Culture House, I think almost as many people came to marvel at the visitors' collection of drums as came to see the performance. Since then, the drum-making here has increased.

There are key huts where the ceremonies take place. One of these is the *macuti* roof-maker's, between the college and

the shore. I lie awake at night and try to decipher the tom-
tom messages, but as with so many other things here, I can
only guess what they mean. Some of these nocturnal sessions are so wild and insistent that I ask around next day
what they were about. The answers always downplay: someone was sick, someone came of age.

'It is nothing. It is our *tradição*.'

It is our tradition. The message is clearer than the tom
toms: it is nothing for you to worry or know about and
everything to us.

I may be lost culturally, but I know what I am doing and why
I am here and I also know where I am. The latter is reassuring and not usually the case for me with my impaired sense
of direction. I know that the latitude is 15°, and the longi-
tude is 41°. I know this because it is in the name of the
lodge that the local builders will erect around the lagoon of
Varanda in 2006/2007. So few people seemed to know where
Mozambique was, let alone Cabaceira Pequena, that 15.41, its
map coordinates, were added by its developer to the name
Coral Lodge.

So I can be as precise as a cartographer or as vague as the
local villagers who know that Angoche is down the coast
and Mossuril and Nacala are up the coast. Naguema,
Monapo and Nampula are inland via the one and only car-
worthy dust road. Nampula is sixteen days' walk away from
the village for an old man and twelve days for a young one.
The spice island of Zanzibar, though farther away, is somehow more familiar. A handful of fishermen have been there
in their dhows. It is seven to ten days' sailing up the coast
and far away. The relatively frail dhows pull into shore each
night and passengers and crew sleep in makeshift foreign
moorings. The return voyage is against the wind and takes
anything from fourteen to twenty-eight days to complete.

Unaided by maps, a compass, any kind of engine, and with the most basic steering and a single sail, several dozen Ilhians and an intrepid handful of Cabaceirians have braved the voyage to see the one bit of the world they can see for free.

Paradoxically, once they arrive on Zanzibar (admittedly without the necessary documents to be there), many of them are so amazed by the sheer size of its port, cruisers, dhows, warehouses, container stacks and streets, that they stay hiding by their boat for their entire stay. The general opinion seems to be that there is too much '*confusão*' (confusion) over there. Once back home, since their attempts to describe what they have glimpsed 'over there' add a great deal more '*confusão*', and since many sailors also drown, such voyages are few and far between.

The rest of the world lies at unspecified and unimaginable distances from the comforting embrace of the shared ancestors. So, when pressed about it, Madagascar will be confirmed as being 'out there somewhere'. Madagascar is 'nearer than America or China' but none can say by how much. Bicycles and batteries, spades and big knives come from China, while America is very rich and Americans have red shiny faces and wear shorts.

When my son, Alex, first visited Mossuril in 2004, he explored the neighbourhood on the back of Morripa's motorbike. Assuming that Morripa had always lived in his compound, and impressed by his insight into human nature, Alex wondered how someone so wise would react to ideas from beyond the confines of his village. Tentatively, and tactfully, he began to probe what Morripa might know of the world beyond by inviting him one day to explore further afield, say to the province of Zambezia or the capital city, Maputo. Morripa removed his blue knitted golf cap, shook his shaven head and announced, 'My travelling days are over. What interests me now is to help my village travel into the twenty-first century without suffering too much on the way.'

There was a long pause and then Alex asked, 'But aren't you curious about what goes on beyond this village? I am going to China next year – you could visit me, you know, just to see.'

'Well, I'm curious to know what is happening in Africa, but not to travel any more.'

Alex told me that while he was trying to find the words to lure Morripa out, the other astounded him by adding, 'You see, I spent several years in Beira and travelled across almost the whole of Mozambique; and believe me, during the war, we got to see a lot of our fatherland close up because we had to crawl across it on our bellies. And when I first went to Russia and China, I was very excited but Russia is unspeakably cold and the Chinese are brutal. I can't recommend your going to China. They'll have you: get you into the army and that is where the brutality comes in.'

Alex covered his surprise and reassured him. 'I'm going to Beijing as a student.'

'That's what you think: it makes no difference. They'll get you marching before you have the chance to unpack your suitcase.'

Without giving him time to reply, Morripa mused on. 'Cuba was nice, though. Cuba was great. I lived there for a couple of years as a military trainer and had some good times; but it took me seventeen years to get home and now that I'm here, I'm staying."

In the ensuing conversation, Morripa described his life as a hostage negotiator and artillery trainer, and his escapades during the war, his tours of neighbouring African countries and his long and perilous trek home once the armed struggle finally ended in 1990.

After that, Alex and I were both curious as to who else, sitting on the stoops of their mud huts in the sleepy village, might have hidden knowledge of the world beyond. We steered talk towards foreign parts but found no more globetrotters. However, whereas most foreign countries other than China and Taiwan rang no bells with the general Cabaceirian public, Malawi was perceived by some as the place where cars are smuggled from and where spare parts can be bought for a song. Between the seven thousand local people, there are half a dozen motorbikes (of which four are connected to the college) and approximately thirty bicycles. With no public or private transport in or out of here, over half of the population has never left the confines of Mossuril District. For the majority of these, Mossuril town (eight kilometres away) with its tree-lined streets, electricity and government offices, is the farthest from home they have ever been.

Morripa's brother has a pick-up truck, another villager owns a lorry, Sr Falcão from Chocas has another, which chugs past the college a couple of times a week, and Mees has a Land Rover. This is just enough cars for everyone to know what cars are. Debates about the scarcity of spare parts tend to be heated and popular. And it was what generated most response to Alex's and my enquiries about what happens 'out there'. Some people knew people who had been to Malawi on the *convolho* (railway train) to Cuamba and then over the hills by road.

Conversation about Europe was more limited, but it was rumoured to be somewhere near Maputo. And Maputo, the capital far to the south, is a name, a place, and some people know someone who has been there or lived there. A few, like Adamji and the ferry captain, have family there. They do not aspire to visit Maputo because it is far away and they don't know exactly where it is. They would like to be able to telephone, and, eventually, for their family to come home. Most new students at the college know the name but don't know where it is other than that it is farther away than Nampula.

Maputo has been the capital since the end of the nineteenth century. Before that, since time immemorial, for at least a thousand years, the capital of Mozambique was Mozambique Island, or Ilha de Moçambique, as it is called in Portuguese; Omuhipiti in Macua. Ilha is only four kilometres away across the Mozambique Channel from the Cabaceiras, but the overland route takes well over an hour, driving along the bumpy dust road in a 4x4.

The overland way from the Cabaceiras to Ilha is via Chocas-Mar and Mossuril, Naguema and Lumbo. Door to door, it is 37 kilometres to Naguema and then back on to the tarmac road to Lumbo, a further 18 kilometres and finally just under 4 kilometres of the single-track road bridge. This has passing places where workmen are constantly repairing the precarious 1960s structure. I have met several engineers who assure me that if I could see under this bridge and see how it is falling apart, I would never cross it again. But I can't see under it, so I continue to cross it along with a few other cars from time to time. For well over a year now, a team of workmen have been laboriously restoring the rusting bridge. But from above, I cannot see what it is the workmen are shoring up.

On either side of the bridge road, clusters of local workmen in overalls nurse generators and winch sacks of cement and soldering equipment over the sides. The most noticeable part of the restoration is the oil drums that have been strategically placed on either side of the already narrow bridge to slow down traffic. They work the way dodgem cars do, and get about the same amount of beating. Meanwhile, no heavy vehicles are allowed on the bridge.

This includes coaches. South African and Tanzanian tours have taken to bringing groups of travellers to visit the island. I don't think they put it in their brochures that all passengers have to get out and walk the four kilometres of road bridge under burning sun, dodging cars like the locals.

Far as it is by road, straight ahead from Cabaceiras' beaches Ilha is visible day and night. When the tide is out, it is almost possible to walk the four kilometres to the island's nearest shore: almost but not quite because of the channel thirty metres deep full of sunken ships and lost souls. When the tide is low, we walk up to three of the four kilometres across the wet white sand to climb into the marooned boats and sail up to a small beach in front of the vast burgundy façade of the municipal museum. For local people there seems to be only one real capital, one real city, and it is the one on their own skyline. No government decree can detract from its grandeur or its history or reduce its popular status. Although via transistor radios, rare newspapers and rarer visitors there is sometimes talk of 'Maputo this' and 'in Maputo that', nothing that ever happens in Maputo is half as interesting to a Cabaceirian as the minutiae of what goes on in Ilha.

'Maputo,' Morripa tells me, 'isn't even its name. It was Lourenço Marques right up until 1976 when our then president, Samora Machel, changed its name to change its image.'

There is scorn in his voice for rival Maputo and a visible softening as he pronounces the former president's name, lingering fondly over consonants.

In the Cabaceiras, life does not revolve around Maputo's or any other name: it revolves around the tide, and around its own fishing fleet of a thousand dugout canoes and battered sailing dhows. It revolves around the market with its baskets of bread and manioc, mangoes (when they are in season) and little fist-size mounds of dried fish, onions or beans. Life revolves around the dilapidated mosques and the *al'mo*, the *curandeiro* and his or her magic powers, the leader or *regulo*, the *feticeiro*, the imam and the muezzin (who calls the faithful to prayer).

And then on high days and holidays and when needs must, there is the metropolis of Ilha, 'Omuhipiti', with its Stone City of restored and ruined palaces and its Macuti City of palm huts packed together in such an unsanitary jumble that it makes the randomly scattered Cabaceiras seem like models of hygiene and planning. Seventeen thousand people live in the Macuti and Stone Cities. Approximately 80 per cent of them are packed into the Macuti City, which teems with activity. Between the mud huts there are mud mosques, market stalls, carpenters, metalworkers, mechanics and shops. Despite its shambling decay, and perhaps in part because of it, it is an exciting city for tourists.

Like Zanzibar, its Tanzanian counterpart, Ilha is in some ways in a time warp. Unlike Zanzibar, though, Ilha is very small, and it is not just an island city but also a city island devoid of any hinterland. And unlike Zanzibar, 99 per cent of Ilha has been untouched by the addition of any modern architecture. Ironically, Ilha's historic buildings and ruins have been preserved by neglect, thereby making the place a must for anyone who loves old buildings. On the other hand, anyone unimpressed by grandiose architecture should give it a miss. Ilha is a living museum with UNESCO World Heritage status and a dire shortage of indoor plumbing and sanitation.

Within that mud-hut maze of Omuhipiti, every Cabaceirian can find a friendly face, a cousin or a former neighbour. But Omuhipiti is another world living at another pace. It is hectic and stressful compared to the peaceful mangroves on its opposite shore. The city has electricity and ice, cars and stereos, squares and streets, shops, televisions, policemen, and even a steady trickle of *Akunha* tourists. People wear shoes and have bank accounts and ATM cards; people have jobs and secondary education. The markets have proper stalls and different prices.

The social and economic distance is too great for most Cabaceirians to bridge on a regular basis. It costs thirty dollar-cents each way to take the packed ferry to Omuhipiti. That is more than most of the villagers can afford, so they content themselves with the very occasional visit and long nostalgic memories of past trips and boat adventures with wind and waves, whales and dolphins, storms and leaks. For me too, trips to Ilha are few and far between. Most of my time is spent in the Cabaceiras, squeezed between the bush and the sea. The villages are held together as though by laboriously mended fishing nets, their inhabitants living by the ancient lore and practices of the Macua.

VI

The Lure of Mozambique

THE MOON RISES TO A mysterious timetable in the mangrove. Some days, a silvery lunar ghost hovers in the afternoon sky. On other days there is no hint of a moon until nearly midnight. So the nights are either pitch dark or hooded by a sparkling canopy of charcoal taffeta flecked with gold. Over the endlessly sea-flooded land, over the mud huts, over the church and the mosque, over the bush and the beach and over the sea itself, moonbeams floodlight the speckled, glowing sky, highlighting falling stars.

Drums beat in the background muffled by ancient trees. A random natural firework of jagged lightning flashes up from the west, silhouetting a baobab, a kapok and a palm grove. It is a dry electric storm and it is the nearest most people in the village will come to Mr Edison's invention.

This land is a net through which stories are sifted from the drama and magic that wash through it day by day. Poetry is as unconscious and as natural as breathing. The mysterious vein it comes from is almost untapped. A great West-African bard said, 'When an old man dies (in Africa), a library is burnt down.'* That is how it is. Things are not written here: they (laws, stories, traditions) are remembered and handed on. As society changes, the generational chain of handing down is breaking. Although the rest of the country and the rest of the world have forgotten this African backwater, through isolation, it celebrates and remembers itself. For decades, the ancient local culture has been barely touched by outside influence. Modern Western values are virtually unknown, even modern medicine rarely encroaches on the traditional cures.

Every day, everyone here sets out with the same dual mission: to eat and to survive. Neither is easy to fulfil. Death lives in the village as an unknown man with no face who steals the hearts of the sick and dying. Some people sleep with a knife by their head when they are sick so that if the Grim Reaper comes for them in the night, they can fight him off.

Others say it is pointless to fight death: it is a predestined event and the shaman (the *al'mo*) knows to the minute and the day when each of us will die. The ceremony of burial and formal mourning lasts for forty days and ends with a celebration. Drums beat for the sick to chase evil spirits away. And drums beat for the dying and the dead and to remember the newly deceased. Hardly a day goes by when the drums are not beaten. The almost continual tom tom strikes me as remarkable but it passes for normal here. Ironically, the word 'normal' is the local Portuguese for 'good' when referring to a state of well-being or health. Every day, dozens of greetings follow the pattern of mutual enquiries into health with the almost statutory answer that I and everyone else are 'normal'. Only when someone is gravely ill or has actually died does this term change.

*A. Hampâté Bâ, *Amkoullel, L'Enfant Peul: 'Quand un vieillard meurt, c'est une bibliothèque qui brûle.'*

The landscape is lush thanks to the twice-yearly rains. From Naguema to Mossuril, most of the bush land is virgin (if a virgin, like a reformed criminal, can regain her former status after a given period of time). The land has not been used for over fifty years and trees, lianas, ferns, lilies and bamboo form a wild tangle beloved of brightly coloured birds.

Around Mossuril, then Chocas-Mar, and then Cabaceira Grande, mud huts speckle the landscape. They are dotted randomly in small mud clearings. The finished product is invariably a two-, three-, or four-roomed hut with a palm roof, two small front windows and a door. In some clearings, a new hut will be under construction, with an intricate double framework of bamboo holding coral stones in place prior to being faced inside and out with the local red mud. In other clearings, older properties sit in a state of collapse as the mud walls return to the earth they were dug from. The huts are unnumbered and unnamed and there are no streets as such. It takes a feat of memory to remember where this or that person lives.

Several times a week, washing is strung out to dry on a sisal line or draped over bushes. Even the laundry is decorative, consisting almost entirely of *capulanas* in bright clashing rectangles of bold patterns. While many of these are Swahili *kanga* inscribed with Kiswahili proverbs, such as '*Jipe moyo utashinda*/If you give your heart you will succeed', few locals could tell you what the writing means. A *capulana* is used as a skirt, dress, towel, sheet, shawl, cover, headdress, coat and almost everything else a piece of cloth can be used for. Even the babies' nappies are cut from worn-out *capulanas*. Women measure their status by the number of *capulanas* they have. Despite the heat, the local women wear two or three of these cloths over each other.

Some of the patterns, like the lurid green tulips on a

yellow and brown background ('Let words be brief and actions great'), do not reflect any sub-Saharan shapes, but many of the others are copies of the patterns found on shells and animals and the intricate weave of leaves in the jungle. The overall effect is always astonishingly bright. Every group of wayside stragglers, every market, every gathering or group of passengers swaying precariously on the back of a *chapas* (a truck or pickup offering communal transport) presents a striking picture. The use of colour is so unrestrained it pushes all concepts of compatibility of shade and tone into oblivion. A painter might strive for years to achieve such an effect and yet a child of five here knows intuitively and effortlessly how to pick out wild and wonderful colours and wrap herself in them. Alas, I have yet to acquire that knack. My attempts to dress in the local style result in my looking like a mad parrot. It is not something I do often, but for funerals and traditional ceremonies, for instance, I try to make the effort. If nothing else, it lifts the spirits of the workers here, particularly the women, who laugh till they double up each time I try to copy their grace and style.

A rose may be a rose, but to a gardener nowadays there are so many roses that the generic term is a poor description. Nor will 'a rose by any other name' necessarily smell as sweet. In fact, there are relatively few roses from among the numerous modern varieties that smell at all. So too the term 'mud hut' identifies a type of dwelling yet fails to take into account the seemingly endless permutations available within such an apparently tight parameter. There are different qualities of mud (*matope* in Portuguese and *mattophe* in Macua) and many different kinds of frame used to support it. Thatched roofs also vary not just from region to region but also from village to village. The various qualities of palm, straw and reeds, the thickness, arrangement, pattern, overall shape, binding and finishing are surprisingly complex. The mud huts of Mossuril that seem to have been thrown together are actually carefully crafted using traditional building methods handed down from mother to daughter. It is the women who build the mud huts here and the women who own them.

Almost every aspect of human behaviour is dealt with autonomously in the local villages. Universities and government departments, Western culture, thought and might, from Plato to Christianity, from Nelson Mandela to President Bush, seem scarcely to have touched anything but the surface of the way of life here. A few of the older men and women, and a few more of the children, can understand and speak Portuguese. Some villagers can also read and write in Portuguese, but it is not the lingua franca along this coast.

For as long as the oldest villagers can remember, the staple diet has been manioc and maize (both originally imported from South America) instead of the indigenous millet. Local markets also sell little sachets of flavouring: Jolly Jus for soft drinks, and Benny, chicken stock in a yellow sachet with a red hen on it; both are imported from or via the Arab Emirates. A typical kitchen is a small outside area of compacted mud where grain is pounded in a giant wooden pestle. Every household has such a pestle and a portable water container (or two or three), one or two saucepans, a knife and a plastic bowl. Food is cooked over a simple wood fire and eaten on the same rush mat that will later be used as a bed. All food is eaten with the fingers of the right hand only. (Woe betide he or she who blunders into the communal pot or plate with the left. Although no physical violence would follow, or even any verbal condemnation, *anyone* who eats with his or her left hand is deemed irrevocably disgusting.)

Sport-wise, the notion of football has arrived. Young men

who migrate to Nampula or Nacala cities in search of work bring home tales of football heroes. Football T-shirts are highly prized from among the charity bundles of clothes that flap for resale in Chocas-Mar's mini-market. The names of players and teams are bandied around the village by boys who have never seen a football game (be it on a pitch or a TV) outside of Mossuril District. Wherever they can, bored boys form clubs and challenge each other on bush-clearings and beaches. And whenever they can, barefoot younger boys kick home-made footballs around in the red dust with passionate flair.

Long before the Arabs arrived to trade and later colonize Mozambique Island, the Chinese were there bartering Chinese goods for gold and ivory. Through the centuries, a few Chinese families stayed, quietly trading. After Mozambique's independence from its Portuguese rulers in 1975, the People's Republic of China stepped into the breach. Ever since, the city markets have been flooded with cheap Chinese goods, some of which trickle down to rural areas. When he or she can afford it, a villager will buy a plastic Chinese torch with fat red and white Chinese batteries. In this land of foreshortened lifespans, the ridiculously short lifespan of such batteries is accepted with resignation. Batteries that die in under an hour are the only available ones. Such things are luxuries; light comes from other sources. It comes from the moon and the stars and from tiny oil lamps recycled from tin cans. Paraffin oil is sold from beer bottles in most markets. It is ladled out and the price is per ladleful. Although no one can recall when it happened, at some point this imported paraffin must have replaced the once locally obtainable whale blubber. The ingenious tin lamps are fashioned locally and yet, despite costing less than five dollar-cents each, few families own more than two of them, and most treasure a one and only miniature lamp. These paraffin lights burn and flicker like fireflies in the mud huts and the night markets.

Yet even imported goods such as paraffin and rubber (which filters into the village as thin strips, called *corda pneu*, cut from a used car tyre and prized by those who can afford it as ties for palm thatch) bring only a general sense of 'out there'. When pressed, a villager will explain that the rubber strips come from Jambeze, Namialo and sometimes Nampula, and paraffin comes from Mossuril, Ilha and Monapo.

'How does it get there?'

'By lorry from Nampula like everything else.'

Only Arabia really has a place in the local psyche. Arabia, where Arabs come from, where money first came from, where rich people live, where Islamic edicts (such as when Ramadan will end) are issued by radio, where there are endless fields of sand and whence dates are sent annually to the market on Ilha to sustain the faithful.

'Alham lililá.'*

The Arab colonization of the north-eastern coast of Mozambique, which started approximately a thousand years ago, has left indelible marks. Every village has a mosque; every graveyard has some crescent moons and sickles carved into its headstones; every village has an ethnic (Arab-Macua) mix. On the executive committee of each village, besides the African witchdoctor and chief, there will also be a local Koranic scholar. And up and down the coast, in mud huts, there are Koranic schools. In the absence of other schools beyond fourth-year elementary education, the latter are often the only place where children can truly become literate. And in a place devoid of libraries or bookshops, or newspapers, the Koran is often the only available

*Praise be to God.

book to study and read. Local men – be they dressed in
flowing Arab-style robes and embroidered skull caps (*kufia*)
or second-hand T-shirts, jeans and faded baseball caps
bought from the charity bundles that find their way into
every street market – always greet each other in Arabic.

'Salaam alaikum.'

'Alaikum salaam.'

Although Arab colonization has left its mark, the changes
wrought by contact with the West and by Portuguese colonization seem to have had much less impact. It almost looks
as though the Portuguese influence was limited to building
palaces, churches and villas and planting trees. The
landscape is full of semi-tended or abandoned cashew plantations sprinkled with giant mango trees and studded with
ruined Portuguese buildings. Buildings and trees alike
merely form a backdrop to the rural African life that takes
place in and around them. So the Portuguese ruins have
become like grandiose termite nests: they are not demol-
ished, nor are they used for anything, although sometimes a
mud hut will be built up against one. Mostly, they will be
left to the elements as ficus and mango, neem and cactus
grow over each ruin and cover it up.

There is a central government in Mozambique, and there
are strong provincial and district governments, but for the
everyday running of the village, not much trickles down
from Maputo or Nampula or Mossuril to hold the fabric of
these rural communities together. There is, on paper, a
Portuguese legacy of laws, rules and regulations.
Theoretically, every step of every day requires written and
stamped approval. But in a place without enough schools or
health posts, housing, water or transport even for government employees, the local (often illiterate) Macua-speaking
population lie beyond the system and the system is too anti-
quated and cumbersome to adapt and bring its lost members

into its fold. Numerous local people do not know what the laws of the country they live in are, nor do they speak or understand the official language of their own country, and some still do not have documents that officially make them members of that country.

It is not the constitution that provides certainties for many, particularly northern, Mozambicans. Certainties are provided by nature and by custom. The sea will fill and empty, the sun will rise and set, the muezzin will call to prayer five times a day, getting through the day will be hard, and if any help is needed, that help will only ever come from family and friends and the guidance of ancestors. And if the going really gets tough, the village chief, the *regulo*, will sort things out, with or without a little help from the *feticeiro*.

The Cabaceiras are small coastal villages ruled from within. The seat of power here, untouched by thousands of years of strife towards democracy elsewhere, is strikingly democratic. As in many other parts of rural Africa, democracy has been achieved by an alternative route which did not start its journey in Greece, nor pass through Rome, London, Paris or Washington, and owes nothing to Rousseau or Locke. Not only have African villages like the Cabaceiras evolved their own democracy (which is so integral to everyday life that it is taken for granted and seems to have no special name, nor to be the rallying point other nations make of their democracies), these same so-called 'backward' villages have a form of democracy that *works*, that truly represents its people, that gives the chance of equality to all members of the community, and pre-empted the notion of a welfare state by several centuries. Without all the razzmatazz of hustings and election campaigns, and the political fanaticism that has devastated the rest of the world for generations, the villagers here sit under a tree, discuss whatever problems they or the villages have and sort them out.

But for the blight of poverty, this could be a political utopia. As 'buts' go, it is a big one. It is a battering ram of a 'but'. It makes a mockery of the culture here, of the people, of their leaders, of their children and of so many of their hopes and dreams. Out of sheer greed, the West, in all its glory, imposed this poverty on these and thousands of villages like them. In a place where words were bonds and land was used but not owned, it was easy for Europeans to steal every piece of land in sight. Desmond Tutu summed it up when he said, 'When the missionaries came to Africa they had the Bible and we had the land. They said, "Let us pray." We closed our eyes. When we opened them we had the Bible and they had the land.' When the Cabaceirians opened their eyes, their land had been tied up via contracts written in Portuguese legalese.

It is impossible to visit any town in north Mozambique without noticing the presence of merchant Indians. Behind the till in almost every shop, the face you will see is Indian. In many African countries this is the case, but here in Mozambique the Indian diaspora dates back to the ninth century when Mozambique Island was, albeit briefly, under Indian rule. In the days when travel and trade were predominantly by sea, Ilha's strategic position on the main trade route to Goa and India lured numerous Indians not only to trade but to settle on the island. Although the overall power of the Indian settlers was later usurped by the more warlike Arabs, the Indian legacy remains to this day. The majority of not only shops but also businesses are owned by Indians. Only a handful of these are actually the descendants of the early settlers; their ranks have been swelled both by Indians from India and also by immigrants from Kenya, Uganda and Tanzania, to the point where the Mozambican-Indian population is a powerful social and economic force.

Particularly in the north, black Mozambicans tend to be poor and Indian Mozambicans tend to be wealthy. When the Portuguese rulers were expelled, they had forty-eight hours to leave and were allowed a maximum of five suitcases a piece. Thus they left behind them enormous quantities of goods and stock, selling what they could en masse in that brief time-frame. The only Mozambicans in a position to buy up such stock were the Indians, who stepped right into the breach, thereby enormously increasing the economic disparity between themselves and their black compatriots.

At a more general level, the Indian cultural legacy is widespread. Rajah curry powder is the most commonly used spice; Indian fabrics and patterns are sold on every market, together with the Tanzanian *kanga*. Local craftsmen carve Indian patterns into their Macua sculptures and local silversmiths along the entire northern coast craft Indian designs (which they believe to be Macua) in the filigree pendants and earrings, belts and necklaces they make. Although the extended Indian families tend to stick together and intermarry from within their group, over the centuries there has been enough Indian-African miscegenation to leave a noticeable ethnic mix. This is evident even in the Cabaceiras. Our mangrove guide, Ibraimo's wife, Sara, is a light-skinned, green-eyed Indian, whose wealthy Ilhan/Nampulese family renounced her for marrying him.

In this dramatic continent, the Cabaceiras are a dramatic setting in which the real world includes a world of spirits, and the mundane and the miraculous constantly interact. Evil spirits, *diavos*, hover in the mangrove and randomly possess passers-by. Once a *diavo* has installed itself in a host body, anything from visiting a hospital to eating a four-legged creature can activate it. Whenever an apparently insane person comes crashing and screaming through the palm groves, bystanders scarcely look up from whatever they are doing, despite the victim's screams and eventual convulsions. Each time I witness such an attack, I ask in alarm, 'What is it?'

Someone will shrug and say nonchalantly, '*Diavos*,' as though no further explanation could possibly be needed.

I am always left wondering if the victim is actually possessed, or if he or she just thinks so. With every muscle in spasm, is there a difference? No matter where in the world we are, we all seek certain truths, sift fact from fantasy, and attempt to define our lives.

When Antonio, the newest of the college guards, asked for an advance on his salary to pay the local witchdoctor to remove the giant stone that he claimed was weighing him down and racking his gut with pain, who could say if such an inner weight existed or not? Antonio had been to the hospital and taken a conventional treatment to no avail. As he insisted it would, the traditional ceremony cured him. How or why it worked remains a mystery. But Antonio is back at his job. He is one of the happiest of all the workers because the leap he has taken has been the biggest.

At the age of nine, as the son of poor parents on Ilha, he was sick and received an injection at the hospital. That injection accidentally paralysed both his legs. For the next eleven years, he hauled himself around on the ground, dragging his chest through the dust as he propelled his torso and withered legs with his hands. Despite his disability, he attended school and is fully literate, conversant in Portuguese and good at maths. In 1995, after the so-called civil war, the government gave him a wheelchair. When both his parents died, he was reduced to begging on the streets of Ilha. He spent most of every day in the bald square opposite the bank, catching people as they emerged from the palatial bank building with a little fresh cash in their pockets. Unlike most other beggars on Ilha, Antonio was always extremely polite and not in the least pushy. Attracted by his gentle charm, I would sometimes get into a conversation with him, which, one day, developed into a plan. Shortly afterwards, he and his wheelchair were carried onto a dhow to sail to Cabaceira Grande.

Working here at the college is his first ever job. I think, as much as the work and the sense of community, he is happy to have his own room, three meals a day, a place to wash, and to have left behind him the humiliation of having to beg to stay alive. He is a devout Muslim and quickly joined the faithful at the mosque that borders the college grounds. As a fully literate storeroom guard, he is extremely useful here and, because of his enforced immobility, he is also learning to help prepare capsules of medicinal herbs for the college pharmacy. His is a Cinderella story: it isn't so easy to make such a huge and immediate improvement in most of the local people's lives.

Socially, he has livened up the local chatting sessions. As a storyteller, he takes some beating. He had to perfect the art to captivate his audience and win them over from a distinct disadvantage. He already has a little circle of younger listeners (Antonio is thirty), who regard him with awe for being here at all. It is as though he had the power to fly, as though some powerful magic has stuck to him because overnight he has joined the privileged ranks of the live-in staff. From being a homeless beggar he has jumped to having sheets and blankets, a clothes basket, a lantern, a bristle toothbrush, his own towel and soap, and a chair. Few of the students have such things at home; their mud huts are bare. In their eyes, Antonio might be crippled but he has got what it takes; so they hover around him and listen to what he has to tell because maybe that way some of his luck will rub off on them.

An established hierarchy is strictly observed here. A carpenter's apprentice will never touch his master's tools other than to hand them to him on request. A builder's apprentice will never get to lay a brick or use a spatula: his job is to carry and watch. In all village disputes including personal domestic ones, the word of the *regulo* is law, together with the joint decision of the community committee. If the latter decides a man must walk 50 kilometres to get something for the village, then that man will walk. Each village is ruled by the fear of the shame of failing it. The pecking order is very complex and the rules of precedence so intricate that I have yet to master the half of them.

The hierarchy of those who toil at sea is easier to discern. Among the local fishermen, at the top are the lucky ones, the captains who have made (or more often, inherited) a sailing dhow. With stitched rice-bag sails and raw cotton caulking, and a coral rock tied to a rope as an anchor, they sail out farthest and catch the most fish in their endlessly mended nets. Someone has to bail out seawater every ten minutes or so with a baobab seed scoop or a severed jerry can, but even though their dhows are rudimentary and small (between ten and fourteen feet long), they are the sea lords of the Mozambique Channel.

Dhows have been built locally since before the Portuguese first came. Many captains today still, *vakháni vakháni*, build boats with the help of their sons. Sometimes a half-finished boat will sit for years outside a mud hut like a beached whale's ribcage, waiting for the cash that will enable it to be clothed in wood, or to buy a handful of precious nails. Though cash is scarce, the fish is abundant and extraordinarily varied, but to get to the bigger fish, fishermen have to get out to sea. The shallows are a nursery and the multi-coloured swarms are babies hiding in the mangroves. Most of the fish consumed locally are no bigger than goldfish.

I have yet to learn their names beyond the basic sword-fish, tuna, marlin, red snapper, stonefish, diminutive sardines, huge and hideous garopa, and the delicious and obliging parrotfish. The latter has big blue bones so bright even a child can fillet one on the plate. In fact, the rainbow-skinned parrot fish would be perfect if it didn't go off faster than any other. Mixed loops of small fishes beaded onto slivers of grass are the ones that get taken home, fried and eaten. Head, bones and all, the usual ration is one per person (as and when available). Given the tiny morsels of flesh on each, it is not surprising that it is always fried rather than grilled. Without these few drops of oil, people would suffer from severe muscle wastage, and the fish itself would shrink and dry on a grill.

Next in the fishermen's hierarchy come the dhow captains' close families, who can join in the daily fishing excursions. Next are the owners of dugout canoes. There are over a thousand of them on this bit of coast. In each one, a single fisherman paddles across the waves. They fish in groups with a shared net, or singly with a simple hook on a stretch of nylon, or a spear or a bow and arrow. What they fish with depends more on what they have than choice. When the shoals are far out (as is often the case), intrepid paddlers can be seen bobbing and bouncing on the waves by the coral reef. Since the majority of fishermen have no boats at all, hundreds of them wade out from the shore and dive with a mask and spear or a mask and pointed stick. Some of these divers are said to transform into sea creatures, which magical power gives them a social cachet.

Dozens more fishermen work in groups, swimming out with a net which they spread and then close between them.

Lower down the scale are the waders. Some of these own the same killing tools as their neighbours higher up the scale but can neither swim nor dive and are thus forced to stay in the shallows. Among this lowly group are some men who have irretrievably lost their boats. Having climbed up the economic ladder, the loss of a boat inevitably plunges the owner and crew back to the bottom rung. Women are permanently placed on the lowest rung because it is taboo for women to go out to sea. They are skilled at gathering shellfish. There are numerous varieties, but they specialize in collecting translucent pointed cones and scooping out their inhabitants. Behind the women are trails of discarded cone shells. Up-ended, the sharp points of these stick out of the mangrove bed like waiting daggers and account for many a wounded foot. Grubbing around among these cones, at the very bottom of the scale, are flocks of half-naked children who paddle over the beaches collecting what everyone else has left.

On most of the days when the villagers eat well, it is a sad day for their economy because it means a catch has not found a buyer on Ilha and the fisherman is consuming his stock. A lack of boats and sails, nets and lines, hooks and masks forces most of the fishermen to take it in turns to fish. A hook costs only a few dollar-cents, but it has to be bought on Ilha on a good day, or in Nampula, 230 kilometres away. Either way, hooks cost money and the cost of the trip makes even a fishing hook yet another luxury item.

It is difficult to describe just how hard it is to get around here; how bad the roads are, and how few roads there are in the first place. Chocas-Mar is a mere six-kilometre walk away from the Cabaceiras, but that relatively short distance is like an uncrossable bridge. On one side, Chocas-Mar is firmly rooted in the twentieth century (and creeping towards the twenty-first), while on the other side, the

Cabaceiras are many decades (and in some aspects, centuries) behind in their economic development. Here at the college, everyone knows that six-kilometre divide too well. We have all walked it so many times, stumbling back at night, bumping into trees and falling into holes. It is hard *not* to be out at night, when darkness falls before six o'clock each day.

Thousands of African villages still subsist in poverty as they have done for centuries. This is not the case in Mossuril District, where much of the real poverty has set in over the past fifty years. Before that, for centuries, this was a place where industrious villagers could thrive. The now mostly barren land was farmed, the abandoned cashew and palm plantations were in full production, markets were full, shops and boarding houses abounded and local industry included a soap and several palm-oil factories. There were schools and hospitals, and substantial wealth in circulation.

With a national average life expectancy of little over forty, there are not many survivors who can remember how it used to be when Cabaceira Grande was a grand little town overlooking the country's former capital on Mozambique island. More local people can remember the last years of the harsh rule of their Portuguese colonizers and the confusing war years that followed.

Some can remember when a lion walked past the gates of what is now the college every day at sunset. Some can remember that the Cabaceiras were full of donkeys until, over the years, the beasts were eaten and their burdens transferred. Everyone knows fragments of their community's past and none knows why the current tide of poverty has seeped into their village, encircled every mud hut and then failed to ebb away.

The baobab tree (*Adansonia digitata*, or *mlapa* in Macua), which is sacred all over East Africa, is said to grow for up to 3,000 years. It is taboo to cut or damage a baobab. The most important village meetings take place under its shade. All there is to know about this place must have been discussed beside a baobab. Beloved by elephants, perhaps, like the elephant, a baobab never forgets. But despite playing an integral part in the *tradição*, harbouring ancestral spirits and advising the village chiefs, baobabs don't talk to foreigners.

PART TWO

VII

How I Found Mees or How He Found Me

ONE OF THE ASPECTS OF African society that I most admire is the intense support, both moral and physical, that family members extend to each other. My own family has been fragmented for three generations. It has enough steps in it to build a staircase. We are a host of stepbrothers and stepsisters, stepmothers and stepfathers, step-aunts and step-grandparents, and there is little love lost between so many of the various branches as to render reunions well nigh impossible. Since my mother died in 1980, I have sometimes felt like a tropical bud-graft that didn't take on a northern tree. I only really feel I belong when I am with my children.

Despite this, I have always yearned for a relationship in which I could be myself and not have to pretend to fit into a society that is, in many ways, alien to my nature. And I have longed *not* to be the eternal support, but instead to find a partner who is equally supportive. Ironically, I only encountered such a helpmeet when I finally gave up searching for one. And also ironically (since I had previously scoured the globe's most exotic places in search of my Mr Right), I met him in Rotterdam. We first met while I was giving a TV interview about my debut into the world of film development, with Amsterdam as my unlikely base.

I discovered later that Mr Right's being there that evening was sheer luck. The interviewer was a friend of his who had asked him to step in and film at short notice. Mees had more or less given up filming and had turned his hand to eco-tourism instead. After the interview, he gave me his card and asked if we could meet up some time in Amsterdam to discuss a number of documentary projects he had in mind. It was months before that happened, but eventually it did and Mees van Deth and I became friends and colleagues.

Long before any romance entered our equation, we worked together (when our busy respective timetables allowed) to develop a documentary film about the northern coast of Mozambique. We named it *Out of the Woods in Mossuril*, and it was to be the pilot for a series of films on places that came into being through their connection with plants and trees. A second project was to be set in Peru and based on the quinine industry; a third and fourth would have followed the course of sugar to the Caribbean and then back to Europe, and would chart how the sugar boom tangentially caused the African slave trade.

We were both based in Holland. He is Dutch and was born and brought up in the TV city of Hilversum: the place where the Philips factory made the revolutionary original television sets. It is where Mr Philips placed the first ever TV reception tower, giving Hilversum the dubious honour of having unleashed TV on to the market, thereby changing the world for ever.

While I was developing movies and documentaries, Mees was making documentaries and developing tourism in the Cabaceiras. In 2002, he asked me to go out with him and help conduct a location scout there for our pilot documentary. But the time was not right, I could not justify the cost, and I let that chance go. Some months later, when he returned and we met for a coffee, he showed me hundreds of photos taken on his trip. I remember feeling quite sick with regret at the sight of them.

I could have gone and visited that idyllic place. I could have had a safe adventure, travelling in the company of a guide who had travelled so much and seen so much in his previous thirty years as a behind-the-news cameraman that my own life looks tame by comparison. Instead of searching for likely subjects and footage from an office in Amsterdam, I could have gone and found all the material I could possibly desire out there on the edge of the Indian Ocean.

Mees was pressed for time that day and had to move on to another appointment. He gathered back his photos and I made him promise to invite me again on his next trip. I also asked him to give me a photo of Varanda: the peninsula with its mangroves and lagoon that he was buying on the northern coast of Mozambique. Back in my office, fired by all the new images of Mossuril, which arrived digitally the next day, our documentary began to take shape, and Mees also began to occupy my thoughts, independently of his camera.

Over the following year, I extracted the following about him. And 'extracted' is the operative word, because it was like pulling teeth. After three decades of filming all the most horrible things that one man can do to another and that the elements can do to man, Mees was on horror overload. He had taken a decision some years before to give up filming wars and earthquakes and civil strife in favour of doing something gentle and positive. He wanted to live in harmony with nature in a place where people were kind to each other. He wanted to build and run a lodge that would also benefit local people and give them the chance of a better life. He had been developing an eco-project in the north of Holland but couldn't quite abandon his own life-long dream of settling in Africa.

His yearning for Africa was a non-specific nostalgia and his wanting to build a barefoot luxury lodge somewhere in the southern part of that continent was a fantasy without any location. What made that vague wish a reality was finding Cabaceira Pequena. Finding it at all, regardless of any ulterior motive, was, if not a miracle, at least a chain of lucky coincidences because foreign investors can't exactly stumble on the Cabaceiras and no film-maker had ever been that way before.

Part of his long experience as a cameraman was filming the Dutch government's official tours. It was thanks to such a tour that he first travelled in Mozambique. The Netherlands is one of the biggest foreign-aid donors here and in 1999, the then Dutch Minister of Foreign Development, Eveline Herfkens, made the first official Dutch visit to Mozambique to see how all the money was being spent and to assess where future funds should go. She and her entourage toured the country in the presidential plane. Mees was the official cameraman for the entire tour. Thus he got to see a great deal of Mozambique in a short time and he realized that he liked it more than any of the many other African countries he had visited before.

When they visited the northern beaches, he was so struck by both their beauty and potential that he decided then and there to up sticks and move. I know very little about the three decades he spent filming, but in a rare expansive mood, he once told me this story.

We were travelling around Angoche in the minister's convoy, and then we stopped for a few minutes to observe the view. When it was time to pile back into the cars, I didn't want to leave, not then and not ever. I didn't want to have to move from that coast to finish filming the tour or for anything else. I was

really tempted just to give up everything else and
stay on.

I've been filming since I was sixteen and I have
never let any network down, never been late or
absent when called to rush out to this or that disaster.
Nor have I ever left an assignment midway, no
matter how difficult, inane or untenable it turned out
to be.

'We need someone to go to Liberia and interview
Charles Taylor. What is he really like? It seems no
one can get to him.'

'We need someone to go to Peru and film the
Shining Path's army in action for a couple of weeks.
There are a lot of reports of arbitrary atrocities and
they are not letting the press in.'

'We need someone in Lebanon tonight.'

'We need someone to get into the heart of the
earthquake/flood/fire/war/epidemic/zone.'

For thirty-one years, I was that someone. I was
lucky day after day and week after week. It seemed
that the last several journalists who had tried to
interview Charles Taylor hadn't been able to get to
him because they were shot in the lift on their way
up to his palatial chamber. A trigger-happy guard
explained this to me as he waited for authorization to
send me up in the same lift.

'You can go up, no problem,' the soldier explained.
'That is not the question. The question is: To which
floor? Our Glorious Leader is on one floor; if you go
there maybe you will also come back down again. But
if my instruction is to send you to the *third* floor, for
example, like that other journalist person last week,
then open the door and: Bingo! They shoot you.
Right there in the lift.'

Further conversation was halted while the candid soldier worked off, and then stifled, his laughter. Although he obviously found the mere thought of the third floor hilarious, I didn't and nor did my crew. As a result, I found myself alone in the sinister lift. Maybe I only imagined it smelled of blood and spilled brains. It was a slow lift and, to add to the fun, the guard had not said which floor I was assigned to. As I ascended towards the mad dictator, braced for a hail of bullets as soon as the door opened, I questioned not just the validity of my quest but also of my being. No one needed to risk their life to tell the public that Charles Taylor is insane. I knew it when I went out to Liberia, I knew it when I made the appointment, and I knew it when I went up in that lift.

As a personal experience it wasn't a waste, though, because it made me stop and think. The Liberian guard understood something about life which I hadn't: we can all go up but the question is to which floor? That was the point and I wanted my life to have a point. I wanted to know which floor in advance, get there myself and pull a few hundred other people up there to safety. I made myself a promise not to take pointless risks again, but instead to do something worthwhile that could bring pleasure and not pain into the world.

Making things happen out here in the north of Mozambique is a dream that Mees embraced long before I could even pinpoint the place on a map. I am a groupie here, delighting in the achievements and findings of others. And because in so many ways I am following other people's plans, the things I do and the way I spend my time are a leap away from the way I lived before.

As a perpetual traveller who has spent my entire adult life avoiding tourists and pretending not to be one, it is ironic that I have become not only a tourism consultant, but also the idea person behind a college of tourism. Anyone who travels in another country in their own time or in search of their own pleasure is, technically, a tourist. For three decades of world travelling, whether I like the label or not, I was also a tourist.

The list of things I don't like about places I visit is enormous and comprises dozens of petty details as well as broader issues. A place that has no tourism, which had no tourism in the past, and which not only wanted but needed tourism in the future, is a tempting blank piece of paper on which to write a new page excluding all the small horrors and errors of other destinations. When I think of all the places I have visited where I have thought how wonderful or more wonderful they would have been ten or twenty or fifty years before, and how I yearned to have known them then, I realize that the pioneer aspect of Mozambique is one that I find endlessly pleasing. It is a great luxury to walk along paths – be they submarine or in the bush – and to know that no tourist walked this way before. No *Akunha* knows this or that place and this or that beach. Even my own confusion about which race I belong to has been unanimously settled here: I am an *Akunha*. My mixed-race status that stands me in good stead elsewhere in the Third World, and which elicits unspoken suspicion and occasional disdain in Europe, counts for nothing here. Foreigners start at Chocas-Mar.

On the upside, whereas anywhere else in Africa I would be doomed to be a perpetual outsider, the Macua are a vast ethnic group with no qualms about welcoming outsiders and foreigners of every race and colour into their midst. Why this should be so was explained to me in Maputo by a scholar called Dr Couto, who grew up in Nampula and knows a great deal about the heartland of the Macua. He told me:

Most African ethnic groups are relatively small and have had to be protective of their bloodlines to preserve their culture. This made all outsiders, no matter what their intentions, a threat. The Macua, on the other hand, are nine million strong. Six million of these are in Mozambique, predominantly in the north, the other three million are scattered across South Africa, Tanzania, Malawi and Botswana.

With a group that size, it would take a lot of foreigners to water down the race or encroach on its culture. Thus, traditionally the Macua have never feared extinction by outsiders. They are not threatened by foreigners, who can marry freely into their villages. If you are not born an Ashanti or Zulu, Yao, Massai, Ngoni, Chewa or Makonde, you cannot become one. But a woman born in London like yourself can become a Macua if a chief initiates you into his village.

Traditionally, there was no higher authority than the village, so each village was like a small kingdom ruled by its *regulo*. Before our independence, Mozambique was never truly united. In places, you can still feel a society trying to find itself. Up north, the social customs are very strongly ingrained. There is no identity crisis among the Macua.

You feel the difference when you are up north. Foreigners are welcome. It isn't put on, it is genuine. Traditionally, foreigners brought news and goods to trade.

I do feel the difference. I felt it immediately I arrived. People stare at me and my family, at Mees and our occasional visitors, with wonder but not suspicion. There is intense curiosity but no feeling of aggression. I would not walk around at night anywhere else in the world as I do here in the Cabaceiras.

For those who fight against hunger, win or lose, there is no shame attached. These are villages that have retained those old-fashioned concepts of honour and dignity. Malice has found no place to take root. Particularly in rural communities all over the world, travellers discover 'the salt of the earth', which just goes to show that even in this corrupt and corrupted planet on which we live, integrity can prevail everywhere. Like a fragment of beautiful old Chinese porcelain washed up by the sea after centuries of lying on its bed, I have found a lovely tessera: a piece of life's mosaic. It is a small remnant from the past, a memory of simpler times. It is my floor, the level at which I want to get out of the lift and stay. I am trying to rise to it. And despite being 'topographically challenged' (as my best friend, Otto, would say), I know where I am going.

The place isn't Shangri-La by any means, but the bad things people did to each other in the so-called civil war didn't happen here. And the bad things done to the native people by their Portuguese overlords in the ten years' war of independence that preceded it didn't happen here either. Bad things happened nearby: they happened less than fifteen kilometres away, but here there is little difference between fifteen kilometres and fifteen hundred, because both are 'out there', out of bounds and happening in the parallel world to which Cabaceirians tend to have no access.

Without a foothold in the economy 'out there' and with such limited access to the outside world, life is an endless barter. Money rarely enters the villages and thus cannot keep changing hands. Fish is bartered for coconuts, salt and palm leaves, favours are bartered for favours, time is bartered for basic materials, as everyone competes to complete the loop, to shore up the protective circle. Help is taken and given freely, compassion is an essential component of daily life, solidarity and generosity are innate. Without them, the community could not survive here in such poverty and isolation. Each and every Cabaceirian must have a passion for life in order to survive. And the quality of all these things is undiluted and unstrained.

VIII

Pioneering in Mossuril

THE NATURAL ENVIRONMENT OF Mossuril is unspoiled. It can boast over 3,000 square kilometres of virgin coast, wild inland woods and seemingly endless semi-abandoned cashew and palm plantations. Devoid of any industry, it is peppered sporadically with mud huts which, from time to time, fold back gracefully into the red earth that made them. The inland vegetation is lush, the climate is good, the native population is unusually friendly, crime is minimal and the vast majority of the population is unemployed.

Part of Mees's long-running dream to build a chain of barefoot luxury lodges in Africa is to exclude all his own complaints from thirty-one years of living almost continually in hotels and eating almost continually in restaurants. He is, without a doubt, the fussiest person I have ever met regarding what a hotel room or a restaurant needs to be just right. He is also passionate about ecology and eco-building and traditional building methods.

As a child and then as a teenage bride, I fantasized about running away to Norway and I daydreamed of pine forests and fjords, thereby gleaning an enormous amount of pleasure from a place I have still never been to. After Norway, no one place ever monopolized my daydreams again until I began to focus on Mozambique. I love travelling, and I love to flirt with places. To the intense annoyance of some of my partners, I enjoy 'armchair travelling' almost as much as the real thing. So I plan endless trips I will never take and then make other trips on impulse without much caring *where* I am going so long as I am going somewhere. My love affair with Africa had shifted from armchair to aeroplane and encompassed much of West Africa long before I met Mees, and yet I was obsessed by the idea of Mossuril for many months before I actually went there. I became infatuated with the place. As with any new love, I found ways to bring its name into conversation and to talk about it (from a standpoint of extreme ignorance) at every opportunity. When Mees went back there in 2003 to complete his purchase of the Varanda Nature Reserve, I was more than ready to join him, although my overt reason was to do a location scout for the documentary/travel project I had been developing sight unseen.

Because of such intense anticipation, I was not surprised when my own reaction to Mossuril was as immediate and overwhelming as Mees's had been: I didn't want to leave it, and I knew that I would return soon and begin to shape my life to incorporate living somewhere on its calm lackadaisical coast. For all that, my first visit wasn't particularly calm because it was packed with things to do and people to see. Gathering information for my Mozambican documentary, I interviewed several local dignitaries, including Sr David Joel, the then District Administrator. Word travels fast in a small world and he had heard that I was a writer. As such, he begged me to help bring schools to his area. I told him, as gently as I could, that I wrote books and developed films but I didn't do schools. One day, far in the future, I might be able to help with a library, but schools were another

matter. He laughed in obvious disbelief and asked me to
think about it. His parting shot was to tell me: 'There are
over seven thousand people there and not a job between
them. I am afraid what will happen to this nice area when
all the children you see now grow up and have nothing to
do. That is a dangerous scenario. I think you could do
something about it.'

Back in Holland, his request weighed on me. I was
already working fifteen hours a day seven days a week on
my other pursuits and I knew nothing about schools. In fact,
the very word 'school' still gave me the shudders. Having to
attend parents' meetings at my children's schools had always
felt like torture. I had hated school for 90 per cent of the
time when I was obliged to attend one, and I had gone to
great lengths to escape the daily classroom ordeal. Yet the
District Administrator's plea continued to prey on my mind.

I did some nocturnal research into existing charities and
aid developers and compiled a vast list of aid organizations
working in East Africa. Then I wrote a tremendous number
of letters, bringing the plight of the Cabaceiras to their
attention. Only five of the fifteen hundred letters I wrote
got a reply and only one (from the then CEO of the
Millennium Challenge) gave any concrete assistance (in the
form of advice) by introducing me to the head of Planning
and Finance in Maputo (Dr Couto, the erudite Macuist). It
seemed that no one wanted to or would help. Yet by writing all the letters (hundreds of which were actually just
copies of the same), I had found a cause I could not let go
of.

Describing to potential donors what could be done to
help, a plan had emerged which didn't actually look too
hard to execute. There were three ruined buildings that
could house three separate schools: primary, secondary and
a tourism college. All they needed was some pretty simple

restoration and each would be ready for use. It wouldn't even be particularly expensive since the buildings were massively built and still structurally sound (give or take the odd corner). If no one else would do something, Morripa, Mees, and I decided that we would do it ourselves.

Trying to sell the idea of helping Mossuril to the experts, I learnt as much about Mozambique as I could, the better to state its case. I confess that when Mees first broached it, I knew very little about the country except that it was opposite Madagascar and once had a guerrilla leader called Samora Machel, who grinned out of the bush in his camouflage fatigues with an incredibly alluring gap-toothed smile. I knew that this very short, vivacious leader became the president of liberated Mozambique and was subsequently assassinated in a plane crash.

Somewhere, in an archive, I knew there was documentary footage of Samora Machel's military campaign, fought by men and women, many of whose leaders were poets, short-story writers and essayists. Jean-Luc Godard had worked in Mozambique on a documentary project. Machel was one of the most filmed fighters in history. His was a literary government and after a long armed struggle, the writers and freedom fighters had beaten the CIA-backed South African Police Force. Other than that, I knew next to nothing about it, except that it was dirt poor and had suffered a calamitous flood.

On closer analysis, courtesy of the internet's limitless gush of statistics and reports, I saw how desperately poor Mozambique had become and what crippling damage its so-called civil war had caused. The invading opposition forces had systematically destroyed the infrastructure: schools, health centres, hospitals, roads, rail tracks and bridges, factories and warehouses. One and a half million Mozambicans died in that war, which is still called a 'civil war', but which was a country fighting outsiders to maintain its hard-won independence. The South African and Zimbabwean invaders left chaos and landmines in their wake.

Despite the enormous damage, and the military and civilian casualties, Mozambique was clawing its way back into economic growth. Seventy per cent dependent on foreign aid, it had a track record of good governance and a long-standing president, Joaquim Chissano, who had been one of the literary fighters and also the first prime minister to Samora Machel's presidency after the war. (In 2006, the 70 per cent dependence on foreign aid finally dropped to 50 per cent thanks in no small part to tourism booming in the south. The country is finally on the road to recovery.)

With a few rather notable exceptions, such as the murder of the journalist Carlos Cardoso, the country also seemed to be actively fighting corruption. Having travelled widely in West Africa where high-ranking government hands seem to be dipping into almost every public kitty, I thought this in itself was tantamount to a miracle, if true.

I gathered great mounds of information and sifted through them in my spare time. As usual, much of what I downloaded was contradictory, but a general picture of drastic underdevelopment emerged and I was able to devise a development project for the Cabaceiras that would try and address some of the contributory factors to its poverty. Morripa and the village committees had given me lists as long as my arm of all the things they and their children needed, which ranged from water to schools, jobs to food, a road to a football pitch. A couple of the projects, such as a sports field, were not essential to other elements of the list working, but most were so inter-related that it began to seem pointless to develop one without the other. The more I looked at what other development organizations were doing, the more I saw how each seemed to focus exclusively on one area without either cooperating or collaborating with another.

The most important goal was to make our plan work and to make its positive results lasting. We were a bit like pirates on the high seas or bandits in the woods. We were unorthodox and out of order (the latter according to many working in the field that stopped abruptly at Naguema and rarely ventured down the dirt road to Mossuril, thereby not touching the Cabaceiras). Some observers pronounced that we were rank amateurs and doomed to fail. One expert, who did take the trouble to visit, but with the sole purpose of sneering, announced, 'Your project will be a piss in the ocean. You have nothing except ideas.'

Putting aside his overt hostility and gratuitous rudeness during the remainder of his visit, his verdict was correct, albeit not how he had intended it. We are not trying to change the world; what we want is to show a tiny part of it how their world can change from within. To do so, what we most need are ideas.

Meanwhile, onlookers from Ilha and Nampula jeered that it would not be sustainable. The word 'sustainable' is not one used in normal daily conversation. Yet it has become the key word in the field of development endeavours. Hundreds of millions of dollars are spent on 'sustainable' projects. Hundreds of millions of dollars are lost and wasted as most of the projects, in the sub-Sahara at least, fail and are reclaimed by bush, dust or desert.

Between us, the villagers, Mees, Morripa and me, we came up with a strategy which reflected the needs of numerous different sectors of the villages plus the overall needs of the villages as a whole. Our plan is a bit like a novel: it has a beginning, a middle and an end; it has a cast of thousands. It is divided into self-contained chapters all of which link into a central story. It is a fairly cinematic novel with a classic Hollywood ending. It has been said that the essence of any film story is the following: 'Somebody wants something badly and is having trouble getting it.' We have so much of that essence here we could bottle and market it. We had our 'goodies' (the villagers) and 'baddies'. The underdogs unite and rise up to beat their cruel overlord. In this case, that overlord (the arch-baddie) is Poverty.

Because the plan grew from inside the village and is designed by the villagers themselves and their hereditary and elected leaders to give the local people what they need and want, it will not be rejected by them as foreign or alien intervention. There are actually some extra bits, like a nursery school, a public library and ornamental gardens, which are ones that I want, but the rest of the project comes from the grassroots, from listening to people like the Varanda workers, the village committees, fishermen and local students, as well as the local government officials in various sectors.

I used all of Mees's contacts, thereby speeding up my access to the corridors of power in Mozambique. And I was able to leapfrog a couple of years of hard slog by using all his research and plans to bring infrastructure to Coral Lodge. Where possible, I have milked my own network of eminent advisors and friends of friends to bring professionally informed advice to bear on each part of our plan. I have been very lucky in meeting experts from all over the world, and they have been very patient and generous in letting me pick their brains.

Morripa has had the benefit of many years abroad and thereby acts differently from, say, many other Mozambicans on the up. Having had to go through the transition himself, he is very aware of how gently his peers must be treated in order to guide them towards having confidence 'out there' in the world beyond the village, and also taking responsibility and initiative for and in the future. To find guides with both the patience and compassion to do this, he suggested bringing in new blood because 'with it could come compassion, a luxury not many Mozambicans found the time for'.

In an ideal world, we need experts here. The entire district is crying out for a medical doctor. There are nearly 200,000 people scattered over nearly 3,500 square kilometres without one. And we need tropical farmers, and people who can teach management skills. And we need English and nursery-school teachers, waiters, cooks, barmen and a football coach. We need a micro finance expert, a librarian, an herbalist, a computer wizard and many other specialists. But the world is far from ideal and we had none of the above as we prepared to start the college. However, we knew that we also needed international volunteers, and they, at least, would prove easier to find.

In the spring of 2004, I began to look for an existing organization with dedicated volunteers to join forces with the community college-to-be. The idea was to bring in groups of a dozen at a time with bursts of energy and enthusiasm to work side by side with Morripa and his team to groom small groups of local men and women for the jobs that Mees and his colleagues, and any other local hotel and restaurants-to-be, would later make available.

Meanwhile, Mees was busy daily with his hotel development, both in Holland and also in Mozambique. Any problems we encountered out in the bush proved minimal besides the endless bickering and nit-picking that went on between the development consortiums behind the scenes back in Holland. The battleground shifted several times as sordid corporate coups sometimes undermined both of our efforts. But we grew closer together by sharing the goal of making things happen in the Cabaceiras. Each time his business partners threatened to abandon the project, thereby breaking all the promises they had made to the village, we found ways to keep it going.

I had started to get involved on the help-the-village projects as a hobby, with a view to eventually and very gradually making them become my full-time work. Given the choice, I would have launched into them full time with my full energy at once, but I couldn't because I was still committed to running my film company.

For some months, I seemed to live in three entirely disparate camps: in one camp there were movies, documentaries and TV, another camp was entirely literary and the third was only for the 'sustainable development' of northern Mozambique. At first there seemed to be no link between them except for the original travel documentary, funding for which was proving hard to find. In fact, funding for all and any documentaries proved hard to find and movie finance wasn't exactly growing on trees.

I didn't enjoy fundraising in the business world and nor was I very good at it. I was, I suppose, better than some because I was able to raise the funds to start one of the only development companies in Europe with any money to spend and also to squeeze a few deals in the private sector for film finance. Selling films before they are made (which has to be done in order to make them) is a bit like selling the fabled emperor's new clothes without even providing the spectacle of the naked emperor.

Millions of dollars change hands on the promise of almost certain failure and the triumph of hope over experience that *your* movie will be the one in a hundred that makes a profit. Without the sheltering canopy of banks that bankers have, or established businesses that most businessmen have, without any bricks or mortar and with a dismal track record, movie-makers and producers go to market every day and still manage to sell their invisible and ephemeral 'product'. To do this requires enormous amounts of energy. So much so that the entire film world survives on a high. When it works (which is not very often), the artificially pumped adrenalin gushes into extraordinary activity.

Selling movie concepts requires endless analogy. A story that can 'green light' will tend to be described in terms of one particular movie meeting another. Sometimes the mind boggles at these comparisons, but the Money People like to hear that a new concept is not all new but really *China town* meets *Apocalypse Now*, or *Ocean's Eleven* meets *The Full Monty*.

I began to wonder what would happen if the energy and creativity of the film world could meet the lethargy and money of the development world. Then in the summer of 2004 I was invited to attend a conference at the end of the year in San Francisco. It was to be organized by the UNDP and it was all about Eradicating Poverty through Profit. The more I worked in the isolated camps of media and development, the more convinced I was that the solution for each lay in somehow merging them. I enrolled for the conference and dived back into work, corporate battles, scripts and schools.

In my office in Amsterdam, I was slowly designing a way not to change the world but to change one little bit of it. Somewhere within the equation of how it could be done, media and aid had to meet. While trying to puzzle out how this could be achieved, unfilmed but not unnoticed, a soap opera was playing out on both fronts.

IX

When Business and Pleasure Are One

BETWEEN THE INTERSTICES OF office politics, some of our projects in the fiction factory office in Amsterdam were slowly taking shape. Despite this, we were still a long way off from actually filming anything. Complex deals were stacked and crumbled and new investors were found and wooed, but, increasingly, no one investor seemed willing to finance an entire budget and to complete each deal we kept hitting the stumbling block of being too new – of not having a track record. So we had to choose one of our projects, make it and sell it in order to make various other bits of our financial jigsaws fall into place. Rather than waste any more time and energy trying to pre-sell as yet invisible products, we decided to auto-finance the first steps of a corporate calling-card.

Most of our projects depended on third parties to be able to start filming even a few minutes of footage. Despite this, by December 2003, we had managed to film some of the material we needed on a South African documentary about Don Mattera, the enigmatic and charismatic hero of Soweto. Several attempts were made to get to the next stage and add some African footage to the Dutch film, but there was no budget to do so. Both the director and the producer/ initiator were Dutch, while the subject and 99 per cent of the material were in South Africa.

Given his decades of struggle, I felt obliged not to let him down. Despite dearly wanting to get the Don Mattera documentary made, to get through financial red tape we had to show a track record and to get a track record we had to show a film. The one film we could make without having to mobilize outside forces was our first one: *Out of the Woods in Mossuril.* The copyright was mine, the script was mine, we could safari camp for free instead of having to pay for accommodation and we could crew a pilot documentary film using family and friends.

While private investors from the business world could be lured into finding the potential gains of feature films a sexy investment, virtually no one from inside or outside the media industry seemed interested in picking up the tab for the probable financial loss of a documentary. Even when the subject was a gift to the genre, it proved well nigh impossible to sell it. Maybe an established company could have done it, but our new Dutch one couldn't. This depressing conclusion has been drawn with hindsight. When we embarked on our Mozambican documentary it was with rose-tinted spectacles and the firm belief that the folders of fabulous documentary subjects that our keen Colombian office cleaner dusted down weekly would eventually be gobbled up gratefully in its wake.

Although this was not to be the case, I gained invaluable insights into Southern Africa via the intense effort to transpose some of Don Mattera's spirit onto film. While I regret not having succeeded, I don't regret any of the time or money spent trying to do so because Don Mattera is such a remarkable man. His Italian grandfather, Giuseppe, jumped ship in South Africa and married a Zulu woman, defying all the social rules of his day. Then, far from being punished for his audacity, he not only flaunted his black wife and mestizo children, but he also started the first bus company in Soweto and made himself a small fortune. His grandson, Don, was sent to a Catholic boarding school where he was beaten and humiliated in the time-honoured fashion of such colonial establishments. As a young teenager, Don joined a street gang and became a formidable fist and knife fighter. By the time he was eighteen he was the leader of the most feared gang in Soweto, where he was the kingpin of the 'kill or be killed' underbelly of that apartheid society.

During the anti-apartheid battles, Don Mattera was politicized. He became the Head of Explosives and worked closely with the ANC. For several years, if a bridge was blown or a railway track detonated, or a car bomb went off anywhere in South Africa, then Don Mattera had a hand in it, if only at an organizational level. As a gangster, he had survived on his wits and his forward planning. As a guerrilla leader, all his past experience kept him in good stead. He was arrested dozens of times, tortured and beaten and placed under house arrest, but he was too smart for the police to ever place him at the scene of any crime.

Meanwhile, he wrote; what had begun as a boyhood hobby became a way of life. He wrote about his own life and about his South African people. He wrote and recited poetry. He began to see that his ability to lead and to make things happen had to go further than it had before. When the battle was won, apartheid was officially ended, and his friend and colleague Nelson Mandela sat in power as the President of a new South Africa, Don Mattera decided to continue battling against evil and to keep fighting for what is good.

Unlike most of his fellow partisans, he refused to settle down. Unlike most of his fellow partisans, he was not a member of the ruling ANC party. He had been a communist for many years and stayed loyal to his party. In the new South Africa this was tantamount to economic suicide. A fraction of the country's wealth was being shared and opportunity was being given to blacks for the first time in the country's history. But both jobs and wealth were for ANC members only, and black ones at that.

Over ten years of new rule, some things changed. The world inside and outside South Africa had nothing but praise for the new regime. It became politically incorrect to breathe a word against the new rule. Don Mattera stands out as a lone figure of dissent. He monitors every step forwards and every step back. He complains that: 'Three per cent of the blacks here climbed up the wealth ladder and then pulled the ladder up after them.'

Although he is still friends with some of his former comrades, he has also made many enemies by being so outspoken and not toeing the party line. After decades of martyrdom on 'the long road to freedom', and a decade of freedom, not much has changed for millions of black and coloured South Africans.

'Coloureds today are too white to be black and too black to be white. They are worse off than they were under apartheid.'

Don Mattera is an internationally acclaimed writer and the winner of numerous South African and foreign honours and awards. He doesn't drive a fancy car or live in an exclusive villa in Johannesburg. He lives in the township where he grew up. He serves his people via over thirty community projects he has founded, such as the Westbury Project, where former drug-dealers, converted to the Good Cause by Don himself, donate their ill-gotten gains and use them to campaign in the streets to persuade kids to stop dealing and using drugs, and also to give food and job-training to the poorest of the poor. All Don's own money goes to support the thousands of people he helps. And not only can he *not* get any government support for his projects, some of them, like the Westbury Project, were under threat from the authorities by means of extortionate rent demands for the derelict buildings they use. Hopefully, the causes and the people he champions are now getting more support, but judging from my own last visit to him, that seems about as likely as World Peace spontaneously taking over from World Strife.

Back in 2003, our mini crew passed through South Africa en route to northern Mozambique to film the first part of our first documentary. We paused to try and tap a little money at source for our Don Mattera project, and then moved on with what was left of our equipment after a thorough mauling at the airport in Johannesburg between being offloaded and circling on the baggage carousel. With what became monotonous regularity, our various bags tended to get torn, bashed or slit open and semi-gutted unless we camouflaged them inside cheap and nasty plastic or canvas sacking many layers deep.

The trip was like a catalogue of Lost and Found. We lost equipment and endless time; we lost our second cameraman before we even arrived. We lost one of the main characters from our script, and we lost the possibility of recharging our equipment on location when the one and only generator gave up its ghost. So the operation became a test in ingenuity. With help from local assistants, Mees filmed while I presented. And Alex and Francesco, who should have been with us assisting on location, made relay trips across the Mozambique Channel laden with valuable equipment to recharge on Ilha. Alex's summer job as a runner for us involved more wading than running. Shouldering laptops, camera batteries, mobile phones and so on in a waterproof bag, he picked his way through the rivulet paths on the long beaches to a waiting dhow. Francesco, a native of Pesaro on the Adriatic coast, has the typical Italian obsession with immaculate clothes, perfect hair and designer luggage. He had never been anywhere in the Third World before, never been confronted by poverty, and he was quite simply horrified by what he saw. He did his utmost to conceal his distaste but I could see from his first day that he would never, through choice, become an Africa Hand.

Despite not being able to stick to our original schedule or even our script due to unexpected absence, loss, interruption and illness, we managed to bridge our gaps, rewrite and re-plan until we got enough footage to make a five- to ten-minute trailer comprising some of the key moments in the film. And in the list of what was Found, speaking only for myself here (although I know that the trip also had a profound effect on our whole group), that was the visit that turned my life on its head. Quite simply, things that I had thought mattered before suddenly became irrelevant and a new set of values filled my head. These values were not entirely new: they were things I had been peripherally aware of. Some were things I had savoured fleetingly and some were ones I had sought but never found.

Having spent so many years in search of a place where I could belong, I discovered the futility of that goal. If I felt like a perpetual outsider, it wasn't because I was in the wrong place, it was because I had cherished being different, and overrated myself to the point of withholding my spirit wherever I went. I looked at, felt for, observed and wrote about places and people all over the world, but I had never actually let myself go. Being in Mossuril released me from my self-imposed bonds.

On the long nights from early dusk until the moon rose

after 10pm, smothered in darkness, I sat on the dunes with the Indian Ocean breeze flittering around me, and savoured direct contact with life. For once, I didn't assess my thoughts or analyse my feelings (or lack of them), nor did I press memories to fill gaps, nor fantasize to fill time. And all the people I had pretended to be and all the lives I had pretended to live opened up enough for me to finally be myself.

It was a great relief not to need to try and excel in all things. In the past, although I had put myself down for certain failures, I never attributed much intrinsic worth to the things I lacked. If I lacked a certain quality, I persuaded myself that the missing link was not of much value and not having it was almost a merit. In all other fields I had, from my earliest childhood, felt obliged to excel. When I moved to Africa, it was exciting to accept myself with all my failings and move on to a much bigger world than I had known before. Enchanted by such new dimensions, I felt that from then on every second and every minute would count. Whatever was left of my life (and I hope that will be many decades more) would be lived out in this remote part of Africa among people wed to the land and the sea for richer or for poorer.

And money, 'that wonderful tester of human sentiments' without which 'we should perhaps never know how undear we are to our dear ones', would never rule my life again. Of course, I would need it to help give the villages a leg-up. But I could live so cheaply in the bush that I would need very little for myself and whatever I could raise would be in direct donations. I was not brought up in a typically English way, and when it comes to money, I realize I am more rural African at heart than London British. I want to share what I have and I want others to help. My big mistake for several years was thinking that a charity had to have an enormous cash kitty in order to get things done in Africa and in trying to raise the relevant mega funds. In fact, what are needed are enormous energy, enormous patience, good will and good helpers, and a very close relationship with the people being helped. Then, and maybe only then (with a very good plan and *some* money), things can happen.

Back in late 2003, I was still unaware that a shoestring budget could change the lives of thousands of people in a lasting way. So once the film work was done, my plan was to stay out in Mozambique for a week or two and see what could be done to tackle the poverty problems of Mossuril by seeking help from inside Mozambique. After only a few days in Maputo, the answer was quickly evident: all the vast budgets available to this or that government or foundation were allocated elsewhere. Mossuril wasn't on the current development maps and they were not scheduled to be pencilled in anywhere in the near future. It was as though the Cabaceiras didn't exist.

X

Home-made Tools and a Giant Learning Curve

AS L.P. HARTLEY OBSERVED, 'The past is a foreign country'. It seems now that my past is another world. I sort over it, sifting memories and translating them into this Mozambican harmony. 'Out there' in the big world that fills the villagers with such puzzlement and fear, my thoughts were scattered and my feelings diluted. Sometimes it feels as though I am being shown a glimpse of the essence of life. It is as though I have the chance to understand something without knowing what. I am a novice, an apprentice: I live on the edge of the earth absorbing age-old African rhythms, learning to actively channel the past into each new day.

While I feel my way in this foreign country, I spend much of my time as the amateur guide to ninety local men and women and their families, leading them into uncharted territory on that enormous map called sustainable development. 'Out there' are thousands of professional guides, many of whom still look on us as a bunch of losers. Morripa is my local guide. Together with his home front he has seen a way forward. Sometimes it is the blind leading the blind, but we always know where we are heading even though we don't always take the best path there.

For this particular journey, we have set ourselves a time
limit of three years (from September 2005). After that, the
results of our experiment must be visible to even the most
hardened sustainable developer. If I had stuck to our original plan for the college, we would have gradually restored
it over twelve to eighteen months and then opened it in
September 2005. Work began in late June 2004 with a team
of forty local builders headed by Morripa. There were ficus
trees growing through the walls and gutters, tearing out door
frames and buckling floors. The 55-metre veranda had a
30-metre-long hole in it and was missing nearly half its
monumental pillars. Whole sections of the roof were missing.
There were no doors or windows, no light or plumbing. Every
wall was covered in green and black slime where the coral
rock had sponged in the annual rains. Most of the ceilings
had caved in and the gardens were a shambles of overgrown
trees embedded in rubble. Yet within three weeks, what had
seemed like a mission impossible was starting to find back
its former graceful shape.

When I first saw the building, draped with purple
bougainvillea, I imagined it restored, and I felt sure that
most of the restoration it required was cosmetic, with only
minor structural work. I wandered around it a couple of
times in between and was struck more by its inherent grace
than its decay. Because it used to be a college, it had most
of the infrastructure a college needs in the way of rows of
loos and showers, kitchens and classrooms. I had bought and
overseen the restoration of several old buildings in Europe
and by casting my amateur eye over the *palaceu*, I persuaded
myself, like Basil Fawlty's cowboy builder, that all it really
needed was 'a lick o'paint'.

One week into the building process, I panicked and began
to realize that I had grossly underestimated the work it
would need. But when I saw how much the builders could

achieve in just three weeks, I was amazed and reassured. It would take time, but it could be done and they could do it. The carpenters and plasterers, builders and craftsmen were surprisingly skilled. They told me that since there was virtually no work in the Cabaceiras, they had all been obliged to move to Nampula and Ilha and they had honed their skills there. Many of them had returned specially to work on the palace – *o palaceu* – and they were very pleased to be back with their families and helping to give pride to their village by restoring a monument.

The atmosphere was exciting. A works kitchen provided vats of beans and rice, and trays of lurid Jolly Jus and bread were carried up and down ladders to combat the heat. During break-times, workers flopped on mats all over the rubble heaps chatting and laughing in Macua. Snakes and scorpions, bats and bees were the cause of hilarity. In the absence of proper tools, the craftsmen made ingenious copies out of scraps. Every morning at 7am sharp, the workers assembled and Morripa made a speech, fanning the sparks of a collective dream into a glowing fire. There is no Macua word for a college, so '*o colégio*' jumped out of every conversation. Some of the builders themselves enrolled as future students and many of their children were shoved through the gateway to have their names added to Morripa's list.

Most of the workers are barefoot. Since much can be learned from observing other people's feet, it was via patterns of scars and minor mutilations, calluses and damaged nails that I got to know about some of the workers. Another nice aspect of mangroves is that everyone's feet are scrupulously clean. The local ladders are made of tall saplings with round rungs nailed across with 5-inch nails. It takes three men to move the tallest ladder. Workmen climb up and down its 15-metre height carrying buckets of cement on their heads

while the ladder wobbles alarmingly. Together with dozens
of small striped squirrels, they run across the rafters and hot
roof tiles, shouting to each other in streams of 'Eeee' and
'Eye-oh' and '*Epa!*' The *mestres* (master craftsmen) keep
inviting me to join them on the roof but I have no head for
heights and cannot bring myself to tackle the trembling ladders. At lunch break, they try to tempt me with tales of how
ingeniously the roofs are made.

'They are works of art,' Mestre Canira tells me. 'There
are rainwater channels built over all the ceilings in a system
so intricate it is hard to believe.'

I cannot be tempted: I get dizzy standing on a chair, so I
explain that roof climbing is not for me. Morripa tries
another tack.

'The view from the roof is unbelievable: you can see all
the islands and all the ruined palaces for miles around.'

I wouldn't go up if the Taj Mahal were visible from the
roof. But the invitation to ascend becomes a daily taunt.
The dozen or so workmen on the roof all call down to the
grounded sissy while their once broken toes curl round tile
ridges. When work begins on it, there is more of a garden
growing through the remains of the roof than in any of the
courtyards. Wild flowers and grasses billow in the sea
breeze around clumps of wide-leaved ficus. Between the
portico and the veranda, clusters of acacia saplings make a
skyline of what, from a distance, look like television
aerials.

Several times a week, like migrating starlings, we gather
in the grounds and meet to discuss our future path. Many of
the workers want to enrol in the college-to-be but they
don't know what a college is or what it is to be. Morripa
and I try to explain that it will prepare people for paid jobs.
This has to be followed by explaining what a 'job' is and the
concept of a salary. The best way to do this is to refer to the

Varanda workers because they are the only local people with steady work and a monthly wage.

Anyone over the age of fifteen can enrol regardless of their current level of formal education. Almost all the recruits are worried by the thought of going back to school. All are aware of their severe lack of education and are nervous at the thought of being shown up in a classroom. This is a country where management by fear reigns. Requests are commanded, instructions are shouted and results are consistently derided and sneered at by the ruling class. Some of the workforce has travelled to Ilha, Nampula or Nacala for work and know how the system works. Their fear of authority 'out there' is ingrained: they were shouted at and beaten at school, shouted at and humiliated at work, shouted at and humiliated by most of the people they come into contact with from beyond the Cabaceiras. Some, like Sumaila, who was in the army, join the college expecting it to be like a boot camp; others, like Victorino and Marufo, join with no idea at all of what it will be, while a few join with a rough idea of what it can do and a longing to be able to do it. The oldest candidate was Muanema, a lady of fifty who didn't understand a word of Portuguese.

The sun beat down. Sacks of cement were relayed from Nampula and Monapo in trucks that charged as much to transport it as the cement itself cost. Giant bamboo canes arrived from Monapo and massive beams from Matibane. Boatloads of smaller timber arrived from Ilha. Morripa took delivery and wrote down each load, running the building site like a military operation. Day by day, he became more and more obsessed with *o colégio*, from the national flag that would have to fly in its front garden to the uniforms the students should wear.

In Johannesburg, a very nice girl called Pipi was gathering a group of volunteers together, vetting and selecting, briefing and equipping them to come out and start the college. In Zimbabwe, Ellie and Ramon had arrived; on standby to reach the college in September. In Kenya, Sieka was drawing up a curriculum and starting planning some of the other school projects. Sieka, the former director in Africa of AIESEC (an international work-exchange organization), would be the project director.

Everything was going well until in July something happened which to this day is a bit of a mystery. Some officials in Nampula (who had been helpful and supportive of the venture) got wind of a visit-to-be of the Minister of Tourism. For the first time ever, he would be visiting Mossuril District and, they said, 'It would be a wonderful thing for the village and the college if His Excellency the Minister were to open the college.' They explained that it would be a publicity coup and would give the college the official stamp of approval such a maverick venture needed to be well regarded in Mozambique.

By the time this came up, I was back in Holland but Mees was in Mozambique. He asked me what I thought and we asked the workers what they thought. The big question was: would it be possible to restore enough of the building in the five weeks left before the minister's visit? Morripa and the workers decided it would.

Morripa explained: 'There has never been such a visit to the Cabaceiras. We want it to take place. It is not only an honour: it is a reward for all our hard work. You are proud of the *palaceu*, but so are we. And it will be the excuse for an even bigger feast and there is nothing the workers like more than a party.'

Twenty-three more builders were hired and we decided to partially restore one wing and the façade.

From then on, everything began to be funnelled into preparation for the minister's visit. Our gentle start-up was becoming a bandwagon and several elements of the razza-matazz were slowly but surely slipping out of my and Morripa's grasp. With hindsight, we should have stuck to our own plan, invited the minister to see work in progress and gone for the down-scaled start-up we had first envis-aged. On the learning curve, we will try not to be roller-coastered again.

Good or bad, we did sort of get ready in time. The effort was much too great and sixty-three workers worked flat out day and night (by choice and with overtime). When anyone complains that the local people are lazy, I know for a fact it is not true. I have never seen anyone anywhere work harder than these builders did. As a result, there are sixty-three people who feel viscerally attached to the college. It is *their* handiwork and they are immensely proud of it. When their family members come to visit, they are given the tour, and the ups and downs, the bee and scorpion stories are retold with relish. Having seen the miracle of conversion from ruin and rubble to the palace as it is now, each of the builders believes in the rest of the dream and are very good rural campaigners converting doubtful neighbours to unite and join the leap forward.

Morripa planted a hybrid palm in the circular flowerbed opposite the pillared portico; Mees and I put two rows of flags on bamboo poles on either side of the path. The vil-lages cooked up enough food for six hundred people; the volunteers whitewashed the college walls and blew up a thousand white and gold balloons, and the workers put as many finishing touches as they could to the palace right up until five minutes before the Minister of Tourism arrived with a convoy of officials. We weren't ready by a long chalk. Ninety per cent of us had been up all night for three nights in a row and the workmen were all high on exhaustion. The chef from Nampula who was supposed to orchestrate the kitchen from the night before and present the banquet on the dot of noon, turned up drunk twenty minutes before it was all due to be served. Since he was also the purveyor of all the salads, fruit and vegetables, there was a lot of improvisation on the various recipes. Everyone, myself included, was covered in lime dust and paint so when the walkie-talkie message from the chief of police informed us that the visiting convoy had just left Chocas-Mar, there was an unseemly scramble to change into our party clothes. From the film taken on that day, I see that in the rush I forgot to shake the dust out of my hair, and I greeted the minister and guided him around with what looks like a powdered wig towering over my head. Fortunately, I was so relieved that we had managed to dismantle the scaffolding and get hold of four kilos of ice in time that I was unaware of my hair.

The party, which had been beset by logistical problems, was further tested by extensive protocol regulations (e.g. a visiting minister has to have ice tongs, and, of course, ice, whisky glasses, champagne glasses, and all sorts of things then unobtainable in the Province of Nampula). We could 'open' the college, but we could not 'inaugurate' it, so the red ribbon that had been tied round the pillars to be cut had to be hastily withdrawn. Little things like the brand new generator breaking down on the day and the third replacement water-pump seizing up didn't help. And when dozens of the gold balloons started bursting in the midday sun, each one sounding like a convincing gunshot, the minister's bodyguard and police escort became alarmed.

We had the required ice tongs and the ice bucket, the correct glasses and even a costly German dinner service for forty people. And in the open kitchen, the local cooks had performed miracles on half-a-dozen hapless goats and a pen of ducks and hens. On either side of the steps, Tufu dancers were singing the visiting minister's praises as he walked up the steps to the main entrance to claim the iced water that was his governmental right. The looks of tension on the faces of the college staff in the video taken that day reflect their knowledge that as the Big Man approached, behind them, three separate cars and a motorbike had headed off into the bush in four different directions in search of ice and not one of them had returned yet. Our joint mission was to delay the visitors for as long as possible on those steps to allow any of the four ice-searchers time to return. Hot-foot from Mossuril, the ice arrived at the moment the minister sat down and asked for a glass of iced water. The remainder of the official visit was easy from then on. Even the drunken chef staggering into the banqueting/assembly hall with a platter of three bananas as dessert for forty people didn't really matter. Everyone was so full of goat and fish, chicken and duck, coconut rice and manioc-leaf matapa, sweet potatoes and prawns that no one wanted the dessert anyway.

The college opened on 27 September 2004, and I left it three days later, basking in its recent glory. Mees stayed on for five weeks and shoehorned it into existence. The really tough half-term was what came after he left. In February 2005, Mees returned to Mossuril for five weeks. Although he was not there to sort out the college, he stepped in and helped out a lot with the organizational work, setting up systems for all the staff and students to follow. Almost as importantly, he also got a team of gardeners going and the first vegetables were sown.

By the time I returned in the first week of May 2005, between them, Mees, Morripa and the pioneers had created something that worked and was there to stay. Having received horror stories of the monotonous diet from Mees and the staff alike, Lolly and I joined the college braced to suffer culinary torture. We took the precaution of bringing out several kilos of spices and dried herbs and two kilos of espresso coffee. Instead of the anticipated mono-diet of beans and rice, though, we were greeted by the miraculous presence of Sofia, the chef, and the equally miraculous growth of a vegetable garden with over fifteen varieties of crops.

Sofia's son, Tigo, arrived from Maputo as a volunteer teacher and stood out from his first moment by being nearly two metres tall and as thin as a stick painting of a Masai warrior. Despite being almost as much of an outsider in the eyes of the villagers as Ellie and Ramon, Tigo tunnelled into the heart of the village by making friends with his students and striding through the bush to visit them in their mud huts so often that he turned the wary stares of their neighbours into friendly greetings. On communal quests for cold drinks, on the six-kilometre walk each way, Tigo takes one step to everyone else's two. On moonless nights, when it is too dark to see where anyone else is on the path, I can always locate him far ahead by his intermittent 'Epa!', which he says as much to himself as anyone else.

At the college, he spends many hours a day practising playing his guitar on the front porch. This area has fitted stone seats that stay cool even during the hottest evenings, and it has wide stone steps down to the medicinal garden overlooking Morripa's hybrid palm. With its view both of the ruined governor's palace and a seashore clogged with mangroves as green and as rounded as a tree plantation, this is Tigo's domain.

Tigo is a 'city boy', as at home in Maputo as Johannesburg. The countryside is a new concept for him. Yet while he transforms fishermen into cooks and waiters and laundrymen, Nature has grabbed Tigo by the throat.

Together with Ramon and two of the students he discovered the joy of growing things. Baskets of fresh produce were taken to the kitchen daily, to the delight of the staff and the consternation of the students and workers, who kept getting (to them, unknown and inedible) things like beetroots and carrots, parsley and celery in their staple beans. When I tried to replace the lunchtime menu with a vegetable soup there was a hunger strike, but by gradual introduction, most of the other vegetables got eaten and even became popular. Students began to accuse the cooks of favouritism for dishing out more carrots to one than another and a handful of students began to ask for vegetables to take home.

We started the College of Tourism and Agriculture somewhat blithely based on the assumption that tourism was arriving in the area (which it was) and vegetables could grow there (which I, for one, did not know, but Morripa and his older colleagues assured me to be the case thanks to the Portuguese market gardens remembered from their childhoods). The success of our back-garden crops was a crucial step in taking everything forward to the stage when a commercial farm could pay for the upkeep of the college.

The founding fathers were all local builders and craftsmen and it was they who led the team of sixty-three peers who worked on the initial restoration of the college building. Having achieved almost the impossible and made the ruin habitable in a matter of only two months, they were intensely proud of their work. More than a job, it was a labour of love. They had all received a salary, but no money can induce a workman to work almost round the clock as they had in the last weeks before the opening. From then on, each one of the builders felt proprietorial towards not just the building but the project and every aspect of its running.

Scratching the surface of these villages unearths something akin to caved-in Etruscan catacombs in which entire pockets have been miraculously preserved. Despite the predominant illiteracy and the profound geographical ignorance of most of the villagers, some, like the *mestres* and a few of the market stall-keepers, and a handful of the older college students, know about some more general Mozambican issues from political meetings and seminars. And some of the villagers have family who have gone south and who return occasionally with fancy phones and proper shoes, wallets, shades and transistor radios. What is gleaned does not always fit together, but enough seeds of knowledge about 'out there' have germinated to convince a small group of local men and women that, contrary to the local popular belief, they can look beyond the here and now to the future. And by wanting it enough, that future can be better than the way things are today.

Fortunately for the college, it was people such as these, such as the Mestres Selimane, Aldi, Tauacal and Canira, Ancha Abacar, Marufo Ussene, and of course Morripa, who have inspired their friends and families to take up the challenge of 'bringing movement to the Cabaceiras'. Without the vision of that hard core of believers, there would be no college, and its building would still be a monumental sprawling ruin smothered on either side of the pillared portico on its façade by purple bougainvillea.

The future, in general terms, is a treacherous concept. The future is a thief. It will steal sons and daughters, parents and siblings. It is the enemy of longevity. When I was a child, because I went around looking very serious and miserable, complete strangers used to come up to me in the street and say, 'Cheer up. It may never happen.' Here, it is as though the same people had gone round canvassing before I arrived. Be it from near or far, strains of laughter abound, together with a profound belief that the future is something that only rich people have entry tickets for.

As the former hub of colonial life in the Cabaceiras, the college is steeped in history, and yet its history is a local mystery. From an Italian priest I know that the building was once a monastery or convent, but we do not, for instance, know which part of it was the chapel. And we know that it was a Portuguese naval academy, but no one yet has been able to describe how it then looked inside. Among the local people, only those who cleaned it or worked as stewards would have ever set foot inside it. In the olden days, no local man, woman or child was allowed past the mango tree that stands guard over the path some two hundred metres from the side entrance (to the middle courtyard). It was there by the mango tree that villagers could state their business. Because few Mozambicans live beyond their forties, there is little chance now of finding anyone who ever went inside the college in its naval days.

Beyond its high walls, though, market gardens flourished and these were seen and have been remembered by two generations of Cabaceirians.

XI

The Workings of a Heart

I SETTLED IN MOZAMBIQUE IN mid-2005. While I stay put, this book is a bit like a fishing boat bobbing about in a raging sea. It gets buffeted by passion, dragged and beaten by the tides. It keeps being washed up on strange shores far away from its proposed course; and then it sets sail again in search of new shoals, fresh supplies, rest, repairs and endless new adventures.

On my first visit to Mozambique, I was hooked. By my second trip I was in love both with the country and the man I was travelling with. Just as this emotional roller-coaster neared its peak, at the end of 2004, I was forced to slow down to accommodate a new and annoying heart condition. I was given the choice of cutting back on stress and giving up my long work hours or dropping dead.

Simultaneously, the company I was running suddenly had no budget and the only way to save it was by increasing my workload and restructuring it. While exploring that particularly dark tunnel, a doctor switched on a light and released me. It actually took me some to time to fully realize this. I had fantasized about being released from my office contract, but when my first chance came, I couldn't bear to abandon the fiction factory without a fight, so against doctors' orders, I tried to keep juggling all the company's projects while I found a way to delegate my work there.

Within a week, I was back in the special paramedic's ambulance and back to the same hospital in Amsterdam. It was only in the ambulance for the second time that I was able to let go of all the things I had been grasping for in the movie world. Literally, by the time my stretcher was carried into the Accident and Emergency ward, and a cardiologist came to my bedside, I had moved on and switched off.

Within minutes, my maladjusted heart began to more fully embrace Mozambique. The possibility of being able to live there full time had been on hold because of business commitments in Holland. But as I lay in the hospital watching the machine-that-goes-'bing' binging unhealthily, I moved to East Africa emotionally. When a second cardiologist tut-tutted about my pulse rate of forty-seven, the shock of suddenly being weak and vulnerable was already mixed with a surge of joy: now I could play truant from my office. When a third and then a fourth opinion confirmed that I must only do the things I enjoyed, it felt as though my prison sentence had been reduced for good behaviour. Which, in a way, makes having a non-fatal heart problem a bit like having a winning lottery ticket. Like a convict with three more years of hard labour still to serve, I was unexpectedly ushered out of my cell and shoved out of the prison gate.

Just a few weeks later, when the palace revolution within my company staged its final coup, the blow to me personally had lost its sting. For the next several months, from the outside, it may have looked as though I was there in Holland, but I wasn't. My heart and soul had moved to Mozambique, and within a few months I would follow them there.

Meanwhile, I transposed every sound into drum beats. In the hospital, I imagined drum taps in the clinking of medical instruments in a kidney bowl and in the slap and squeak of the nurses' shoes on polished floors. After being released, everything crept into Macua rhythms, from the thuds of crates being unloaded from trucks on the street, to the chug and hiss of passing trams.

Having been advised to take long regular walks to increase my sluggish pulse, I trudged through Amsterdam and finally got to know the city I had been living in for some years. During those wintry promenades, I became both closer to and farther away from it. Discovering its back streets and hidden places, a fondness for that small, noisy, sweet and stubborn city returned. Yet with each step, as my heart pounded, I recalled the drum beats of the Cabaceiras and looked forward to the many years ahead in which I could aspire to understanding what each rhythm meant and which drums are used for which ceremonies.

After a two-month frenzy of restoration during the summer of 2004, and after the opening day, and after I left, the restoration of the palace's fabric had stopped. Window frames that were half painted when the Minister of Tourism's convoy turned into our parking lot the previous September had stayed half painted. Doors that were missing then were still missing. Rooms that had been hurriedly painted and occupied like indoor camping sites were time-warped to that opening day: not a shelf or hook had been added, not a poster had been put up or a mat put down.

The struggle to survive had been too time-consuming to continue with any improvements. To all this there was one exception: the main kitchen, which had been a roofless ruin when I left, was well on its way to being a professional training kitchen by the time I returned. And the derelict storeroom beside it was finished. Mees had got a building team started under Morripa's guidance and left them to it. He had warned me not to expect much to have happened when I went out, so it was a welcome surprise to see how much work they had just got on with and done while we were both away.

Morripa and the master plasterers showed me around each shelf and ledge, pointing out the special design of the built-in grill and oven, the charcoal bin, the sink, the new gables and the roof frame. Despite their pride in the new kitchen, the workers were not happy: the college was not looking smart enough for all the hard work they had put in the previous year. I had promised them that we would make the building look splendid again, and yet apart from the kitchen it was not progressing. I apologized for my long absence and confirmed what they already knew about my recent battle with my recalcitrant heart and the months I had recently spent convalescing.

Several of the workmen asked me how long I was staying and what was the exact date of my return flight to Holland and then how long it would be before I came back again. Mestre Tauacal told me, 'A team is a team; and if someone leaves they leave it in the lurch. We liked it when we were all working together. And we think you should stay and . . .'

He looked at Morripa rather shyly. Some of the other workmen were also nodding to Morripa, as they do when they have met and discussed something and delegated him to forward their findings. I began to get a bit worried because they were all looking so anxious. I dreaded what he might have to say. Morripa cleared his throat as though to make a speech and then he blurted out, 'We all want to paint it yellow.'

'What?'

'Yellow.'

'Yes, but paint what yellow?'

'The *palaceu*, the college. In the olden days it was yellow and we want to paint it yellow again.'

'Great,' I said, much too enthusiastically for it to sound at all sincere and my voice took a sudden squeak.

Having feared the worst, e.g. that they were fed up with our learning curve and were leaving, or that the government had scheduled a new airport in the village and the college was standing on what had been designated as runway two, I started laughing. I have a nervous laugh that sometimes comes at the most inappropriate times. I laughed alone for a few seconds and was then joined by first one and then another of the workforce until the yellowness of the building and laughter itself become a joint focus of hilarity.

For several minutes we laughed our way back to their place at the top of the hierarchy in that strictly hierarchical place. Some students came to see what the big joke was about and then gave up, shaking their heads.

'Eeh! It's going to be yellow,' several workmen spluttered at once, pronouncing the yellow (*amarelho*) in a squeak similar to my own, thereby setting everyone off again.

The students stared, puzzled, and left. But outside, I could hear them retelling the scene and starting a second wave of laughter as a counterpoint to our own.

The college sits in three walled compounds. Its central compound is about eighty metres long and has buildings on three sides. The main wing is the oldest and was built at some time in the eighteenth century. Because the Portuguese left Mozambique in such haste in 1975, and because there were seventeen years of war after their departure, the historical documents and plans about a monument such as this college have disappeared from the national archives and (as yet) have not been tracked down anywhere in Portugal. Apart from the fact that the derelict palace building was a beautiful 'silent mansion' begging to be saved, it is also ideally suited to house a college because it used to be one. There are dormitories and bathroom blocks, kitchens and storerooms, a refectory (now used as the *Casa Cultura*/Cultural Centre) and numerous classrooms, a huge assembly hall and even a grand ballroom (now my office).

Despite its sorry state in 2004, 90 per cent of it was structurally sound. And last but not least, its walled gardens are protected from the salt-bearing winds and are perfect for growing herbs and vegetables and even delicate medicinal plants. Potentially, the palace has room to take two hundred non-residential students and some twenty to thirty residential staff. To have built somewhere like it from scratch would have cost a small fortune. Whereas by restoring the existing building, we have managed to keep our costs down *and* save a beautiful building for posterity. After so many centuries of oppression, there is also some poetic justice in the local villagers having their community college in what is undoubtedly one of the grandest buildings in the province.

When we first painted the building white, the painting turned out to be a huge effort in which everyone concerned joined in, from students to staff to volunteers and workers. The impression, midway, was good. The pockmarked, crumbling façade had lost its coating of green slime and the palace no longer looked abandoned. It took two coats of lime paint all over and then the main wings were ready in time for its opening on 27 September 2004. Yet after all the effort, the final result was disappointing. Mees and I didn't dare say anything at the time because everyone had worked so hard, but white didn't really suit the college. The sun is too bright and it produces a glare; the expanses of walls are vast and all the detail of pillars and cornices are lost in white. I sometimes thought that the beautiful *palaceu* had actually looked better in its ruined state. Yet the fact of the matter is that whatever I think about how its decoration should and shouldn't look, the building isn't mine, it's theirs: the villagers.

Luckily, in this case there had been a misunderstanding and both we and the villagers wanted the outside to be darker. Since there was a bit of extra cash in the building kitty, we went for their yellow, and where the palace's walls first stood out like a sore thumb, it now sits quite naturally among its palms.

One of the reasons I had been worried when Morripa approached me about repainting the college was that I knew there were tensions between the workers and various members of the college staff. On arrival I had felt the underlying tension, mixed with relief that I was back and grievances would be able to be aired. I had been away a long time: too long really for a project that was still locked largely inside my own head. The workers, in particular, had felt abandoned, and not understanding some of the actions of the volunteers, they had pulled back emotionally from the college they felt was theirs. Also, with virtually no funding, it had not been possible to keep buying materials for the restoration, thereby enforcing the lull in the main building work.

Pleading poverty in a poor African village doesn't really work: no one believes it. Westerners are all so rich compared to the local people that the idea of money running out is hard to grasp. Shoestring projects and vastly funded ones all seem the same. When money is not forthcoming, the general assumption is that one has *chosen* not to spend it, rather than imagine that a wealthy foreigner does not have the money to spend. And all foreigners *are* wealthy compared to all local people. A dead-broke backpacking student is wealthy compared to them. So I knew that the workers believed I had chosen to withhold materials for continuing to restore the main building, and they wanted to beautify their college.

The following week we bought a hundred kilograms of yellow pigment in Nacala and four local painters began the huge task of painting the college. The home-made scaffolding went up on the portico steps and vats of lime were soaked in water and mixed with yellow pigment, to be hoisted up and down from the painting platform in cut-off jerry cans.

We laughed about the paint and the pattern of our mirth was unusual because I started it. Yet every day, several times a day, the college rings and echoes with peals of laughter. All the workers and all the students manage to find subjects of intense mirth.

While the eighty-metre-long and ten-metre-high façade was undergoing its facelift, I embarked on the inside. Since there were bags and boxes of miscellaneous decorations and decorating materials in the storeroom, my own first job was to upgrade the interiors of all the rooms, be they bedrooms or classrooms, kitchens or halls. Lolly, with her teenage knowhow of styling, was the first to join my new campaign to beautify the college. As each room was upgraded, the students and the guards learnt how to paint skirting boards, how to hang curtains and pictures. Ramon and Tigo developed a flair for painting window frames. Tigo turned out to be the only one of us tall enough, with the help of a table to stand on, to reach the top arch of each window and finish off each job. As each giant window frame was completed, he would step down the home-made sapling ladder three rungs at a time and exclaim, '*Epa!*' Tigo tends to start and finish most of his sentences with this exclamation, imbuing it with myriad meanings from satisfaction to despair.

Sofia, the chef, who I don't think had ever held a paint-brush before, became a demon painter. Each afternoon she would leave the kitchen and clamber on to chairs and tables with a pot of paint in one hand and a dripping brush in the other and attack the window frames with gusto. When we ran out of frames to paint, she started painting her bedroom floor, and when that was done she would sneak out at dawn to tackle door after door. Each day, as new curtains, cushions, pictures, mirrors and furniture converted cell-like rooms into something more resembling a home, Sofia blossomed, becoming more and more talkative and skittish, despite her fifty-five years.

Eighteen-year-old Isabel, Sofia's youngest child, had been living at the college for the past four months but had left the week before I arrived for hospital treatment in Maputo. As each improvement took place, Sofia would tell me how pleased Isabel would be to see it when she returned. And then Sofia would talk wistfully about the husband whom she had loved so much and who had died not long before, and she told me about the religious order she had cooked for in Maputo, and about her father, who disappeared from the face of the earth one day when she was a girl, and about Mattola, the place outside Maputo where she had lived all her life and which she had left to come and help breathe movement into the Cabaceiras. Still grieving for the recent death of her husband, she was another travelling soul finding her own life through helping other people.

Painting and sewing cushions and curtains and cooking together, Sofia and I grew close. As she described her childhood, the mystery of her father's disappearance, surviving twenty-seven years of war, pre- and post-independence, while bringing up her eight children, I realized how courageous she was. At the point when she and her son Tigo and daughter Isabel arrived at the college, they had travelled into the unknown. None of them had ever been to the north of Mozambique before. None of them had lived in such isolation, none of them spoke Macua, none of them had lived away from their very extended family; and yet they had all come to help.

While Sofia made things nice for her daughter, I began to make things nice for Sofia as a way of saying thank you to her for giving up so much and giving so much to the village. At night, after everyone was asleep, I worked on. Every morning, she would notice even tiny nocturnal improvements like a soapdish in the shower, or a new ovencloth, or a rack to put the saucepan lids on.

Having my own daughter with me also spurred me on to make life in the bush as acceptable as possible. For any teenager, the jump from sophistication to bare necessity, from consumer overload to below-the-breadline poverty and, most of all, from hectic social life to imposed loneliness, would have been enormous. For Lolly, who (unlike her shy and rather reclusive mother) has always been an intensely social person, the change was almost immeasurable. Having problems attending school in our fifteenth and sixteenth year seems to run in our family. And from what I see of friends' children is not uncommon in general. Lolly is no exception to the pattern. Having switched schools in Holland in the hopes of settling better, she lost her foothold after a long illness and the concurrent absence and begged me to give her a year out and home school. Probably because I wanted to move to Mozambique anyway, but also because her brother had done it before her and managed notwithstanding to slip back into the system and get to university, I agreed. During the first months, before she found new friends, it was incredibly tough on her emotionally. Without MSN messaging, email or the daily routine of actually going to school, she was thrown very much on to her own resources.

Four years before, when we had first visited Mossuril, she had begun to make friends with the village children. But the difference between twelve and sixteen is huge. All her points of reference were different, the ideas, books, music and things she liked that were the mainstay of her social life in Holland, England and Italy came from another world. So she spent a lot of time reading and writing, and a lot of time composing songs. Interlaced with every day, somewhere in the college, Lolly can be heard singing. At New Year 2005, she went back to Amsterdam, Paris and Italy for two months to spend time with her big sister, in Umbria (where her father lives, and where she was born and grew up) and with Mees. It was only after she returned in the spring that she managed to find a balance between the world she had left and the African world she had come to. When she moves on to complete her formal education, she will have left an indelible mark on the students she has helped here, and she will also have some valuable things to take with her. Her vision of life has changed. Her horizons have broadened and burst that egocentric adolescent bubble so beloved of teenage girls. She speaks fluent Portuguese, she is writing a novel and has enough material to fill another three, and whatever hardships she may encounter in the future, she has a scale to measure them on. Rather in the way I was rudely awoken by my sojourn in Venezuela at the age of eighteen, at sixteen, Lolly has woken up.

Not least, the chance to go to school, which she spurned in Europe, is every child's goal here. Their hopeless dream was her right. What she once turned her back on, she now wants to embrace. And money, which she once spent like water on designer knick-knacks, has gained a value here. Her weekly pocket money was more than a local family's monthly budget. And things she used to throw away would be their most coveted and prized possessions. Whatever she goes on to do with her life, she will do with conscious appreciation for its many gifts. No one who has lived in the bush takes things for granted again: even little things like turning on a tap or switching on a light remain miraculous. Our time here, being often thrown back on to our mutual company for want of any other, has given us a unique and intense year together. But more importantly for a teenage girl, Mozambique has wrapped itself round her heart. It was here that she became a woman because it was here that she fell in love. An unlikely and chance encounter in Chocas-Mar resulted in a tumultuous and passionate relationship that has taken her across the length and breadth of northern Mozambique in its wake.

Bob Dylan wrote a song called 'Mozambique'. It was actually about a town in America, but it could have been written for me. It is more like an obsession set to rhythm than a song. I moved here with an obsession wrapped in a drum beat and then the place and its rhythms swallowed me. Whatever I write about it, the place, the people and their history are inextricably bound up. And my own personal life and that of thousands of Macua villagers have become linked. It is my story and their story. It shows and tells the transformation I am undergoing and it does the same for a swathe of virgin coast and the lush bush lands behind it. And it shows how Morripa, the *mestres* and a handful of their peers are turning the tide in this African village behind God's back.

XII

The College

WHEN THE COLLEGE OF TOURISM opened to fanfares of pipes and drums and ecstatic troupes of Tufu dancers, delegations from Maputo, 2,000 kilometres away, and Nampula, our provincial capital, 230 kilometres away, arrived and walked through an avenue of flags up the main steps and onto the portico. Over a thousand villagers came to watch, together with hundreds of schoolchildren. The international volunteers were there, Morripa and all the workers were there, Mees and I were there, Sieka and Pipi the project leaders-to-be were there, the *regulos* and traditional leaders were there dressed in their official regalia, two dozen local and provincial dignitaries were there, the Minister of Tourism was there, the national radio, TV and press were there, and tucked almost out of sight in all the photos are Ellie and Ramon.

In the first six months, it was Ellie and Ramon and Morripa who held the college together. Ellie Greenwood is my niece. Born in Arequipa in Peru, she was adopted as a tiny baby and brought back to England where she grew up in the quaint Devon village of Chagford. As a teenager, she moved to London and began to work with a youth project affiliated to the Home Office. It emerged that she had a future in Human Resources and her career was one of rapid promotion. I saw a lot of Ellie when she was a very little girl and then I hardly saw her again for more than an hour here and there in London and Devon. I remembered one of the few proper conversations we had, when she was about fourteen, in which she said it was her dream to work in charity.

By chance, just after Teran Foundation started, I met Ellie again. She asked me a lot about Mozambique and the college-to-be and told me that she would like to go out and work there. I explained that it was pioneer stuff and not for the faint-hearted: we were planning to do something new. I didn't think it had ever been done before so we didn't really know what to expect. There was Morripa who was the key to everything and everybody out there, but then there were some huge gaps and imponderables. Ellie was adamant: she wanted to go, and she asked me to give her good warning when it would start.

Fourteen staff members and volunteers foregathered in Johannesburg in early September 2004 to travel in a group for the razzmatazz opening. Ellie and her boyfriend, Ramon Reeves-Whit, were planning to join them via Zimbabwe (where Ramon has family). Ellie emailed to say they would make their own way directly to the college. The first group arrived but there were still no signs of Ellie. Her 'directly' was wishful thinking; she and Ramon travelled overland and by boat and raft on an African odyssey, the arduousness of which must have prepared them in some ways for the inevitable culture shock which knocked out so many members of the first team of helpers within the first few days of arrival.

As the workers were struggling to get the building ready for the grand reception on 27 September, the staff-to-be invaded Morripa's compound and camped there out of the path of falling tiles and cement dust.

I arrived three days after the volunteer group and their leaders, Pipi and Sieka. I couldn't stay for long, I had been juggling work to come out beforehand but there were problems in the Dutch fiction factory and it was becoming clear that if I turned my back on my office for more than a few days someone would stick a knife in it. I arrived at night with a carload of fresh fruit and vegetables, crates of bottled water and sacks of food, bags of ribbons and balloons and boxes of delicacies for the coming feast.

Arrival in Cabaceira Grande or Pequena is always via a stop at Morripa's compound. Communications are a constant challenge in Mossuril District and the usual mainstay of the M-cell mobile phone network had been playing up for days. When this happens, a cloying female voice informs you that the network is down and asks you to please try again later. The message is in Portuguese and the last words are '*Liga mais tarde*' delivered in a jolly sing-song. They are the most annoying words in the world.

Lolly, Tigo and Victoria Salmon (who came out for a beneficiary script-writing course) formed a group called Random Drop and wrote their first song about it, using the '*Liga mais tarde*' as the chorus. Random drop is a particularly African phenomenon and it is the arbitrary and random cutting off of telecommunications be they phone, fax and internet. It occurs mid-sentence, mid-email, and mid-fax. Its cause is mysterious: no one can explain it, and it is very irritating. On the rare occasions when internet is available on Ilha or in Nampula, entire documents disappear into cyberspace without so much as a by-your-leave or a nano-second of warning.

In Europe we have road rage; in Africa there is internet rage. A newcomer succumbing to apoplectic fury is quite a normal sight in any of the four internet-access places open to a public of up to a million potential clients. On Ilha, where there are only three computers, only two of which work, the fits of frustration tend to turn into general discussions. It takes an average of ten minutes to open each email and an average of ten minutes to send one. Only people who have been here understand that with the best will in the world it is not possible to work and keep up a regular digital correspondence.

For over a year, there was no postal service available to the college. The District Administrator informed me that no post had ever been delivered. There was no post office at all and no one in his area had ever received a letter. We compromised and gave his office as our c/o address and asked as many people to write as possible. The central post office had confirmed that there was no postal service to anywhere in Mossuril, but they added that it was because none had ever been needed. A post mistress told me, 'If you get enough letters to justify a delivery, when the sorting office has a sackful, then someone will travel to Mossuril and deliver them.'

We obviously didn't reach our quota because the delivery never happened. However, one volunteer, Mauro from Italy, received a letter, a postcard and also a package of edible goodies from home. These were delivered to the District Administrator and duly forwarded to Mauro. I can only deduce that someone in the sorting office had a soft spot for Italians and a friend or cousin travelling our way who acted as courier.

Since then, we have had a postal revolution. The college now has a post box on Ilha. Our address is:

Caixa Postal 81, Ilha de Moçambique
Provincia de Nampula, Mozambique

The amazing thing is that letters get through. Letters arrive. Parcels arrive. Books arrive. Mosquito nets arrive. The difference is fantastic. Sailing to Ilha and receiving a new book to read is the most enormous treat; as is being able to take back a book in Portuguese (for those students and workers – like Marufo and Morripa – who read but are starving for books). As with so many things, the postal box option was there from the start but its existence seemed to be yet another piece of classified information issued on a 'need to know' basis and none of us knew it was there.

While skills and information are transferred to key local people so that they can eventually take over most of the management, we depend quite heavily on volunteers. Some of these volunteers need to be specialists, such as agronomists, chefs and waiters, barmen and housekeepers, stock-keepers, and gardeners, English-to-foreigners teachers, and health and hygiene workers, but we also need a lot of willing hands. There is useful work for dozens of willing hands here, whether they come for a month, three months, or longer. The more help we have, the more we can do. The college runs on a relative shoestring and it will keep running, with or without me. It has a market garden to help support it. And thanks to the Dutch charity Moments of Joy, which gives just that, we have a restaurant kitchen and storeroom and a community restaurant. The opening day of this restaurant has kept sliding forwards, but it had a trial opening in July 2006 and it will be officially opened when Maurice Eykman, whose charity paid for most of it, will come and see the moments of joy she has given the village. We hope that in years to come it can pay its own way. That would ensure that 2 Coqueiros is here to stay. But even though it is still in its infancy, the local people are so fond and proud of it that I think between them they would find a way to keep it running no matter what.

Students Mugiva and Sergio and their two teams of waiters (of whom there are ten men and women divided into two shifts) received a baptism of fire when it opened. Most of the waiters had never seen a restaurant or bar before and really had no idea how it would work. To get them started, Jason, Lolly's boyfriend, came from Nampula to head both teams. He has experience in the business, knows the area well, is bilingual in English and Portuguese and cares enough about the local people to first carry and then guide them through this new world. Since we now live at the mercy of tyrannical generators, Jason's skill in repairing engines has been invaluable. We may be on our fifth generator, but without all the repair work that he and also Tigo have put in round the clock, we would probably be in the high twenties. From the minute he stepped in, he became a key member of the team.

The training restaurant didn't open its doors because it doesn't have any. It is open plan, so that customers can sit in the breeze and eat and drink surrounded by nature. Due to a slight hitch in the building schedule (caused by the usual problem of materials not arriving when they should), there was no time to do restaurant trials in situ before opening to the public. The twenty-fifth of June is a national holiday, the day when the whole of Mozambique commemorates its hard-won independence from Portuguese rule. The workers and students were determined to open 2 Coqueiros on Independence Day. The training bar and restaurant sit in a palm grove surrounded by dozens, rather than two, coconut palms (*coqueiros*). But built into its structure and protruding from its roof are two tall palm trees.

When Independence Day dawned, despite months of lessons to prepare student waiters for just such a day, everyone froze as the first cars arrived. Tigo (who had helped teach the students for the previous twelve months and is the teacher closest to them) was bedridden with a massively infected cut. As our resident (and only) electrician, notwithstanding the pain he was in, he valiantly offered to be carried into the new restaurant before breakfast to direct the wiring of it, being lifted up and down by the students to do the intricate bits himself. When everything was ready, a surge of guests arrived and cookery and restaurant students alike froze. On that first day, for the first several hours, Lolly was run off her feet being head waitress to show the others how it should be done. Jason ran the bar, and I ran the kitchen. Halfway through that first day, the students began to get the hang of it.

On day two, when Ancha got a four-dollar tip from a tourist impressed by her grasp of English, word flew round the village. It would take ten mornings of carrying sacks of salt in the salt flats to earn four dollars. Jason and Lolly continued to struggle from dawn till dusk and were rewarded when Mugiva, one of the newest and quietest students, got the hang of how to run the bar. Mees, having designed the restaurant and ferried much of its equipment over from Amsterdam, completely missed the opening by being (like Tigo) bedridden with an infected wound and an alarmingly high fever. I ferried news of how the restaurant launch was going back to his sickbed, but he was too ill to be able to savour either the news or the offerings of miraculously upgraded drinks and snacks.

Notwithstanding some breakages, loss of drinks, an entire 10-kilogram marlin, a client being served a glass of rice pudding instead of a drink of Amarula, and another client getting a side order of chocolate mousse with his chicken saffron, some tears, and some frayed tempers, the restaurant was a success. In fact, it is an ongoing success, climbing from strength to strength and even luring some curious tourists to Cabaceiras's shores. And within two weeks of opening the training restaurant, twenty-one new students enrolled for Teacher Tauacal's orientation class, swelling our numbers to seventy-four students.

With fourteen people in the kitchen and ten in the restaurant, 2 Coqueiros tends to dominate the college. As dominatrixes go, a provider of cold drinks, ice, good, mostly African food, a selection of African music, a pretty garden and pleasant company is not a bad one to serve. I never thought I would be a restaurateur ferrying crates of 2M and Coca-Cola back and forth or stock-taking liquor or menu planning, but it is not so different from running a very large villa full of house guests as I did for nineteen years in Italy. The most significant difference is that all the guests have to pay in a restaurant; and in this case, all the money goes to help the village.

We do not aspire to great profits, which is just as well, because even if the restaurant were full six days a week we couldn't make them with our low prices. It will be enough in the future to do a little more than break even. Local people cannot afford the tourist prices of Mozambique and we want local customers. The more clients we have, the more training the students can get serving them, so we have priced everything very low and some things at silly prices so that the village can have a focal point and anyone with a job or grant can afford to drop in for a tea or coffee or a cold drink.

Vakháni vakháni seems to be our motto as we take two steps forward and one step back. Despite having had a few ups and downs with missing stock, Mugiva and Sergio now run the bar and the drink storerooms on their own. And with two students expelled for petty theft, the bar is working and making enough money to keep going. The real thief, as Morripa calls it, is the generator, which consumes petrol like an alcoholic on a constant binge. Not only does it knock back over five hundred US dollars per month, but our generators also keep burning out and breaking down, and, on one memorable day, imploding. Everyone here has become generator-sensitive, asking after its health as though it were a sick child. If the lights flicker, everyone braces for imminent disaster.

No matter how many ups and downs there have been, and no matter how many wrecked appliances are piled up in our storeroom, we now have some visible and lasting results. Two years into the project we cannot just say that it is working: we can prove it. Out of all the things I have embarked on and failed in over the past thirty-five years, I thank the stars that this is not one of them. There are seven thousand people needing it to work, seven thousand people praying to the gods, to Allah and to their ancestors that it will work.

Over the past three decades, I have spent enormous amounts of time and energy (and a couple of small fortunes to boot) restoring castles, villas and palaces as a sort of hobby. As hobbies go, my penchant for collecting and restoring beautiful ruins was a lot more cumbersome than, say, stamp-collecting or bird-watching. Mossuril District indulges this hobby to the hilt. Cabaceira Grande is littered with ruined palaces, as is Mossuril town and its environs. Beyond the college, between the mud huts and arid strips of manioc, the incongruous remains of grandiose buildings are the nesting grounds of genets and iguanas, owls and crows. They are built so solidly that only their outer walls collapse. Built out of coral rock in monumental Mediterranean style, they have porches and balconies, massive doorways and chipped, red-tiled roofs. Peeling lime stucco in a palette of pastels pokes out through palms and strangling ficus trees. Beautiful as many of these ruins are, there is no money to restore them, so they tumble down a little more each year as squirrels dislodge the tiles and the rains take their toll.

While thousands of children in Mossuril have no school buildings, dozens of stately ruins stand abandoned to the elements. Back in 2003, when the derelict *palaceu* was donated to the community-college scheme, I started on a restoration binge which looks set to continue for many years to come. Talks with Morripa and the community leaders revealed that local builders and workers could restore the palace and that local villagers would be keen to enrol in the college-to-be. But as well as the *palaceu*, several other historic ruins were also available for eventual restoration, to house a primary and secondary school. Of these, the most magnificent (but alas, also the most expensive to repair) is the Governor General's former summer palace. Thankfully, the Dutch national post-code lottery has pledged to restore this silent mansion and to equip it as a secondary school. This project is very dear to me, but to make it happen depends on it having a sponsor.

Owned by a husband and wife team, the Dutch lottery (Nationale Postcode Loterij) has a great deal of money to donate to charity each year. After a first successful meeting outside Amsterdam in September 2005, both owners arranged to fly out to visit the Cabaceiras within a few weeks, thereby putting the development of the Cabaceiras on a roller-coaster. Unfortunately, at the last minute only one, Annemieke, could come. Yet come she did, like a knight on a white horse, to help this neglected place. Alas, the portfolio of potential projects that we had hoped to do together fell by the wayside, but two or three remained, of which one was guaranteed to be the secondary school in the summer palace by the sea. In meetings with Annemieke and the local leaders, the District Administrator and provincial officials, Mees, me and Annemieke's entourage, the promise was repeated and gratefully accepted because what the village needs more than anything else are schools.

It has taken much longer than planned on that whirlwind tour to get this secondary school off the ground, but after a great deal of toing and froing with applications and documents in the Netherlands, phase one of our joint venture can finally start. Stichting DOEN, another Dutch charity founded by the dynamic duo at the lottery, will pay for the development of the secondary school and a number of other proposed projects. So the experts who have sat patiently in the wings waiting to make their drawings and plans can actually get started, and 2007 should see the realization of every Cabaceirian's dream: a secondary school that their children can get to. Dozens of villagers who have sent their children to Nampula can then bring them back home, and hundreds of parents whose children have nothing to do and nowhere to go will have the chance to see them get the education they long for.

As I keep saying (as much to myself as to anyone else), I never planned to start a training college although I did plan, eventually, to start a foundation. It was all something for later that took off prematurely under its own momentum. Even after Mossuril District became the chosen place, it only happened as it did because in April 2004 the Mozambican Ministry of Culture informed me that the government of Mozambique was now ready to hand over the ruined *palaceu*. While the government was ready, I was not. I still needed to create a legal entity, a registered charity for it to be handed over to. I had been told that everything official was painfully slow in Mozambique, and yet suddenly any delay was threatening to be on my part.

In one day in Holland, Teran Foundation was founded and Morripa's college dream began to become a reality. It was a dream that happened to be not so far away from my own long-term dream of starting some community work in Africa.

I had, and have, no qualification whatsoever to start a training college, but Morripa and the villagers wanted and needed it. At least I was older and better trained in the University of Life than I had been when I started farming in Venezuela. And I was certainly better qualified than any of the villagers were to get such a project going. I could combine it with a Faculty of Agriculture to bring fresh food into the area. Were it not for the vitamin C from the odd lime, tomato and piri-piri pepper, the villagers could add scurvy to the list of diseases caused by the widespread severe subnutrition.

It certainly isn't a qualification for running a training college, but I do have strange childhood memories of the one my mother attended in Tooting Bec, South London, starting when I was five years old. She stayed there for three years as a mature student and I often went with her and sat in the library or common room waiting for her lessons to end. I was sick and off school and she didn't want to leave me at home alone, so we took the bus together and I sat in on what seemed like endless bickering, coded courtships and common-room dramas. So it shouldn't have come as quite such a surprise that certain aspects of college life are like endless reruns of a Brazilian soap opera. Tiny grievances escalate and fester and romance blossoms and dies leaving trails of rancour in its wake. Even some of the elements of hardship which have hallmarked the setting up of this particular training college were echoed in my past.

When my mother quit the dead-end job she had taken to make ends meet in the aftermath of her separation from my father and enrolled as a mature student, our family skirted the nearest we have ever come to actual poverty. As a student in London in 1968 she was entitled to a student grant.

This was just enough for a teenager to get by on in digs and a meagre diet. No allowance was made, however, for my mother's four ravenous daughters. So for three years she eked out her grant to try and sate our prodigious appetites. If one of us ate a little more than her share of the porridge, mashed potatoes and tinned pilchards that were our staple diet, another of us went hungry.

Since my mother's pride never allowed us to admit to the semi-permanent emptiness of our stomachs, she insisted that whenever we were out, we all had to refuse any offers of food three times before we were allowed to accept one. I can still remember the anguish I felt in other people's houses where proper food was on offer. Out of respect, I turned down all the tempting offers once, twice and then thrice, praying fervently to the powers that be that a fourth chance would ensue. And I can still remember each of the disappointments when it didn't. Nearly five decades later, such memories allow me to understand how little anyone can concentrate on other things with an empty stomach.

By the time I arrived to actually live here, one of the three walled gardens was an oasis of fresh salads and vegetables. Also, against all the odds, the crows and foul pest, a batch of scrawny home-bred Macua chickens were making regular appearances in a curry sauce at the long refectory table. Ludicrous as it may sound, even buying fish on this seashore isn't easy. Even after two years, keeping up a supply of fresh fish is so Kafkaesque that Morripa is starting his own fish farm.

One day, a fisherman might bring a 30-kilogram marlin or tuna, but then several days can go by without there being any catch at all. The local fishermen are not used to selling. They subsist. Even when the fishermen are prepared to sell their catch (which is not often), five little fishes the size of my index finger cannot feed the fifty to ninety people who

lunch and/or dine at the college every day (excluding visitors to our training restaurant). With no refrigeration, no
ice, no electricity, no car and a very low food budget,
buying an entire marlin or tuna was out of the question for
a one-off feast and none of the cooks were able to repeat
the miracle of the feeding of the five thousand with the mini
fish.

I used to think the hundreds of fishermen had joined the
ranks of our enemies – which we do, of course, have – and
were starving the college out by refusing to sell us their
catches. It was only by ferrying backwards and forwards to
Ilha by dhow that I realized that without proper nets or
lines or hooks and with so few boats, there were hundreds
of fishermen but, like the rest of the population, most of
them were unemployed. Day by day, someone in the family
would scrounge around in the shallows casting a short line
into the rich waters in the hopes that some intellectually
challenged fish would ignore the fisherman's presence and
shadow and bite his crude bait-less hook anyway. If a man
waits in the mangrove for long enough, he can guddle or
grab enough little fish to take home. Since money hardly
circulates here and there is no way out to any other market
where it does, a bigger catch would go to waste. If anyone
is lucky enough to get a proper catch, he sails to Ilha to sell
it rather than take it home. It has taken over two years to
persuade the local fisherman to bring those lucky catches to
us.

Since July 2006 when the college training restaurant '2
Coqueiros' finally opened, we have savoured the culinary
treats we now get there every day and never take the fish
and chips that are the mainstay of our menu for granted.
Each meal feels rather like the day when my mother grad-
uated and got a job and put nice food back on our table.

Having survived the first two years and its giant learning

curve, we have learned to stand and are learning to walk so that in the future we may have the strength to run. Looking back, though, I see that for the first six months it was touch and go whether we would make it. We had a big plan and a big concept. We had a ruined palace on the edge of the Indian Ocean and the tacit support of thousands of villagers. We now have the active support of about six hundred local people, ninety of whom are already on our payroll. We have restored 65 per cent of the college building; we have the training restaurant and three market gardens, a poultry farm and a medicinal plant garden and pharmacy. We also have several satellite projects in health, micro-finance, culture and literacy. And last, but not least, we also have a few friends 'out there' and a few more enemies.

XIII

Varanda: A Slice of Paradise

I LIVE TWO LIVES HERE: that of Varanda, the nature reserve on the beach where home is an *Out of Africa* camp, and then there is my life at the college. Although the two are linked in a joint effort to bring some movement to two otherwise still villages, and although there is only a distance of eight kilometres across salt flats, mangroves and dunes between them, life in one and the other is very different. Not least, a day at Varanda is hugely relaxing, while a day at the college is one of continual small actions.

Varanda is the sort of place Europeans dream about. It is both a peninsula and an island with over four kilometres of virgin beaches. It has white sand and warm, almost transparent waters streaked with aquamarine and turquoise. Protected by a coral reef and frequented by dolphins, the sea here is safe and gentle. There are no sharks or dangers beyond the occasional sharp coral underfoot when wading through a meandering lagoon.

Twice a day, at unfathomable hours known only to the local fishermen, the sea streams into the lagoon and turns it from a series of natural swimming pools into a churning saltwater river flooding the surrounding countryside. When the tide is out, ivory-coloured sand ripples towards the neighbouring islands, and halfway to Ilha itself. When the tide is high, thousands of hectares of mangroves stand in two metres of water, and part of the one road and all of the footpaths lie underwater. Then no one can get into the local village of Cabaceira Pequena and no one can get out, except by boat.

Varanda is inhabited by plants, birds, fish and various animals. The only people who come here are the local fishermen who stash their dugout canoes on some of the beaches. Occasionally, a lone prawn fisherman from Cabaceira Pequena will come to scan and scour the sandbed of the lagoon. A boy will stand for hours knee-deep in the still water waiting for the transparent prawns to feel at ease with his presence. From a distance I used to wonder why someone would appear to petrify and stare glazed-eyed for so long. I thought it might be yet another of the thousands of traditional ceremonies of the *tradição*. However, it was not about religion, just common sense, not to frighten his prey away.

On the whole, though, Varanda is more about not meeting people than meeting them. There are mangrove cuckoos and herons, storks and egrets, bluebirds with turquoise fantails, parrots and blue and scarlet finches. In the rainy season, the dunes erupt with lilies great and small. What looks like tufts of short grass are actually miniature wild orchids. When the rains come, everything bursts into flower. But it hardly ever rains.

In November there are the so-called short rains in the form of intermittent torrential showers, which stop and start abruptly. Within half an hour of one of these drenchings, there is no sign of it having been. Then, in December and January, there are the long rains. By the time they come, the land, the wells and the people are desperate for water. The long rains fall in sheets and can last for hours. It is the long rains that sustain all the trees and the manioc and fill the wells and waterholes. There are no sweet-water rivers here: only endless rivers and rivulets of seawater, streaming in and out of the Indian Ocean.

The previous owners of Varanda were a Dutch couple who lived in Nampula and were shown the beauty spot by friends. The land was owned by the local community with little segments here and there pertaining to various local families. The Dutchman was working as the director of the Dutch charity SNV and he and his wife felt confident that they could get land title if they put enough time, energy and patience into the process. To that end, they started a Mozambican company and went through all the bureau-cratic hurdles required to get it registered and running, and then they set about buying the land (which, rather embar-rassingly, they got for a song and then sold on to Mees at an enormous profit before heading off to the other side of the planet). When they finally got the necessary documentation in 1999, they began to run a community project together with the village of Cabaceira Pequena. A group of sixteen workers under the command of the ubiquitous Morripa were enrolled as nature guards.

These were the first proper jobs in the village. At the end of each month, sixteen people took home a salary sufficient to support up to thirty family members. It was the first time that anyone had taken the time to help local people, to bring the supplies unobtainable locally so that carpenters could have nails and glue, and metalworkers could have zinc plates and iron. For his services, which in the early years were (by his own wish) always donated, Morripa got a motorbike and a mobile phone.

It has been said that the combined salaries of all the local guards and the sum total of all the bundles of palm leaves

that have been donated to the village and the cement blocks
and other materials for the health post in Cabaceira Grande
amount to far less than the profit the Dutch couple made on
the land sale. But in a land of endless injustices, that may
just be one more notched up on the poverty totem.

The previous owners planted eight thousand trees on
Varanda between 2000 and 2002, many of which died
almost instantaneously while the remainder have been
struggling ever since. These coconut palms and various local
trees are not dwarf varieties, they are just dwarfed by the
lack of water, the continuous sea breeze and zero protection
from hot sun. When we started the college, I took it upon
myself to do a bit of gardening at Varanda, mulching the
trees and weeding round them, erecting bamboo windbreaks
where the coconut palms were suffering most and generally
tinkering with the plants.

Like a lost tribe, the Cabaceirians have had to look after
themselves. By looking after each other they have preserved
and in some cases distilled an essence of what is good in life.
Their staple diet of corn and manioc flour may cocoon
them in lethargy, and some solutions that seem so simple to
a Westerner as to be ludicrous not to implement them may
have passed them all by, yet let's not forget that despite
stuff dropping down since time immemorial, no one noticed
gravity until it was pointed out by Sir Isaac Newton. In
Nampula, it is the custom among some of the foreign aid
employees and well-to-do locals to mock villagers for their
lack of what might be taken for granted as common sense.
Among the expatriates in the cities, there is little allowance
made for the fact that common sense can vary from place to
place. What is second nature to someone born and bred to
the sea or the bush may elude a foreign expert.

One of the more striking aspects of living in this particular so-called 'backward rural community' is the virtual

absence of crime. If something does get stolen, the local *al'mo* sits on a mat under a mango tree and writes out cabalistic signs, which are supposed to make the offender either return the goods, confess, or both. Failure to do either will result in the thief's belly swelling up and for him, or her, to be racked by pain. Although most of the college goods are safe in the hands of its students and workers, there was a string of petty thefts which lasted for nearly a year. Most of what went missing were little things, but here in the bush, those same little things are often crucial. Morripa tipped me off that one of the newer students was a suspect in these crimes and should be expelled forthwith. In the absence of proof, and trying to follow in my mother's footsteps of always giving the maladjusted a second chance, I stubborned it out and let the student in question remain.

One surprisingly chilly morning in March 2006, two policemen arrived in our courtyard. They explained that they were chasing a criminal who had been caught red-handed robbing his neighbour's storeroom the night before. With no transport and no telephone, the victim of the theft had tied up the young thief. At dawn, a runner was sent to fetch the police from Mossuril. Meanwhile, the robber had escaped and fled, and was believed to be hiding out in the mangroves of Cabaceira Pequena. After all this had been explained to me, I asked what I could do, and one of the policemen told me, 'We just thought you should know because he is one of your students.'

Sure enough, he was the same one Morripa had tried to expel. Two days later, some of the villagers from Cabaceira Pequena caught the run-away and delivered him battered and bound to the roofless police station in town. I asked if he had been badly hurt and was told, 'Badly enough ... We can't have thieves here. We are poor enough as it is. And the storeroom he robbed was his best friend's uncle's. It isn't his first time, either. He was caught and beaten by the community last year. His family are good, but he is bad.'

The reluctance that Anglo-Saxons have to gloat does not exist here. When someone is right about something they underline it, frame it and tell it to the four winds. So I got a lot of 'I told you so but you wouldn't listen' lectures over the next week.

That was the worst thief we have had. The temptation here is enormous: very poor people have daily contact with hundreds of items, any one of which could alleviate their own dire straits. I see it more as a triumph that relatively so little has been stolen. To date, not counting the one in prison, two students have been expelled for repeated petty theft. One kept stealing food from the storeroom and the other stole clothes from the laundry and sold them. The latter was another opportunity for Morripa to tell me that I had been warned. The young man in question is a very bright, sweet person who looks much younger than his twenty-one years. He is popular with the other students and had done everything he could to attract my favourable attention by bringing plants for the gardens and helping to tend them in his spare time. He learnt English quicker than most of his peers and showed every sign that he would make a star pupil. That is until he was arrested and thrown into jail for stealing three coconuts.

It turned out that the theft had occurred before he joined the college but his case had been complicated by a gang from Matibane, who carried out a jail break on the day our student-to-be was due to leave the jail. He had walked out with the escapees and was subsequently re-arrested. At the point I became aware of his problem, he was stuck in Mossuril jail and facing an eight-month sentence.

Every day his mother trudged the sixteen kilometres to Mossuril and back to take her son some manioc porridge.

And every day she came to the college in tears to beg me to help her boy. I hated the thought of him in the dark smother of a cell with nothing to do but pine and weep. From the little I have seen and heard of prisons here, they are not the sort of place where a nice young boy should be. I also knew that poor people ended up in jail for very petty thefts, such as stealing a chicken or falling foul of a wealthier neighbour. And I felt sure that, given the chance, he could turn out well and be a credit to the community. So I paid two hundred dollars to bail him out and allowed him to join a team of trainee waiters. But in the intervals between serving drinks, he slipped in and out of the walled garden and stole clothes from the washing lines. I was actually very sorry to see him go. The village committee expelled him, though, and despite his and his mother's tears, this time there was nothing I could do.

If this were somewhere else, and if there were not thousands of people who don't steal and who need help, and if there was enough money to invest a little in bringing someone back from the edge, I would still like to help him. Every child I have ever known, myself included, used to be a petty thief. It is part of our growing-up process to leave theft behind us. This particular student hasn't done that and instead he has thrown the chance of a decent future away. I wonder how it would have felt if, for instance, on one of the (many) times my sisters and I took a knife to slide sixpences out of our mother's piggy bank, or when we stole stationery from school, we had been caught and thrown into jail and ostracized as thieves. Would or could we have gone on to contribute something positive to society?

But this is a poor underdeveloped country where chances are few and far between. And his two-hundred-dollar bail could have bought two families a new house each, or sent several children to school, or bought fifty mosquito nets and saved hundreds of lives. The fear that the former District Administrator had, when he begged me to bring schools to the area, was precisely this sort of story: a good boy goes to the dogs, turns to petty crime and then spirals into never-ending trouble. Meanwhile, I cannot appear to condone his crime and neither can I go against the wishes of the community. But nor can I forget how dazed and broken he looked when he was in jail. Without the college, his is a hopeless case.

We don't have any programmes for helping to bring lost sheep back into the fold but, since Don Mattera in South Africa can turn the most hardened criminals into ministering angels, maybe we should. Meanwhile, the Cabaceiras continue to police themselves and provide their own Macua welfare state, feeding the five thousand with their little fishes. There are no beggars here, and despite severe sub-nutrition, no one actually starves. Nor is there a single homeless man, woman or child. Not many places can say the same.

The villagers rarely come into contact with the police or the courts, but if they do, their innate submission and lack of education keep them at a constant disadvantage. By law, they are entitled to a duly qualified counsel for their defence, an advisor who can explain what their rights are and how they should plead. In practice, there is none of that. With so few local people being able to understand, let alone speak, Portuguese, and with the florid legalese of the courts, they are doomed. The only way they can avoid the brutal prisons is to pay a fine and the fines are far beyond their means. Despite never having been much of a rider, I find myself leaping onto my high horse all the time now, deflecting sneers aimed at my new neighbours and sticking up for the rights they don't even know exist.

Morripa has a way of shrinking back into himself like a sea creature retreating into its shell whenever the college falls under verbal attack. I should probably do the same but have not yet mastered the technique. As he quite rightly points out to me when a verbal skirmish is over, within Mozambique we don't have to defend ourselves. Anyone can come and see, and the success of what the village is doing can speak for itself.

Vakháni vakháni, I am trying to reserve my weaponry for outsiders who occasionally visit under the false banner of pretending to help while actually adding to the woes of the local people (who need such cruelty like they need a hurricane). Three times now, outsiders who are no strangers to spite have actively undermined the project. Each time my paternal grandmother's Carib blood and its legacy of non-forgiveness rises in my veins. Since it is I who have guided these outsiders in, I would joust for the villagers' success if need be.

Before Mees came here, back in 1999, there was no health centre at all in Cabaceira Pequena. Since the village regularly becomes an unreachable island, some kind of autonomous medical post was a priority. Even when not cut off from the tides, there is no qualified doctor in the whole of Mossuril District, with its 189,000 souls. But in Cabaceira Pequena, when no one could get in or out, people died of gangrene from infected cuts. And people died of malaria and gastroenteritis for want of treatment that was readily available elsewhere.

To this day, people die and are wrapped in their winding cloths and buried and no one really knows what they died of. The cause of death on their certificate will give some cause or another, but sickness/disease (*doença*) is a general term. It would be more honest to write 'neglect' as the cause of most deaths here.

In a tropical village with a population of over three thousand people, a simple health post is only a first step towards
dealing with the serious local medical problems, but it is a
big step in the right direction. With a health post, wounds
can at least be disinfected and covered, malaria can be
treated, fevers can be lowered and diarrhoeas and vomiting
curbed. Eye infections can be cured, and so can numerous
skin diseases. Even though all the above treatments are
administered by a nurse and not a doctor, that nurse can, at
least, recognize the most common and recurring complaints
and treat them. In the absence of any other health facility of
any kind, under the previous owners the Varanda Project
paid for a health centre, which the villagers then built.

In 2003 (in fact during my first ever visit), this was officially handed over to the Mozambican Government. There
was an enormous amount of Tufu dancing. This local dance
is typical of Ilha, Mossuril and Angoche. It is performed by
women only, in troupes. Each troupe dresses in identical
capulanas and is thus easily identifiable by colour. The
groups then compete with each other. Tufu is about song
and dance. The songs are African ballads. And as a commentary on recent and past events, they can both protest
and praise. In the Tufu lyrics, women can air any grievance
including ones it might be taboo to bring up in a more
formal meeting. The dance troupes are rigidly organized by
the local women and each group has a chief, a secretary and
a treasurer.

The first time I saw this Tufu dancing, I thought it was
wonderful and exotic and exciting. Now, innumerable Tufu
spectacles later, I still find it all the above but it wanes in
direct proportion to its duration and the amount of available
shade to watch it in. The dances I attend usually take place
outside in the midday or afternoon sun, so one stands in 30,
32, or even 34 degrees Celsius nearly passing out from the

fierce rays. Far from admiring the dancing, after about twenty minutes one is just dying for it to stop, for there to be shade. Fantasies about ice, cool coconut water, chilled mango juice, lemonade, a cold Coke, take over from any kind of aesthetic appreciation.

The Philistine in me goes into ascendance and the cultural aspect is lost in the mirage of shade and refreshment. Feeling like a complete freak on the day of the health centre celebration, I noticed that all the government officials were sweating profusely and every visitor was standing in a dripping shirt. Centre stage had been given to the Director of Health and the District Administrator and their entourage, and they were getting the real brunt of the sun. The slight overhang of the tin roof of the health centre provided a very thin line of shade. There was quite an unseemly scuffle to get into this, which I am afraid I joined. It wasn't much help but it just prevented the alternative of fainting into the magic circle.

And then the dancing stopped and thoughts of diving for cover and dashing into fabulous Chocas-Mar – as we like to call the place – for a cold drink began to seem like a possibility, when out of nowhere a different-coloured troupe stepped in and began the whole performance again with variations. It may be a modern addition to the dance, but plastic football referees' whistles play an important part in latter-day Tufu. The District Administrator wasn't looking good and the Mayor was swaying as though prior to passing out. I saw later that they had years of experience in similar events but took the precaution whenever possible of having a few palm leaves arranged over their heads to get through the dancing and speeches. With the handing over of the health centre being a first official occasion for Cabaceira, no one knew that this was the expected protocol.

Sheik Namana (whose name can be and is spelled at least

five different ways) is the traditional hereditary leader of
Cabaceira Pequena. He is old and frail and wears thick
bottle-end glasses. His light skin, straight hair and beaked
nose are his Arab legacy. He is a fine, wise man with a
tough job. His village has no money and its chance to compete in any way was cut off and thrown away at birth. The
ruins of Arab warehouses along the shore are thought to be
over eight hundred years old (and are said to have been
destroyed in a punitive raid by Vasco da Gama). The rest of
the dusty village is a straggle of mud huts littered with
shells. Sheik Namana himself, though the owner of a flock
of goats and a dozen chickens, lives in a simple mud hut
furnished with four chairs and a couple of rush mats.

For years he too has been dreaming of a better future for
his people. He has had the forethought to get all the official
documentation to build a jetty and he has hardwood stored
for it. With a jetty, the fishermen could get in and out at
will. They could fish every day. They could sell their
catches on Ilha. As he describes such future opportunities,
decades fall from him and he smiles ruefully. He is a man
who has suffered with his teeth, most of which have given
up the struggle and fallen from his troubled gums.

Sheik Namana has been hovering under a tree, reflecting
odd flashes of light from his enormous, green glasses. When
he sees that his guests can bear the heat no longer, he
instructs the village committee to serve coconut water from
a stash he has been keeping out of sight.

The effect of that cool coconut water was instant and
miraculous. The District Administrator gave a rousing speech
on the strength of it; the former Dutch owner of Varanda
gave a speech, Mees, as the new owner of Varanda, gave a
speech. And then just about everyone present gave a speech
and there were enthusiastic cheers for all of them. At a certain
point the cheers became so enthusiastic that entire speeches

were lost, but no one seemed to care. A good thing had happened and it was the herald of more good things to follow. Varanda had paid for a community meal and the food was being stirred in pans the size of washing cauldrons. Everyone would eat. The longer I spend here, the more I see that speeches are great but they are only words and Portuguese and Macua are both florid languages. Meanwhile, food is food. The success of all events big and small is measured by what there is to eat.

There is a saying here that in the West people have money but the Macua have time. Everyone here is incredibly patient. They are patient with each other, with the government, with the elements, with hardship, and with me. Sheik Namana has been patient all his life but now that his great age shows how close he must be to death, he has become impatient. He is quite blunt about it.

'Look at me,' he says. 'My time has almost come. I have waited my whole life to see a jetty and I want to see it with my living eyes, so please don't wait too long.'

In this ancient trading place we are exchanging speeds. While I help to make some of the things they want happen quickly, at another level, I am also learning to slow down, to harmonize with the mangroves and the sea. When I walk through the bush, I try to feel the grasses and the trees, the stones and heat in the way that the locals do, letting it all flow through them so that they can walk for twenty, thirty or forty kilometres effortlessly. The word '*esikula*' means 'the inclination grass makes when stepped on by someone'. The phrase '*othikila isikula*' is Macua for 'what goes around comes around', or more literally: 'to thank someone for a gift or good deed by repaying it with another', and more literally, to repay a gift or deed by bending towards the giver like grass that has been stepped on.

The give and take of life here allows me to blend. Even

though I will always stand out as an *Akunha*, this is where I belong. I do not aspire to be able to transform myself into a lion like the old man at Naguema is said to do, or even to carry a jerry can of water on my head the way local women can, but I have come to know the feeling of being an extension of the red matope earth, and to find my own way sometimes through the mangroves, although not yet across the inland seas.

XIV

Beachcombing

I KNOW EVERY STEP OF the beaches on Varanda 8, and Varanda 9. When I think about the numbers, it seems like a strange way to refer to a beach, but since that is how all the locals call them, it has come to be a habit. Varanda 1 has a long classic sandy beach, Varanda 8 has labyrinthine rock pools and Varanda 9 has the lagoon, pristine white sands and a little cluster of rock pools as well.

I walk up and down all their tide lines gathering shells. While scanning the sands for cowries and conches and dozens of beautiful speckled and spotted shells whose names I don't know but whose forms and settling places I have become familiar with, I see the constant changes along the beach. There are stretches of the finest white sand and stretches of coarser grain. There are slabs of coral rock ground smooth by years of passing waves and there are clusters of sharp grey coral where the sea has played architect and left rock pools and towers, bridges and caves. From week to week the sands shift, alternately hiding and revealing the coral beneath them.

Sometimes there are footprints in the sand. These are mostly the barefoot prints of fishermen walking to and from their dugout canoes. Five of these battered dugouts are moored to an old casuarina tree on Varanda 8. Beside them is a mound of hundreds of giant clam shells. When I first visited Varanda, I spent hours searching for single giant clam shells and over a week I gathered a dozen, which I stored with the guards by the water tank. They seemed very unimpressed when I showed them my find but they smiled politely and asked if I wanted more. I tried to explain in my Hispanic Portuguese that the pleasure lay in finding the shells myself. Only later, when I discovered the remains of the fishermen's lunches dotted along the entire coastline did I understand the patronizing nods the nature guards had given me when I started hoarding my shell treasures.

For the villagers, everything that the sea has to offer is interesting if you can eat it. Even some of the really beautiful shells that wash up only rarely on the beaches here are varieties the local people eat. The first time I walked through Cabaceira Pequena in daylight, I saw that the narrow sand streets were littered ankle-deep in places with the same shells I had laboriously collected one by one. Now that I have been here longer, I have become more selective and try to find only the prettiest examples, along with fragments of old Chinese and Portuguese porcelain that sank to the seabed when the ships they were ballasting went down.

Over the years, I have collected innumerable basketfuls of shells. I have collected so many I am running out of places to put them. The worn and chipped specimens I gather do not appeal to others in the same way that they do to me. The rare and perfect specimens sold by the fishermen are the shells that others can most readily admire, but the fishermen dive for their shells and I am no diver, so I hoard my flotsam, curbing the desire to bob down every few seconds to scoop up yet another battered fragment as it signals to me from the sand.

Most days, though, when I walk on the beach now, I gather nothing but impressions of the sand and the sea, adding my footprints to those of the sandpipers and egrets, gulls and pelicans, flamingos and storks, and the intricate maze of crab tracks. Deep in the mangrove beyond Varanda there are giant black crabs. They are bigger than my feet and can look quite sinister, especially at night. Out on the more open beaches and in the lagoon, there are innumerable species of designer crabs flaunting as many colours as the local *capulanas*. At night, thousands of them dance on the sands, chasing the waves.

There are two points on Varanda where giant sea turtles lay their eggs. I have yet to witness this, but everyone else has seen them. They come at night and leave several-metre-wide tracks in the sand. Part of the guards' job is to protect the eggs and, when necessary, to help the baby turtles reach the sea. Tortoiseshell is forbidden here, but it is still sold as bracelets and hair combs. It is fairly easy to persuade people not to kill the turtles and not to traffic in their shells, but it is much harder to persuade hungry people not to eat the turtles' eggs. For hundreds of years, turtles' eggs have been part of their diet. Once a year, local children glut on them. In a land of severe sub-nutrition, telling people not to eat a protein-rich food because it is unecological to do so isn't enough to change a lifetime's habit. Meanwhile, Varanda guards protect two of the nesting places. Each turtle lays her eggs in various spots. If predators come and raid a nest, another will survive. This works for some predators, but knee-high local children know the ploy and dig indiscriminately all over the beaches in search of hidden stashes.

There is nothing sacred about turtles, big or small, in the local culture. Fortunately for dolphins, to catch one is taboo. No fisherman will kill one, and if a dolphin accidentally gets into their fragile nets, a fisherman will go to great pains to extract the entangled dolphin and let it go.

Ramon and I were once sitting in one of the two beach bars on Ilha looking out to sea when a young man in a dugout canoe caught a dolphin. One minute he was paddling slowly along the coastline, and the next minute like a cartoon character he was whizzing across the sea. His dugout was raced to the end of the derelict pier and then back towards the fortress. The fisherman had to struggle to stay upright and yelled to a neighbouring canoe for help. For several minutes, the first man was yanked this way and that with the trapped dolphin leaping out of the sea from time to time before being dragged under again by its nylon harness. The second canoe managed to pull up alongside and the two grappled together. More slowly, but still at an unnatural speed, both canoes raced up and down parallel to the beach until their living engine tired and they were able to extract the dolphin and let it go.

Opposite Varanda 7 and Varanda 8, by the desert island of Sete Pãos, dolphins come regularly to play with the local fishermen. Children from the village go out and swim with them in the still, transparent waters of the western beach. The island got its name because it has seven windswept trees (*pãos*) clinging to its beaches. The remainder of the eleven-hectare island is bare beaches, moorland or sea-smoothed coral rocks scattered with millions of coral stones and fossils. From a distance the southern tip of Sete Pãos looks like a moonscape. At certain mysterious times of the year, when the tide is fully out, it is just possible to walk and then wade to Sete Pãos from Varanda, but it is not possible to walk back without being cut off and probably drowned. I have not yet been able to find out when exactly it is safe to walk there, so a plan to do so and then camp overnight sits on a back-boiler. On the days when I visit the island, it is by sailing dhow, safely steered into port by one of the fishermen and his sons.

Mees is an experienced sailor and takes to the sea without any qualms, guiding the dhows into this and that wind as we tack across to Ilha or the other islands. If a dhow captain insists that we be dumped miles away from our designated destination, Mees tells the sailors how to land us where we want to go. When I am alone here, I am never more than a passenger at the whim of the captain. I cannot tell the difference between having to land in the wrong village or on the wrong island because the wind or the waves really don't allow us to do otherwise and being dumped arbitrarily because the captain wants to go home or to go fishing or for a hundred and one other reasons.

Morripa and Ibraimo are the arrangers of our boats, most of which come from Cabaceira Pequena. Despite there being hundreds of available dhows, most of which would be happy to take passengers and get a fare, only one particular boat was ever contracted. Many hours were spent contemplating the fortress wall on Ilha, waiting on the coral rock carved into sea steps, for 'our' boat to arrive. No matter what time we arranged to be met, we always seemed to end up waiting in the burning sun.

The gigantic fortress of São Sebastião is on the tip of the island. It took the Portuguese sixty years to build it and innumerable slaves lost their lives dragging its coral rocks. It has never been successfully stormed or besieged. Inside, there are the remains of a small autonomous city and two massive rainwater tanks, which were built a thousand years ago by Arab conquerors. As though to belie its military nature, the fortress has an ornamental doorway. Despite watching it from across the channel for month after month, the true scale of it only really became clear from the inside. It is almost alarmingly huge and empty. Given its violent history, I had expected it to exude some of the sadness and despair of some of the thousands of slaves and hundreds of prisoners held there through the centuries, but the place has a surprisingly peaceful air, as though all the sighs of the lost souls have been swallowed up and dispersed by the sea breeze.

Week after week, the diminutive and wizened sea captain rocked me into the small harbour by the fortress steps. During each crossing, as his son attended to the sails and tiller, the captain sat doubled into the bowed wood by the mast, knitting a new fishing net in lurid orange nylon. This activity gave him an old-womanish look, denied only by his sinewy forearms. Intuitively, every time the boat needed his expert attention, he uncurled like a hermit crab and tightened or loosened a rope while ticking off his son in a stern whisper.

The captain seems so at ease with the water that he gives the impression he could sit and knit on the ocean's surface without the intermediary of a boat if need be. I cannot say that I have found myself to be completely at one with the water yet, but then I came here late in my life and was not initiated into its mysteries as new-born babies are here. Every time a wave made our old dhow lurch, or the leaking, curved side planks dribbled more than the usual amount of water onto the floor, I wondered whether we were near enough to either shore for me to swim to safety if our boat capsized. When there are more passengers on the boat I feel less nervous because they treat every crossing like a works' outing or school trip and fill the dhow with animated chatter.

One day, while sitting on the regular ferry dhow waiting to set sail together with a dozen villagers, I witnessed a traditional ceremony without having been first guided to it by Morripa. Among the passengers was a young couple with what had to be their first child: a new-born baby they were cosseting as only new parents can. The father was holding the baby girl in his lap while the mother angled a blue and green striped umbrella against the morning sun. After the muezzin had called to tip the captain off that it was time to get under way, the captain asked the baby's parents something in Macua and then told them off. Both mother and father apologized sheepishly. At which point the usually calm captain leapt across the dhow and seized the baby. For a moment, it looked as though he was going to throw the infant overboard, but he merely took possession and marched round the rim of his dhow, balancing on the worn planks as he held the baby out to sea to all four compass points, lowering her towards the water as he mumbled an incantation. Then he stepped into the middle of the boat and knelt over the slimy bilge that always seeps through the raw cotton caulk and very delicately wet his fingers and then wet the baby's lips with sea water as he whispered 'mother's milk, mother's milk' in Macua. Whereupon he gave the baby back, everyone smiled and the boat was poled out of the mangrove with an infant on board on its maiden voyage.

When I returned, I learnt that all children are thus presented to the sea god in the hopes that he will spare them. It seems that the sea god is like a dragon that preys on young flesh. As though to prove this, on the next weekend two local children were stolen by the sea, trapped by the massive tide and drowned. Girls don't learn to swim here because girls don't go out to fish. The women and children only gather crabs, clams and cone shells. It is impossible to learn to navigate all the sea paths through the mangroves because the tide redesigns the landscape on an almost daily basis. One week the water can be shallow in one point and the next it can be three metres deep. The sailors and fishermen feel their way through the water, trusting their instinct to guide them.

I hope by the time the baby on the boat is old enough to gather shellfish, there will be a proper school in the village and swimming lessons for all the children. With a double death, all the drums in the village beat out their ghostly tattoos. But all the drums in the village were not loud enough to drown out the mothers' wailing. I could hear their grieving cries from dusk till dawn from Saturday to Sunday when the sun came up and life moved on with the daily trudge to the well.

That weekend when the children were stolen by the sea god has frozen as a moment in time. It will stick in the time-frame of the village. Time hangs like clothes on a line of events. Last weekend, next weekend, today, yesterday and the various weeks and months are timeless. Only events are remembered, and life is measured from one to another.

Some people come to Africa and they adore it. It excites them more than anywhere else in the world. They don't see the squalor so much as the riotous colours and the bursting energy of street markets and the buzz. When I first came to Africa, many years ago now, it kidnapped my heart. I know that when Mees first visited as a young cameraman of seventeen, he promised himself that one day he would come back and live in Africa. Wherever one travels, there are people like that who came to visit and could not tear themselves away. There are those who came and went home as though infected in their blood with a need to return, who sold up all they had in Europe or the States and headed back never to leave again.

Africa is full of mysteries. Mozambique is full of mysteries. I unravel one, understand another and decode a third only to discover more and more layers, more and more depths. I live here and I know it quite well now, but it never ceases to surprise me. There is no room for monotony; it will always continue to surprise, to disturb and delight. It is unpredictable, the people are unpredictable, the weather is unpredictable – except that here in the north of Mozambique there are always varying degrees of heat.

Every day is a voyage of discovery. Every day is an adventure. Sometimes that discovery is no more than finding the place where the mongooses stand each morning on their hind legs worshipping the sun. They gather in a half circle in attitudes of prayer and look up to the early morning rays as though giving thanks. They stay like that for nearly an hour. They go to the same place every day. They are not disturbed by human presence so long as one remains a couple of metres away. They just stand with their gingery coats and their thin bodies greeting the day.

Some days the discovery is in the sea. Sometimes it is on land. Sometimes it is to see the star-shaped siri siri flower making a puce carpet on the mangrove floor where before it was only succulent leaves. Some days, a new Macua mystery unfolds. I know that at least four of the workers at the college are powerful and form part of the group of shamans. One, I think, is the head of heads, the shaman of shamans for our area. Once, there was a secret sect meeting into which I was inducted. It was very strange and rather spooky. I felt honoured to have been drawn in and I know that I was included because I was trusted to keep secrets. Without fully understanding what many of those secrets are about, I see that within the tight hierarchy of the village and its sects, it is not my place to describe everything I see.

The Varanda workers have a hierarchy and swear an oath of allegiance to their fellow members to enter the Varanda team. Even the college workers and students are forced by the community to swear an oath of allegiance. It matters to the community that the projects we have will work. It is the projects that will provide the jobs so needed in the village. It matters to the villages that the forthcoming lodges work. To ensure future enterprise, it matters that in this infant stage no equipment be stolen and no visitors upset.

The Cabaceirians are proud of Varanda and proud of the lodge that will be built there. The community's share of the profit will transform their economy. And there will be eighty jobs. Eighty jobs are enough to feed 2,400 people. Each time Mees returns from Holland, hundreds of villagers come out to greet him, chanting and Tufu dancing and banging their drums to say thank you for the chance of a better life. Mees is very uncomfortable with all that. In fact, he hates it. He says, 'Let them say thank you *after* Coral Lodge is up and running. I don't want to be thanked for what I haven't done yet. It makes me feel like an impostor.'

I have translated this into Portuguese for Morripa who has translated it into Macua and relayed it to the village, but the chanting and the dancing processions continue because, they say, what Mees has given them is hope and they never had that before.

PART THREE

XV

The Tradição

AMONG THE VILLAGERS IS A tiny Catholic congregation of thirty-nine souls, which exists without any regular priest. The last incumbent, Padre Cirillo, 'went native' many decades ago and abandoned his duties. The Catholics, headed by Victorino, foregather in the dilapidated but grandiose church of Nossa Senhora de Remedios: 'Our Lady of the Cures'. Ironic, because there are numerous maladies here and virtually no patent medicines. Most of the cures are from medicinal plants; much of the hardship here is from a lack of cures. Long ago, this area was famed for its herbal remedies. It lured trading ships from around the world to trade with the local *curandeiros*. Nowadays, although the mangrove and surrounding bush are still full of herbal remedies, they are for domestic use only.

Victorino, the church's key-keeper, is also one of the foundation students at the college. Aged thirty-nine, he has found a late vocation as a chef. He is meticulous, proud and often silent and he takes life and loyalty very seriously. Highly regarded within the community, he is one of the few locals to have ever had a job before: for many years he served at the District Administrator's table in Mossuril town;

and the sense of protocol he gleaned there has remained
indelibly. Despite being an ardent Catholic, Victorino follows the pagan *tradição* closely and sees no contradiction in
so doing.

During his training shifts as joint head of kitchen he runs
the storeroom and cooking areas with ruthless precision and
takes personal offence at any slackness. Having been taught
to chop and slice by a visiting five-star chef, he has subli-
mated both into an art form. His often stern features relax
into an expression of such bliss while in the act of chopping
that no one (myself included) dares interrupt this ecstatic
communion. His manner is very grand and almost as con-
descending as an old-fashioned English butler. The
similarity does not stop there, because like Bertie Wooster's
Jeeves, Victorino can be counted on to come up with a
simple and sensible solution when problems escalate.

Be it for the Catholic minority or the Muslim majority,
statistics about religion here are semi-redundant because
while closely following either creed, everyone simultaneously follows another. Yet adherence to both Islam and
Christianity is truly felt, it just isn't the Christianity or the
Islam that others know: it is a local, more tolerant version of
both. Apart from the small number of Christians, everyone
else is a Muslim. Islam here dates back hundreds of years to
before the Portuguese arrived in the wake of Vasco da
Gama (who first landed on Ilha and then at Cabaceira
Pequena in 1498). Along this northerly coast, most of the
population is nominally Muslim. Inland, Catholicism pre-
dominates, neck and neck in places with Jehovah's
Witnesses and a handful of other evangelistic sects. But the
coast, with its mixture of Macua, Indian and Arab, is dotted
with numerous tiny mosques.

Throughout the day, the muezzin climb the steps outside
what look like small white farmhouses and face Mecca to

call the faithful to prayer. At 7am the muezzin from the mosque next to the college gives an extra yodel out to sea to alert the ferryman that it is time to punt out of the mangroves and set sail to Omuhipiti with the last boat of the day. But at 5 and 6am, when the first ferries leave, there is no yodel from the mosque.

When the sea is calm and there is no wind to fill the patchwork sails, the captain and his sons will row the whole way. When the sea is rough, though, or the wind is contrary, no ferries or fishing boats can leave at all. There seem to be many such days.

Apart from the muezzin and the occasional crescent moon carved into a gravestone or stick marker, and the handful of mosques with minarets, it is hard to see that this is a Muslim community because the outward signs of other Muslim areas are absent. Cabaceirians are socially relaxed and easy-going. Local men sometimes wear Arabic skull caps (*kufia*), yet the women usually show no hint of Islam in their garb. They wear their traditional *capulanas*. These exotic-coloured fabrics wrap around the waist, strap babies to backs, transform into fantastic headdresses (*lenzo*) and also act as windcheaters, and as both shawls and blankets. Women tie their housekeeping into a knot of *capulana*, which they tuck into their waist; they make a great performance of secretly tying and untying as though each had discovered a unique hiding place. As a skirt, the *capulana* has a tendency to work loose. Unlike in other Muslim settlements, where the women cover up, Cabaceirians and Mozambicans in general have no compunction about rearranging their clothes in public, wrapping and unwrapping *capulanas* to hitch them back into place.

I have never seen anyone wear a veil here or a headscarf other than in the flamboyant traditional style, but Momade, the tomato-grower, says there is a woman outside Mossuril who 'wears the hooded sack'. Women and girls wander freely around the village and on the ferry to Ilha. The girls tend to be loud and giggly. Men and women openly tease each other and flirt. Many men have more than one wife, but many women also have more than one husband. Officially, a man can have several wives at the same time; officially, women cannot have more than one husband. But marriages are both easily made and easily broken.

When the local girls are courting, they roam hand in hand with their boyfriends, kiss and cuddle, dance and date as they would in London or Amsterdam. Make-up is local style and consists mainly of a rather unnerving white mealy facemask made from a pounded tree bark (mussiro). Although not the most attractive cosmetic at first glance, it works, because the local women have beautiful skin in varying shades from ebony to beige, reflecting a thousand years of interracial mix in the times when Cabaceira Grande and Cabaceira Pequena were important trading posts and Ilha was the empress of the Indian Ocean.

There are other cosmetic products squeezed or concocted from local plants. Atija, who was one of the first class of students in September 2004 and is now employed by the college as deputy head of kitchen, knows every local recipe there is for beauty products. Despite having five children, Atija is still disarmingly youthful and pretty. She is also one of the few local women with a high energy level. A lifetime of sub-nutrition has slowed many of the local women down to the point where speech is a whispered drawl and even walking is a slow shuffle. The only time when all the women and girls seem to be injected with adrenalin is when it is time to dance. Girls who find it hard to stand up for more than an hour at a time will dance in the traditional ceremonies for six or seven hours at a stretch without showing any signs of fatigue.

Atija and a small team of local woman form a tireless team of work and social commentary. This is probably enhanced by having had nearly a year of cooks' perks and thereby beating the almost endemic anaemia and poor diet of her peers, but the team in question also stood out before the extra food graced their palates.

While unflagging in their pursuit and performance of the *tradição*, none of the local women, be they lethargic or energetic, seems to devote much time to the pursuit of Islam. They fast during Ramadan and always wash after going to the loo, but other than that, they hold on tenaciously to their pre-eminence in this matrilineal society and take full advantage of the liberties this entails. Very few of our students have all their children with the same man or stay with one husband for more than a few years. If a man goes away, such as to seek work, his wife or wives feel at liberty to switch husbands. With one notable exception, all the women I know in the villages have few problems with being one of two or even three wives.

It seems that the problem of survival is so universal and paramount that little else can distract from it. Most families live in harmony with their neighbours; about half of the families share a two-room mud hut between two wives, four or five children and one husband/father with a lot less bickering than an average Western family. Even in the cemeteries, visible from afar by a halo of frangipani blooms, Christians and Muslims lie side by side and have done so for centuries. Perhaps one of the reasons why there is no religious tension here is because underlying everything else, the people are of one faith. For one and all uphold the *tradiçµão*, and the pagan beliefs go hand-in-hand with whatever other religion is upheld. Overall, it is the *tradição* that rules. Where the customs of the ancient ancestor worship contradict either Catholicism or the Muslim faith, then the latter are adapted.

These villages are microcosms of the old Macua way of life. For instance, Macua women are traditionally powerful. But further inland, customs have changed, swinging towards women being more like active chattels than depositories of power. Yet within this matrilineal society, women can do very much what they like, restrained only by the strict parameters of poverty. So women continue to own much of the property, to have both control and the custody of their children, and they also have almost complete sexual freedom. Women sit on the village committees, and hold office in the local and district government. This tendency is reflected nationwide: at regional and national level, there are many women in the government. It is hard to know how much of this is due to the innate matriarchy of the predominant Macua, and how much is thanks to the late President Samora Machel's championing of women's rights.

Many of the *curandeiros* in Mossuril District are women, as are some of the *al'mos*. Each category is immensely powerful within a given village. The Cabaceiras do not have their own *curandeiros* at the moment, although there are women training now with a female master *curandeiro* in Lumbo, fifty kilometres away. When their services are needed, a troupe of twelve ladies arrives by boat dressed in white robes with red sashes and carrying mysterious luggage. Each time they come, preparations begin weeks before their arrival and a buzz of excitement circulates from hut to hut and through Atija's kitchen. Since the traditional healing and exorcism ceremonies take several days and nights to perform, I will reserve describing one to another chapter. Suffice it to say that enormous homage is paid publicly to these women, and their elevated position within the *tradição* overrules any stipulations on the lowly place of females in society decreed by the Koran.

Another contradiction is the local attitude to alcohol.

Most people don't drink any, but that is more because they cannot afford to than on religious grounds. A few of the village elders abstain on religious grounds if it is offered to them, but most men and women will drink a beer when they can and see no reason not to, despite the Holy Koran specifically forbidding it. And yet, with a few notable exceptions in Chocas and Mossuril, a general sense of the Muslim disapproval inherent in the religious ban does seem to curtail the consumption of alcohol. The shabeens and hooch distilleries to be found in almost every other African village are not a part of life in the Cabaceiras. As with many Western 'home brews', it is not so much the alcohol per se as the toxic substances which adhere to it in the slapdash home brewing that corrode livers and brains. In East Africa, proffered home brews are best politely avoided since battery acid is added to give it that extra zing, with deadly side-effects.

The combination of public drunkenness being socially frowned on and the local poverty which prohibits most people from buying alcohol at all has resulted in much happier homes than in other equivalently poor communities. Beyond the village, there are a handful of notable and noted drunks with the salary and the inclination to sit morosely nursing quarter litres of gin. They alternately stare at their trophy and drink from it until they fall comatose across the table and have to be carried home. The most popular brand is called Travel Gin. As some of the villagers learn English, when the irony of the name dawns, there is much joking about the 'travellers' and conjecture about where they are travelling to as they stare red-eyed into their yellow cartons; and how, if they keep travelling in the same way, they will end up nowhere.

Despite such upstanding remarks, I noticed when we opened our own training restaurant and bar that our first stock of Travel sold out with indecent speed and some peripheral tipplers seemed to be losing their sense of reality a little more regularly than could be any good for either them or their families. From our first stock-taking it was clear that the amount of 'travelling' in July 2006 was threatening to get out of hand. Since all supplies have to be brought in from over one hundred kilometres away, it was possible to curb this tendency by simply not bringing back the beloved gin (a quarter litre of which is cheaper than a beer). Before we opened the first bar in the Cabaceiras as a training vehicle for the college students, there had never been a bar, café or restaurant here.

There is a local mad woman who rants in the early evening, weaving between the mud huts and shouting whenever she can run away from her anxious family, but there were no drunks sprawled in the dust, no fighting, nor beating up of their wives and children. To be fair, nor were there such scenarios when we opened our bar, but with our entire stock of Travel (for what we had assumed would be six months) consumed in three weeks, we didn't want to turn this spiritual village into a gin shop. So, if only for the sake of the livers of the four customers who, virtually unaided, accounted for our gin sales, it seemed better to teach the trainee barmen how to stand firm when asked, '*Tem* Travel?'

One of the hardest lessons for the student barmen (who as hitherto jobless villagers are lower in the hierarchy than the relatively wealthy customers whom they know and respect) is to admit that our new and lovely bar, once again, is gin-less. We have had many meetings about it because all the students would like the gin to flow in unlimited quantities so that their bar, 2 Coqueiros, which is their pride, and which is stocked with so many other exotic drinks, sweets, appetizers and bottles of mysterious beverages, never has to announce the humiliating phrase, '*Não*, Travel *não temos*.'

In the first month their community bar opened, I noticed a lot of salaries and subsidies from our project spiralling into its kitty. By the second month, ninety sobered staff and students were beginning to get over the marvel of ice and cold drinks and home-made cookies. For most of our team, the presence of a freezer at the college was much more alluring than the stocks of alcohol it chilled. The luxury of a cold drink is hard to convey to anyone who has not lived without refrigeration for a prolonged period of time in a tropical climate. In the summer of 2006, I was also bloated with Coca-Cola and joining the local craze of savouring the many flavours offered at 2 Coqueiros by way of fizzy drinks, from the lurid crimson Sparletta to the E-colorant bonanza of Fanta (a local favourite now replaced by the gentler blends), and the sophisticated Ananas, Lemon Twist and just plain Limão.

In this 99 per cent Muslim community, the two most popular national beers are the lagers that are served all over Mozambique. They are called 2M (pronounced 'doys emmy') and Manica. The two brands engage in a constant marketing war which includes giving away posters, mats and all sorts of propaganda. Even a devout Muslim will use a metal 2M sign to repair his roof, or to cut up into a pot or bucket, funnel or watering can. Apart from the occasional 'traveller' though, bars here are more places to meet and talk over a cold drink than places specifically designed for the consumption of alcohol. Beers are what rich people drink. And the students are amazed at the capacity of an *Akunha* to consume alcohol.

One group of South African visitors downed six bottles of 2M each, provoking a local debate as to how such a feat could be possible without any ensuing vomiting or passing out.

'How do they do it?' Morripa asked me. 'I mean, I have travelled and tried it, but I can't get past a bottle and half without virtually falling off my chair. *Six* bottles each. We counted them, and then they stood up and left without so much as a stumble. I always thought that colour was just about your skin and a certain hardness of heart, a lack of compassion, but now I am wondering if it isn't a lot more than that. *Six* bottles in just over an hour! I fought for my country for seventeen years and I've lost count of how many battles I survived, but I couldn't survive *that*, none of us could. So we must be made differently.'

I think I find the paradox of religion and drinking more intriguing than the local people do. Alcohol isn't really an issue here: it is a luxury, and luxury is a phenomenon that occurs 'out there' beyond the frayed edges of these twin outposts.

No one can say for how long harmony will continue to reign here, but while it does, there is an almost tangible gentleness about the village. Occasionally there is a petty theft, but it is rare. There is a lot of gossip but it is mostly devoid of malice; rejoicing in the misfortune of others is also rare with so much misfortune to share. Criticizing the rise of others is a trickier subject, but such is the way in many post-colonial societies. The students find it hard to take orders from leaders chosen from among themselves. As a result, getting chosen for the management courses is a mixed blessing. Students who complete such courses will not only get much better jobs, but they could, theoretically, set up their own small businesses in the future. The down-side is an instant loss of popularity and solidarity among their peers. Success is a lonely journey. A few of the men and women who have started on its road have managed to regain their place in the social hierarchy at a higher level. This has been easier to achieve in the kitchen than anywhere else. Atija is accepted by all as deputy head of the kitchen. Her successful transition from student to staff acts as a good example to the many student cooks. They get a student subsidy, she gets a wage.

Having joined 'the other side', the teaching staff, Atija can also see more clearly the very long road we need to take not only to train cooks and chefs but to introduce and maintain essential standards of hygiene in the kitchen. Part of every day is consumed in the battle with dirt. In our sanitized, pre-packaged world in the West, we tend to take hygiene for granted. In Africa, in a place with very limited water, devoid of storerooms, refrigeration or even furniture, the level of ignorance on hygiene – apart from that which pertains to each scrupulously clean person – is high. Instilling hygiene is a slow and laborious process. Everything has to be repeated and shown not once, but a hundred times. And everything has to be checked and checked again. Hand-in-hand with fighting sub-nutrition, it is our daily diet. Out of the battle I have gleaned that common sense varies from culture to culture, and what may be obvious to me is a complete mystery to people here.

More than providing skills and training, more than providing jobs, getting the local people to truly understand the importance of home hygiene and better nutrition are two simple things that can save their lives and the lives of their families.

Village life is a hand-to-mouth affair: days are about surviving, nights are about discussing the daily miracle of being there and staying alive when almost everything conspires for this not to be the case. After the talk and the laughter, the tears and even the drumming either ceases or pauses; there is sometimes a profound silence interrupted only by screech owls, nightjars, the plangent wails of bushbabies and the occasional furtive movements of genets.

XVI

Natural and Supernatural

IN THIS PLACE OF BASICS, where everything has to be conjured out of what is available, and where so little of what we think of as basic materials in the Western world *are* available, even the trappings of traditional ceremonies are about as simple as such things can be. At the beginning and at the end of life, the voice of these rites is that of beaten rhythms and whispered prayers, beaten rhythms and whispered spells, beaten rhythms and cabalistic signs written on scraps of paper. Until the Mestre Canira began his clandestine drum upgrades, all the local drums were four pieces of wood stuck together with resin glue with a piece of brittle goat hide stretched across them. An unskilled drummer will split this hide within a few minutes; a skilled drummer will wear it out with his fingertips and the palms of his hands. When someone is sick, or when someone dies, the drums are beaten all night. One drummer sustains the rhythm in a thinner solo while the others tighten the skins over hot charcoals. There is shame in a slack skin, shame in a badly kept drum. Caring for the drums (*batoke* or *nlapa*) is an honoured position within society.

When a child is initiated or a baby is born, when

someone reaches puberty, marries, sickens, dies, leaves or returns, then drummers pound out their quick rhythms for hour after frenzied hour. Since there is hardly a day one or other of the above events does not occur, the drumming becomes part of the night. Only during the month of Ramadan, when drumming and dancing are not allowed, or when goatskin breaks putting a drum out of action, is there really any silence in the village at night.

There is no easy way to learn about the traditional Macua ceremonies, not least because all questions regarding them are answered identically: it is the *tradição*. The word is like coming up against a brick wall without any apparent fissure, let alone a window, through which to glimpse a little further. As a spoken language with an oral culture, learning has to be from people and not from books. The Portuguese colonists came to Mozambique to make money from ivory, gold and slaves, they did not come to observe or record the local customs. Few Christian missionaries came and most of those who did were more intent on stamping out the local culture than preserving it. Some of the more recent Italian Catholic missions have gathered valuable information on various aspects of Macua culture, but it remains largely unpublished and unavailable (such as to me, a novice Macua scholar).

If I trespass into the more secret realms of the *tradição*, it is with the knowledge that TV and Western values will, inevitably, change this area, and when they do, the rich cultural treasure currently stored in the elders' heads should be preserved for future generations to come back to when the joys of soap operas and advertising eventually pall. By chance, courtesy of its long isolation, the Cabaceirians have an undiluted version of the *tradição*. For all that, it is not my place, nor do I have the right to intrude. But since I have been *invited* to observe the traditional rites, I hope to repay that privilege by recording what I see and learn.

However, my invitation comes from village elders and not from the rank and file of their disciples. The latter guard their secrets jealously. Only with the elders (several of whom are the local *mestres*) can I dig deeper into the culture. Gradually, though, bits and pieces of the old religion are unfolding thanks to the patience and erudition of my guides. Morripa, who is virtually the key to the Cabaceiras, is foremost among these. Without him, I don't think I would be living here. He is my guide and interpreter, colleague and friend. Just as in real life, wherever I go, Morripa either is there or just was there or is about to arrive, so too, in these pages, Morripa is never far away.

Magic is practised daily by the Macua, but there is no longer anyone to keep its more powerful and darker side going in Cabaceira Pequena since the old *feticeiro*, Alpino, died a few years ago. The septuagenarian hereditary chief, Sheik Namana, is said to know all there is to know about Macua magic but he has not handed his knowledge down. Some of the village elders do not see this as such a bad thing. Whereas a *curandeiro* and the other village leaders work for the good of all, a *feticeiro* can work for both the powers of Good and Evil. The late Mr Alpino, apparently, was 'a bad man who hurt a lot of people, making them sick so that he could cure them for money'.

However, not many tongues loosen on the subject of Alpino, whose bad habits are feared and whose powers are believed to reach from beyond his grave. His lurking spirit has much to do with the general reluctance to enter the mangrove at night and also a general reluctance to discuss the *tradição*. When I try to find out more about Alpino's bad spells, I am advised to take my interlocutor's word for it that he was a nasty, spiteful, greedy and embittered man whose goal in life was to hurt others. When I asked, 'But if he was so harmful, why couldn't the rest of the village do something to stop him?', this elicited a look of sympathy, as though to wonder how I could be so stupid.

'He was the *namirrette.*'

The crack closed and the talk ended. A *namirrette (feti-ceiro)* has superhuman powers, he can see into souls. He can read thoughts, pre-empt attacks and provoke sickness and even death. A bad *namirrette* in a village is a liability, but also, it would seem, a cross the villagers just have to bear.

Less powerful members of the village still concoct benign spells and there is at least one transformer said to be able to become a fish at will. But the old days of powerful spells and curses have gone. Since 2003, I have wandered through the village freely; but in times past, no one entered it without permission from the *regulo.* Anyone who ignored this rule was doomed 'to see the sun set but not live to see it rise again'. During the 'civil war' in the 1970s and 1980s, the village was a safe haven for hundreds of refugees from Chocas and Mossuril. The war itself never reached the village, but all who entered it with permission of the *regulo* were safe for as long as they chose to stay there. Some of the villagers now are former refugees.

Scraps of cloth and small clay pots filled with roots and leaves balance at the feet of sacred baobab and mutholo trees. Under the latter, small sacrifices of flour are offered to the ancestors, some of whom were buried under mutholo trees long ago. Frayed ribbons and stick arrangements are tied to twigs in the bush. Some of these are calls for help, some are to give comfort, and some are warnings to put the fear of angry gods into the community. Cabalistic warnings are written out on the torn pages of children's exercise books and stuck in unexpected places or tied with strands of banana palm. Banana palms are good and their leaves and fibres are used in many ways in the ceremonies. But there is

also a bad banana, called munhepiri, the fruit of which is
never eaten and the leaves and fibres never touched. So bad
is this palm believed to be that it is never transplanted even
by *feticeiros*. Where it grows it grows wild and it is watched
warily from afar.

There is also a phantom called Makhuru who occasionally visits from inland. Makhuru has to be exorcized. Here
on the coast, this bad spirit is only a danger when anyone
travels and inadvertently brings it back with them, or when
outsiders visit. Makhuru has only one arm and one hand,
one ear and one eye. In fact, of all that a normal person has
and is, Makhuru is a 50 per cent clone. It even has only one
of each organ such as kidneys and lungs. Out in the bush, it
shoots animals and then offers their meat to passers-by.

'Never buy meat from a stranger.'

Such meat is contaminated and the bad spirit will climb
inside you when you swallow it. Alone, or via a possessed
victim, Makhuru will spoil field crops and start bush fires.

'Muluku' is the Macua word for God. It means the one
God, singular, and can never refer to 'the gods' unless it is
specifically pluralized as *Muluku Mwanène* or *Mwanène
Muluku*. All the local people will tell you that 'there is only
one god and his name is Allah'. Yet in the same breath, they
will tell you that there are many gods. To name but two:
there is *Muluku a Wirimu*, God of the Sky, and there is
Muluku a Vathí, God of the Earth.

This is a place of enormous contradictions and also of
enormous tolerance. Since time immemorial, it is a place
that has survived by everyone getting together and sitting
under a baobab tree to resolve problems by reaching a compromise. Just as Christianity compromised by incorporating
pagan festivals into its own calendar (most notably allocat-
ing the birth of Christ to 25 December to accommodate
an ancient fertility rite), so has the *tradição* adapted and

absorbed Islam. So, locally, there is one God, Allah, and there are many gods. There are prophets and there are the ancestors, there are good spirits and angels, demons and bad spirits, and their combined wisdom and strength forms a sacred consortium.

Democracy rules here, no one person can be right alone. Rightness is a joint decision. Thus, no one god can decide alone, all the gods must have their say as well. The *idea* of one God is accepted, but the *belief* is in many gods. In the Koranic schools (one per village), a teacher interprets the Holy Koran. The style of learning by rote of other Islamic countries is less important here than an understanding of the text. What exactly happens when that sacred text contradicts the local beliefs, I don't know, but the upshot is that nothing changes.

There is another sacred tree called a *murruku-ruku* (*Kigelia pinnata*), which has fruit that dangle down like sausages. These fruits are the object of prayers and oaths. When a prayer has been said or an oath taken, a cut for each is made in the fruit. I used to wonder if, on those puzzling days when a young Koranic student is first confronted with the dual nature of his village creed, he asks the sausage tree for guidance by praying for enlightenment as to which is right: the Holy Book he is studying or the *tradição*? As time goes by, though, I see this is unlikely. The *tradição* is rarely dogmatic. Apart from certain taboos, there are no set rules. Its rules are as flexible as the tides. More than any dogma, it is a way of life, and since it is the only way of life anyone knows here, it gathers up and integrates everything and everyone for as far as feet can travel and drum beats can echo.

There is no border between the natural and the supernatural. The world is a magical place wherein the weird and the wonderful uplift the drudgery of everyday. Birds are rumoured to sleep on the seabed. All creatures from the land are mirrored in the water, breeding their marine equivalent. Over the centuries, fishermen have sighted them all. Only a few years ago, two fishermen were surprised to hear a woman singing in the mangrove during a high tide. Mussagy, the driver, knew the story from his father, Ibraimo.

'When they went to investigate, they found a strange fat woman swimming among the mangrove stilts. More people came to see and the more they observed her, the less human they found her to be. She was naked and had large breasts, but she was half woman and half fish. When she stopped swimming, she couldn't or wouldn't speak. Before they could analyse her arrival any further, she swam back out to sea and stayed underwater longer than any diver could, longer even than the ones who can transform so thoroughly that they hardly come up for breath.'

We discussed this apparition one night at the college and then again the following morning around the well. When I told Mussagy and the guards that the creature was a manatee (of which there are many in, for instance, the Caribbean) and imitated its singing voice, none of the local staff said, 'Ah, so that's what it was.' Instead, I could see them thinking, 'Respect! Dona Lisa obviously knows a thing or two about magic.'

In a place were old men become bats at night and hang upside down from palm trees, and drummers induce a frenzy of shrieks and cheers round firelight, summoning rain or ancestral intervention, respite or health, rational explanations are neither wanted nor needed. The *tradição* has an explanation for everything. With or without their own *feticeiro*, the local people live within its rigid restraints.

The tide comes in and out. Birds find their way into the rock pools within the lagoon. From raucous crows (which it is taboo to even shoo away) to tiny scarlet finches, all have a home on Varanda. There are fewer birds at the college, but from time to time, as though to make up for this lack, a fish eagle perches on the top of one of the derelict pillars and watches superciliously as we struggle to make a garden out of a pile of rubble. Even though he has one eye closed, I know he is watching our chickens, mentally measuring the ingredients before swooping on one for a snack.

So far, the fish eagle and the giant African crows between them have snapped up over twenty of our chicks. After each raid, there is a long talk about birds and beasts between the kitchen staff and the guards. The conclusion is that strings must be criss-crossed over the courtyard high up in the trees to confuse the crows. No one ever suggests anything like chucking stones at the marauding crows because that would be taboo. Like wayward children in a hippy household, they can do whatever they want; it is for us to defend ourselves against them.

On their report card, the crows have black marks for killing our chickens, having incredibly loud and unpleasant voices, frightening away songbirds and stealing innumerable bars of aloe vera soap from the shell soapdish on the veranda.

XVII

Macua Rituals

PIECES OF CLOTH AND STONE, twigs, roots, feathers and bones, powdered bark, powdered wood, powdered shells, powdered stone and powdered spice are all used for spells. The quantity and variety of ingredients can give no clue as to the importance of a spell. Some of the simplest recipes are used for the most potent magic or intercession with the spirits. The power of the person relaying the spell is crucial. Mere mortals can only hope to achieve results through fervent prayer. The more heartfelt the prayer, the more help it can bring. In cases of extreme sickness or calamity, many Macua elders must join together to pray specifically for the afflicted so that their prayers may be answered. I have been told here that all prayers are heard but only some are answered, thus the supplicant must petition loudly and forcefully to compete with the millions of other prayers that fill the ears of the Lord.

For traditional ceremonies beyond the realm of the mosques (despite being administered by most of the same elders), certain places are sacred, certain trees are sacred, certain plants and animals are sacred and certain people are too. I first became aware of the sacred spots here by virtually stumbling over one when I lost my way returning from the dhow ferry beach. Unwittingly, I was stumbling towards an acacia tree with a very small clay pot half hidden in its roots. A handful of stones were scattered in the grass beside this pot and a ragged scrap of ribbon was tied to a low twig. The ribbon flapped its grey tatters in the wind, thereby drawing my attention to it. When I stepped nearer to see what it was that had caught there, my village guide warned to me to step back, shouting, 'Not there!'

'Where?' I asked, not having seen the nondescript pot or stones. I moved closer to the short grass by the tree instinctively, imagining a green or black mamba poised in the longer grass to strike me down.

My guide lunged forward and grabbed the edge of my jacket, gently but firmly guiding me back.

'Our way is over here,' he said.

By that time I had seen the array of offerings round the tree and stepped hastily away.

'What is it for?'

'Nothing,' he muttered.

'*Tradição?*'

'Nothing,' he repeated and hurried on, forcing me to hasten to keep up.

I could judge the significance of what I had seen by his change of pace. There is very little that can do that. Every movement including walking has its own pace, its own immutable rhythm. By altering his pace and hurrying, my guide betrayed his own fear. It was early days for me in this largely benign society and the hair stood up at the back of my neck and on my arms; I was fearful for what would happen if by unwittingly trespassing on a sacred place I had incurred the wrath of the shaman.

I tried to dismiss the thought on the grounds that decades of movies have implanted irrational fears in me. I walked on; hurrying along a path of trampled grass, African mint and a pretty creeping plant with yellow flowers and seeds like sputniks, whose thorns can drive right through the sole of any normal shoe. Returning mentally to the Macua shrine, I told myself I hadn't actually touched anything. Approaching the place of spells had been an accident. Hmm, I also told myself, such accidents didn't help travellers in West Africa or Haiti or even Brazil. I had heard too many stories on my own travels and seen too many unpleasant things where careless accidents occurred and encroached on matters of the occult.

When I got back to base, rather than keep my fear of waking up the next day as shrivelled as a snakeskin, or even – I luridly imagined – not waking up at all, I decided to consult on the matter with one whom I knew to be high up in the secrets and spells of Cabaceira. More than any *Akunha*, Sofia and Isabel harboured great fear of the local spells. They are both staunch Catholics, aware, as any Mozambican must be, that there is a dark side to native culture. In Maputo, this dark side must have been much more sinister than it is out here because both were terrified of offending the local people lest they cursed them into a state of paralysis. Sofia was fond of telling me about the traditional ceremonies in the south in which 'everyone came out spattered in the sacrificial blood of chickens and goats'. Apparently, while under a trance, dancers would bite the heads off living chickens.

'Anyone who got on the wrong side of those witchdoctors could go to sleep and never wake up.'

When Sofia explained her fear of local spells, it seemed that some of the old myths and clichés about savagery in 'darkest Africa' were more prevalent in Maputo than they were abroad. One of our visiting Christian Mozambican staff takes a ritual bucket bath every night in a concoction designed to give protection from curses and evil spirits.

It was easy to laugh at what Sofia believed would be the consequence of her crossing any of the local people, but it did little to calm her troubled mind. I was an *Akunha* and obviously didn't know what I was talking about. However, locked away in the middle of nowhere, I spooked too when I inadvertently invaded a sacred spot. A small world magnifies emotion.

I remembered an incident earlier in the year when Isabel had a heated discussion about something with one of the locals and fell into a high fever the following night. Scared witless, she and Sofia fled to Ilha and stayed in a hotel whence they sent frantic text and voice messages to inform me that Isabel had been bewitched, poisoned and cursed by her opponent who was, Isabel assured me, 'trying to kill her'.

Too terrified to return to the college, Isabel flew back to Maputo. On arrival she was whisked into hospital where analyses showed that she had a bad bout of malaria. After standard treatment, she recovered completely and eventually returned. I was in Amsterdam at the time and could only try to calm all and sundry by phone. Long term, the person who remained most upset was the supposed assassin.

Not wishing to let my imagination run away with me, I hastened to find the *mestre* who could help me. We sat down and completed the obligatory ritual greetings, then I invited him to hear my story and advise me what to do. He laughed at my fear, wondering, no doubt, what kind of barbarian society had bred me. I learnt with great relief that the small clay pot contained the evil spirits that had been tormenting a young girl. Had I inadvertently knocked this over, I would have released them. Since I did not touch this pot, no harm had been done.

'If, however, you had released the banished spirits by mistake, no harm would have come to you. But the poor girl's life would have been in danger. Bad spirits hate being trapped and banished. If they escape, they invariably seek revenge on the recent host.'

On the following day, perhaps after some consultation with his fellow spiritual leaders, my advisor invited me to step aside and sit with him to learn a little more about the *tradição*. Bad spirits, fever and pain were regularly taken from the sick and placed in a pot. Ribbons were tied to the trees to honour the guiding spirits and alert them to a new call. The ribbons had a ragged appearance (which was the main thing that made the site sinister to my eyes) because in that poor village, what were there but rags to offer? Each stone had a deep significance. What that significance was or is was not for me to know. What I should know is that the *tradição* is a force for Good. As in all things, there is scope for a bad practitioner to pervert power, but such things lead to isolation and ultimately ruin. The *tradição* is an unharnessable force. A few wise men can try to channel a fraction of that force, just as a few engineers might be able to channel a river into the sea. We can disrespect the sea but we cannot change its mood. We cannot anger it. We are too insignificant; all we can do is hope to add another drop of water or matter to its massive volume.

Feeling decidedly silly, I went back to work. But from that day on, I began to notice many more scraps of cloth and stone, many more of these calls for help. These are not, as the sage *mestre* pointed out, attempts to appease the wrath of any spirit or ancestor but to appeal for their intervention. Like anonymous phone calls from a hapless crowd, they call the ancestors to alert them to their plight.

The Old know more than the Young and have more mental force. The Dead are stronger and more numerous than the Living. The Dead are untroubled by the fight to survive and can therefore give up all their thought to wisdom and contemplation of the world. The Living are advised and guided by the Dead. The Living should strive to emulate the wise men and heroes of the past. The Living have a duty to care for the legacy of the Dead. The Living are offered many paths and each must strive to find and keep to the true one. All living things have a spirit and all living things must respect these spirits, be they in a fly, a man or a baobab tree. Some species, such as rats and mosquitoes, are messengers from bad spirits, and as such can be killed without much penance. But other species are sent as messengers from the *cherifo* – the sheriff – to guide and protect us; their spirit is more powerful than ours (for example, crows, dolphins and baobab trees). To harm one of these messengers is strictly taboo and will result in dire consequences. Mankind has been sent by the gods to interpret and carry out their wishes. In order to do this, each person has a potentially powerful spirit; thus to hurt a fellow man is also taboo. Punishment for the deed can be immediate, but can also take years to visit the offender.

Curandeiros also practise preventative medicine. This is called *Mapithela*. This word probably comes from the Mapitti tribe, who invaded Mozambique in the second half of the nineteenth century. Arriving from the southern territories of the Zulu and Angones, they attacked the Macua and enslaved many of them. Although their activities never reached the more settled, Arab-influenced and Portuguese-ruled northern coast, news of the invasion travelled, as news will. Now, a century and a half later, Mapithela is medicine to prevent marauding sickness from taking its victim unawares, like the Mapittis took the Macua long ago. Although the *curandeiro* can stave off disease, his preventative measures will only work if the patient is predestined to go on living.

It is firmly believed that all life is predestined in some

ways. On the day we are born, it is written in the stars the
exact time and day when we will die. Within that time
(known to the gods, the *cherifo*, his many servants and our
ancestors, but not to us directly), we must incur no shame.
Great things achieved beyond our community are of less
worth than great things achieved within our community. A
man or a woman has lived well when he or she has the
love and respect of her family and neighbours. The man or
woman who offends the community must redeem him- or
herself. Failure to admit failure and failure to make
redemption could, in the most drastic of cases, incur banishment from the community. No fate is considered worse
than this. Death, torture and agony are as nothing to the
terror of banishment. When someone dies far from his own
native community and is buried on foreign soil, his soul is
doomed to wander for eternity. For Cabaceirians, anywhere
beyond Chocas-Mar (six kilometres distant) counts as
'foreign' soil.

So when anyone dies, family and friends make every
effort to take the body home for burial. In a tropical country where funerals occur within twenty-four hours of death,
and where transport is scant and expensive, and where over
90 per cent of the population is grindingly poor, the
expense of moving a corpse is usually prohibitive. Thus,
people from the villages tend not to go to the hospitals in
Nampula or Nacala at all. If they do go to a hospital, as
soon as death seems probable the patient is hastily removed
and bundled onto the back of a truck or squeezed into an
overcrowded minibus and taken home. That last and, for
many, agonizing journey is worth the sacrifice because it
ensures home burial. The idea of dying far from home is so
frightening that those who do die beyond their native community die in fear, thereby adding to the future unrest of
their soul. A 'good' death is important. We should not fight

'the call'. When our predestined time has come, it has come, and we should go peacefully into the light.

As soon as someone expires, a stone is placed under the deceased's head, both eyes are closed and water is sprinkled ritually over the closed lips. The body is then ritually washed by a family member, who has also ritually washed in order to perform the duty. The body is then wrapped in 5 metres of white cloth (7 metres for a woman). Rolls of this white cotton are sold on Ilha in the general store on the corner of the market square. Like so much else here, it is made in China and has purple Chinese characters stamped on the end of each bale. While the death rites are being attended to, simultaneously a messenger will set out to alert the village that so-and-so 'has been called'.

Family and friends gather round the deceased to keep him or her company on his last night at home. The funeral will take place on the day after the death. Funerals are always well attended. No matter what someone is doing, they will stop, down tools and leave to attend a funeral. In the early days, particularly after the rains when people in the neighbourhood died like flies from malaria, the college kept emptying out completely as all students and workers left en masse to attend another funeral. This was making such a huge dent in the curriculum, the construction schedule and the struggling farm that Morripa and the village elders made a chart for who could attend a funeral. Thus students can attend funerals of immediate family members, next-door neighbours and village elders. A further two students and two workers will be delegated to attend any given funeral to represent the entire college.

Although there are several cemeteries, some people are buried in their own compounds and, in the past, some were buried under sacred trees. There is a strict and intense mourning period of ten days during which rigid rules are

observed in diet, dress and behaviour. On the tenth day, the
departed spirit is helped on its way by an all-night ceremony of drums, prayers, chants and grilled food. Thereafter,
a further thirty-day period of ritual mourning is observed.
On the fortieth night after a death, the drums will beat from
dusk till dawn in a last farewell. This is the *arumaíni* rite for
the dead. '*Arumaíni*' means 'forty' in Macua. Sometimes it is
called by the Arabic '*ekoti*'. No matter how poor a family is,
food and tea (*matapapishu*) must be offered to the numerous
guests to accompany the departing spirit. Whatever can be
scrabbled together, borrowed or sold will be done to provide this last terrestrial act of respect.

When the time comes for someone to join their ancestors,
he or she will enjoy a life eternal in the village of their
birth. Once elevated to the rank of spirits, each will take
their place at the great community meeting in the sky
according to their wisdom and goodness during their brief
passage on earth. It is an honour to be called to join the
ancestors, but it is never an appointment one can make one-
self. We are each obliged to pass the test of life and to enjoy
whatever pleasures and endure whatever hardships the Lord
and Sheriff (*cherifo*) sends our way. Suicide is seen as an
unforgivable crime against nature and disrespects both the
Living and the Dead. Mourning is about the loss endured
by the living, who must continue to find their right path
without the love and help of the deceased, rather than about
the loss of life itself. The one who dies will never suffer
again; the one who dies has been released and will live on
forever. Thus the ones who have survived weep, wail and
pray for themselves and each other because they have to
continue their journey without someone they love.

With a population of seven thousand souls, hardly a week
goes by without a death, so the drums echo and resound
through the bush, carried on the wind from the mangrove

into every compound and every mud hut. Sometimes the insistent beats are so loud they seem to be coming from inside my head. They throb as I fall asleep and they wake me up in the small hours as the rhythms change.

Sometimes, between the doleful cries of bushbabies, the nights implode with the eerie sound of women ululating. This *elulu* vibration is a uniquely female African sound reserved for moments of joy. Its outpouring of happiness carries further than any shout. It is the primitive, spontaneous sound of women when words fail and the normal range of voice becomes redundant. The unique sound is made with the tongue and the lips. It is caused by the tip of the tongue creating vibrations and it has a truly alarming volume.

The nearest we come to it in our society is the visceral grip of the *squillo* some opera singers can produce at the end of a held note. A *squillo* causes glass to vibrate and hair to stand on end while throwing its listeners into emotional tumult. Yet when an African woman ululates, the effect is far more emotionally churning. It is a sound that cannot be ignored. As it surpasses a whoop of sheer delight, its effect is exciting and the raw emotion shocks.

It is the women here who vocalize pleasure, and it is they who most vocalize grief. This is a society where men can and do cry. But it is the women who wail. In bereavement, the sheer volume of such cries is sickening to hear. Without the trappings of material riches, wealth is measured in terms of human relations. Thus, when a local person dies, their extended family loses a chunk of everything and it is the women who express the enormity of that loss.

XVIII

A Visit from the Curandeiros

WITHIN OUR TEAM, ADAMJI the guard is one of the people closest to me. By day, we often work side by side gardening. He watches me as I start a new job and then wanders over from his post under the kapok tree by the gate and joins in. Making a garden out of a wilderness is uninspiring as a spectator sport until the positive results have time to show. Most of the agricultural students regard ornamental gardening as a complete waste of time, but Adamji understands and appreciates flowers. It is his pleasure to outdo me in the garden, and mine to be outdone. The college courtyard is gradually being converted from a rubbish dump to a formal garden with stone paths and flowerbeds, fruit trees and a herb garden. Each bed is enclosed by a low stone wall and each stone has to be found and dug into position.

The college grounds are littered with hand-cut stones, in blocks and slabs. Most are still buried under sand and weeds, but Adamji has a knack for finding them. From early on, he sensed that a way to my heart was via these walls. I have mentioned that I like to garden, but 'like' doesn't really describe the obsessive nature of this activity. It would be correct to say that I delight in gardening. In the days when

I and the local people were mutual mysteries, Adamji was the first of the team Morripa and the village committee assembled to find some common ground with me. We bonded building walls together in the early hours after dawn and the dead hours of the afternoon. We didn't talk much: we just fit stone to stone and then drank tea together, admiring our handiwork from afar.

From there, we moved on to conversation. Adamji works on alternate nights, and gravitates from the gateway to the kitchen to sit and talk, keeping me company while I make jam or chilli sauce or bottled fruits. He has become adept at holding an oil lamp at just the right height for me to see what is cooking on the charcoal stove; and he anticipates my need for a new spoon to stir with or a new jar to fill. If a week goes by with no night cooking, he will find papaya or guavas or piri-piri peppers [chillies] and bring them to sell so that the process will restart and we can team up in the outside kitchen under the stars again.

Over the months he has told me about all his family, scattered across the length and breadth of Mozambique: about his daughter in Nampula who has a peanut farm, and his daughter in Quelimane who has invited him to visit, and his daughter in Maputo whose husband fishes for tiger prawns. And he has told me about his first and his second wife and his divorce from both; and about the plot of land by the former governor's palace that he inherited from his father.

When the other workers and students are around, Adamji is popular and a key person within the village. He is the one who knows all the fishermen. And when no one else can get peanuts or maize flour, he will know where to find them. He has a bicycle which he calls a 'rooky tooky' and with which he has a love–hate relationship. It is an old bicycle that keeps breaking down. On many days, he sets off on an errand sitting straight and riding high, ringing his bell as he leaves, proudly flaunting the red and black Dutch postman's hat which is his favourite part of his uniform. But he sometimes limps back hours later, pushing his bike with savage shoves as though it were a delinquent son. When we are alone, his descriptions of the new bike he will buy one day are almost lyrical.

His dream is based on his memory of a gleaming new Ruff Tuff bicycle. This brand is known in Mossuril as a 'rufi tufi', and has filtered down to the Cabaceiras as a 'rooky tooky'. This new rooky tooky will have dozens of accessories and extra-wide tyres and the almost unthinkable luxury of its own pump. It will travel at speeds unknown to other bikes and will have a basket at the front and a box on the back; it will have a padded seat and gears and it will be painted sky blue with silver lines. When the time comes, we will go together to Nampula to buy it, and while we are there, we will also buy a mattress for his new bed and a china mug for his tea. The contemplation of these future purchases gives him so much pleasure sometimes that he clutches his stomach and laughs out loud.

When not plotting for his own future comfort, Adamji spends a lot of time running around ensuring the comfort of others, including his two ex-wives. Apart from a bad case of malaria, and the occasional headache, he seems to be one of the healthiest of the workers, and yet he was the one who most asked for medicines. After a few months he admitted that these requests were not really for himself: one of his ex-wives was ailing and the pills and potions, liniments and infusions were for her. In the early spring, her cluster of minor ailments stopped and she became seriously sick and fell into a mysterious decline, the escalation of which he updated me on from day to day.

Her condition worsened to the point when she could

hardly stand; then the *curandeiros* were brought in. Their boat glided through the mangroves on a high tide and delivered them to the hem of the village on the edge of the palm grove behind the two-room health post run by the nearly round 'Dr' Rocha, one of the most powerful men in the village. Rocha owns land and coconut palms, he owns cashew and mango trees, he owns one of the four motorbikes in the village, his house has electricity and he owns wonders from 'out there' such as a fridge, a widescreen TV, a hi-fi sound system with speakers, a DVD player and a veritable library of kung fu movies and Bollywood 'weepies'. Twice a week, in a purpose-built mud barn beside his home, he charges a few cents for his neighbours to come in and watch either a Chinese kung fu or an Indian weepie, or a double bill of both. The soundtracks, particularly of the latter, drift through the bush and linger in curious echoes in the palm groves. Sometimes, when Rocha's 'cinema' is in full spate, no sound escapes from it at all, deadened by wind, then, out of the blue, on the edge of the shore or in the mangrove or by the church or in one of the ruined places or in our Culture House or in one of the classrooms or on our veranda, ghostly bars of piano music play, or there is a demonic laugh, or, more often since most of the movies come straight from India, there is incredibly high-pitched dialogue bursting into song.

Beware of what you wish for. After longing for and lobbying for light for over a decade, a small part of Cabaceira Grande finally got its wish granted. EDM, the national electricity company, installed poles and looped cables up to and including Morripa's house. For no apparent reason, the EDM activity stopped a tantalizing 800 metres from the college. When we asked when the work would continue and the college could also have light, we were told:

'You will have it by the opening.' (i.e. Sept 2004.)

'It was not possible for the opening but will be installed by the end of 2004.'

'They are coming in February 2005 to do the work.'

When February 2005 came and went with no signs of EDM in the neighbourhood, a delegation from the college traipsed back to Ilha to do some more lobbying. Eventually, we were told that we would get our promised *energia electrica* by the end of March. Extorting this information was a bit like pulling out a strong tooth and required trips to Nacala, Nampula, Ilha, Mossuril and Chocas. Information about what was going on re electricity and the Cabaceiras seemed to circulate on a 'need to know basis' in a hierarchy in which neither I nor my niece Ellie nor Morripa obviously had clearance. While a small percentage of the villages luxuriated in the benefits of light (and in the case of Morripa, his brother, and Rocha, a fridge), most villagers cannot afford to pay any electricity at all let alone the cost of installing a meter, and so the cables string over their palm roofs, passing them by.

It all went very quiet on the electrical front until April 2005 when Morripa called me in Amsterdam to announce that the light was finally coming and would be installed and ready to switch on in June of that year. June came and went without any sign of such happening. By September 2005, I had taken up the crusade myself with zero effect. However, just as we began to make serious enquiries into installing alternative energy, an EDM fanfare announced June 2006 as the definitive date when we too would be able to switch on a light, plug in a phone, have ice and music, electrical tools, fax, computers, and the one hundred and one things we take for granted in the West, but which without electricity in the bush I had come to yearn for.

Meanwhile, the happy few, 800 metres up the path, enjoyed their privilege. My laptop was ferried daily to

Morripa's house to recharge. Rocha played eerie films through the late afternoons, alternating this activity with a weekend disco. Depending on the caprice of the wind, this too could sound as though it were emanating from under my own pillow.

Beware of what you wish for indeed. The tom-tom nights whose sound was wrapped only in singing, laughter and silence with the occasional natural shriek of bushbabies has, when the wind dictates it, given way to tunes blasted out of amplifiers. Magical moments in and around the college become surreally framed by Rocha's soundtracks, which incorporate the worst legacies of Hollywood with absurdly over-emphasized musical scores.

Meanwhile, on the dark side of the village by the shore, a boatload of *curandeiros* arrived to the more traditional welcome of song and dance Macua-style. Adamji and his ex-wife's sisters were the joint masters of ceremony on the greeting committee. Amid much cheering, shouting and shuffled dance, the Sisterhood of twelve healers arrived and clambered out of a dhow, hitching up their matching robes to wade to the shore. They were under the leadership of a grand-master healer, a woman of about forty-five whom her own apprentices and hosts alike treated like visiting royalty. Two of the sisterhood were seriously fat and they had serious and unseemly problems disembarking. Another pair of apprentices was from the village and they were welcomed home as returning heroes.

After the *curandeiros* came baskets and bundles of food and fetishes. The food was to be paid for, in part, by Adamji, who had proudly itemized the exorbitant (by Cabaceirian standards) costs. A goat had to be bought and killed, and three chickens and a sack of manioc flour, jumbo-sized mats, macuti to cover the stage, coconuts, spice, salt and also much of the hidden contents of the incoming luggage, including the twelve white robes and headdresses, plus extra white cotton to dress the patient.

For such a stupendous outlay, and for such an event, hundreds of villagers had gathered to watch. Preparations would be made for the same evening; then at 7pm the 48-hour-long ceremony would begin.

Back at the college, Sofia told me that all of the college staff had been invited. Jorge, the head of orientation, and Tigo decided not to attend. Teacher Tauacal (no relation to our deceased builder) was going down with a fever, which left Sofia and me to do the honours.

During the afternoon, Adamji returned, dressed in a lurid Hawaiian shirt, to ask if he could borrow the Petromax. This is a power light that feeds on petrol, hissing all the while it sends out a staggeringly bright light for a radius of approximately 30 metres. If that were all it did, it would be a miraculous alternative to electricity, but one doesn't casually light a Petromax, because it is a potentially deadly apparatus that metamorphoses into a wonder lamp. Like the butterfly which has to pass through a much less attractive phase as a caterpillar, a Petromax starts off as an incendiary bomb and then either explodes and burns itself out (destroying its insides in the process) or burns with an astonishing glare. A column of flames up to 2 metres high always leaps from its cap and would certainly burn through the average mud hut's palm roof. Apparently, the original lamps didn't do this, but all the new 'made in China' ones I have seen, do. Ours was a particularly vicious model with a batting average of nine out of ten burnouts.

Adamji assured me that it was not going into a mud hut and also that there were experts on site to deal with it. The ritual was to take place in his wife's family house. This partly ruined but still splendid villa queens it over a palm grove on one side and the sea on the other. With a grand

Portuguese external staircase to the veranda, it looks more like a stage set than a village dwelling. Adamji had taken the task of set designer to heart and described how such a light as mine would stage light the set and enhance the night.

'Because there is no moon and it will be pitch dark no one will be able to see a thing without it. With this, though,' he said, proudly tapping the giant lamp's umpteenth replacement glass, rather harder than glass usually likes to be tapped, 'it will look like something out of Rocha's cinema.'

He set off swinging the metre-high lamp, chuckling to himself. Close encounters with a Petromax are infrequent here, with less than a dozen of them in the joint villages. Even holding one, it seemed, was to be in possession of a trophy. I heard him stop and explain to several colleagues and then passers-by how he had borrowed it from me for the grand ceremony.

On the evening of Adamji's family's traditional healing ceremony, Sofia and I walked from the front of the college to Rosalina's. Although Adamji had been unceremoniously divorced many years before, his first wife was well connected locally and the joint owner of a beautiful, run-down villa on the edge of the mangrove beyond the governor's palace. The ceremony was to take place in the villa's front garden and the public could watch it from the wide, semi-circular steps of the impressive Portuguese staircase that led up to the stately villa's porch. By the time we arrived, there was already a clot of children on the steps. The girls wore their hair newly braided for the occasion and some of the boys had newly shaven heads. As Sofia and I approached, the chatter subsided to whispers and then burst into animated comments and laughter as we passed. Both of us were wearing *capulanas* and college uniform *lenzos* on our heads as a mark of respect. Sofia regularly dressed like this, but I do so only rarely and although the students insist it is appreciated, the result invariably seems to be that I am mocked.

By the time we arrived all the actual seats had gone, as had all the good viewing places. Whether it was because we were respectively the president and the head of kitchen from the college, or whether it was because we had lent the ceremony our treasured Petromax, a space was found for us near the top step with a perfect view of the palm-leaf palanquin that had been erected the day before.

Based only on my ability to dress wounds and lower fevers, Sofia insisted on calling me 'doctora'. When I insisted on our living and working together on first-name terms, the nearest she would come to it was to call me 'Doctora Lisa'. On the way there, Sofia had warned me: 'Be prepared for anything, Doctora Lisa. Remember what I told you about those traditional ceremonies in Maputo. I tell you, there is blood everywhere from chicken and goat sacrifices, and severed chickens' heads flying around like tennis balls. The screaming is deafening and it all gets very out of hand.'

Since the ceremony was to last forty-eight hours and neither of us was up to seeing it through to the end, we prearranged a signal so that if it got either too wild for us or we got too tired we could sneak away together.

Adamji was the meeter and greeter who ushered us up to the front porch and introduced us to a couple of dozen local people, who listened politely while he explained to them who we were, until a stern-looking older man with sunken cheeks and elbows so knobbly that they looked like implants pointed out that everyone already knew who we were. Adamji paused for a moment and seemed to be weighing up whether to take this as a rebuke or a compliment. For the sake of harmony, in the spirit of the evening, he visibly swallowed whatever retort he had been about to make and

returned to his post at the foot of the steps after ostenta-
tiously checking on the progress of the Petromax. The latter
was throwing out a light so dazzling it was impossible to
look into its glare.

We had been told to be there for 7pm and had actually
only managed to arrive by half past seven, with Sofia assur-
ing me, 'The ceremony is bound to start late because they
always do.'

Apart from the odd white-robed, red-sashed *curandeiro*
appearing on the porch to take a wand from the wand
basket or a bandage from a bandage box or paint from a
paint basket, nothing happened on the palanquin's stage
until nine o'clock. The audience swelled steadily, the steps
filled, the porch filled, the garden filled, the Petromax hissed
and there was a great deal of whispering, but the troupe of
healers remained inside the patient's bedroom while we all
stared at the floodlit empty stage.

At nine o'clock, three drummers appeared from the
crowd in the garden. They tempered their drum skins over
a glowing charcoal fire and took their places centre stage. At
9.15pm, they started drumming. By 9.20, the rhythm had
almost silenced the audience. At 9.30, accompanied by hand
claps and foot stomps, the *curandeiros* appeared from the sick
woman's bedroom and began to shimmy across the porch.
Unasked, the crowd which had refused to part to let anyone
else sit on the steps, parted and the *curandeiros* shimmied
down the steps in a healing conga. Last but one in the dancing line was the sick woman, who was also dressed in red
and white and who wore an outsize *lenzo* cloth wrapped
round her head.

The head of the conga was the chief *curandeiro*, a woman
so fat she had rolls of flesh juddering as she danced. While
her apprentices carried small red batons, the head *curandeiro*
carried a fancy red wand double the size of any of the

others. Their entrance into the exorcism ring on the palm stage was accompanied by their own ululating battle cry and a tin whistle, which one of the chief *curandeiro*'s two hench-women blew with the insistence of an outraged referee.

Like a piece of theatre, what followed was divided into acts and scenes. The protagonist was always the chief *curandeiro*, her chorus were her eleven disciples, the maiden in distress was the sick woman and the antagonist was the invisible evil spirit or spirits who had possessed her. The plot consisted of a series of complicated ploys to trick the bad spirit into appearing, the better to be exorcized by the healers.

Many of the scenes required props which the *curandeiros* had brought with them in a series of baskets. All the scenes were accompanied by frenzied drumming but each had a par-ticular tempo. Each scene incorporated a set of dancing, often in the conga form and always ending with all the *curandeiros* and the patient exiting back up the steps in a dancing line. This continued for hour after hour with no sign of exhaustion from any of the participants or the audience.

The drummers, who had worked themselves into a trance, broke many lizard- and gazelle-skin drum tops during the ceremony. Between each session they would re-temper their drums over the waiting charcoal fire, helped by a small group of assistants who let no one else near their open-air workshop. As one drum burst, one or two of the assistants would sit and repair it for the next session and the drummers meanwhile would use another from what appeared to be an endless supply of small hand-drums. Such was the rapid passage of drums on the stage, such was the whirling of white-robed women in front of the drummers and such was the rapid and intoxicating rhythm, that from my vantage point at the top of the steps I was unable to identify exactly which of the many ceremonial drums were in use that night.

Approximately every half hour, a member of the audience would be seized by an attack of *diavos*. Thus possessed, the victim (who was usually female) would leap from her seat and throw herself on to the stage there to thrash and convulse in the grip of her own evil spirit. The audience was very unimpressed by this and the *curandeiros* even more so. As the conga of healers and patient circled the stage, the presence of an outsider in the throes of a convulsion interrupted their carefully measured dance steps. At each turn, the healers and patient would step over the intruder, but the lack of invitation to the stage did nothing to deter the possessed gatecrashers.

At one point, there were three such uninvited women on the stage. I asked Sofia in a whisper why the healers didn't extend their healing to the afflicted gatecrashers. She told me that traditional ceremonies had to be requested and paid for. This one was for Adamji's ex-wife. It wasn't for anyone else. If any of the *diavos*-afflicted audience wanted to be exorcized, they had to apply for the treatment separately and pay for it themselves. I whispered back to ask why, if everyone knew this, were those of the public who were possessed throwing themselves onto the stage.

'It's the drumming,' Sofia told me. 'It brings the *diavos* out. And some bad spirits are like people, they are show-offs. Look at that one down there,' she said, scornfully pointing out a young woman in a yellow T-shirt who had been writhing on stage for nearly twenty minutes without a break, convulsing, frothing at the mouth, jerking up and down from lying to sitting in the most alarming way.

When the *curandeiros* and patient abandoned the stage and conga-ed back up the steps and into the ceremonial bedroom, the young woman continued to writhe. Her spine arched almost to snapping point and then flopped back to the rhythm of the drums until she passed out, presumably with fatigue. She lay on stage unattended for a few minutes and then came round. She looked up, dazed and shaking. Her face was covered in dust and foam, which she attempted to wipe away with the back of her hand. She had long since been separated from her yellow T-shirt, which was lying in the sand beside her. She picked it up and shook it out and put it back on before staggering to her feet. At that point, an older woman stepped forward to help her back to the empty seat by her embarrassed husband. As she sat down, her husband grabbed her firmly by the lower arm. Later he would try to maintain this grip to no avail because no sooner did the *curandeiros* appear for the next set than his possessed wife leapt up shrieking and threw herself back on stage.

Whatever jerks and convulsions, writhing and rolling she had done before were as nothing to her own second set. On her return, she monopolized the show to such an extent that neither the *curandeiros* nor the patient could get past her. The chief *curandeiro* frowned and gave the interloper a powerful stare, which calmed the *diavos* momentarily. But by the time the conga came around again, the gatecrasher was thrashing up a cloud of dust. The chief *curandeiro* stepped out of the conga and signalled for it to continue without her. Then she pointed her large red wand at the gatecrasher's back and touched her in the small of her spine with the tip. The effect was instant. The possessed gatecrasher stopped moving and appeared to be dead. Two of the drum assistants hauled her off the stage, where she came round and went back sheepishly to her husband. The chief *curandeiro* resumed her place at the head of the conga without even looking at the woman she had just commanded to be still. Like Sofia had said, this was not the interloper's ceremony.

Later, I asked Adamji if the interloper would have been cured by that wand touch. He shook his head.

'Eee! No chance! She didn't even buy them a chicken, let alone a goat. It doesn't work like that. They didn't come for her. She was just in the way with her *diavos*.'

The first two hours were a sensual feast. I felt bombarded by sights and sounds. Deciphering what was going on, what each scene was about took a lot of concentration. At first, Sofia and I whispered to each other what we thought was happening and why, but after the first two hours, most of the scenes seemed to be action replays so I took more to marvelling how the sick woman, who had scarcely been able to stand for over a month, was able to dance round and round that stage and up and down the many steps in and out of the ceremonial room for so long. I wasn't sick but I would have been exhausted after the first hour. The idea of the ceremony continuing for forty-eight hours was daunting.

Sofia and I whispered our determination to leave at around 3am at the latest. Meanwhile, the thirteen white robes with the red sashes kept shimmying past us on their way down to the stage and on their way back and the drumming did not stop for a second. Apart from some children who were asleep on rush mats on the porch, splayed out like drying fish, no one showed any sign of flagging. Tin plates of rice and beans or rice and a bony chicken stew and portions of grey manioc chima appeared from time to time in the hands of spectators, who sat and balled the food into bite-sized chunks which they chewed and swallowed without taking their eyes off the stage.

Four hours into the ceremony, the *curandeiros* reappeared from the room and shimmied past us with a basket of food which they took to the stage and began to lay out on a mat in a (to me) new ritual. Then, together with the patient, they sat by the food and washed in a traditional Macua ritual I had seen before. Water was splashed seven times on their foreheads and then faces, on each hand and then on each lower arm. Then water was splashed seven times, on their necks and upper chests. When this was done, each woman dipped the fingers of both her hands back into the water seven times shaking them dry each time as they incanted a prayer.

After that, it was ritual supper time on stage. However, the food was not recognizable from where we were sitting. It seemed to consist of many small roots and blobs of paste. The paste was rolled into balls and partaken by the chief *curandeiro* and the patient alike. Each food was proffered by the one to the other. It looked a little like a mother bird feeding her young, and the young returning the favour.

After about half an hour of this particular ceremony, the chief *curandeiro* touched the sick woman's forehead with her wand and instructed her to stand up and take a small dish of one of the foods to share with the audience. The sick woman did not seem to understand so the action and instruction were repeated three times. Eventually, very much in a trance, the sick woman stood up and stumbled towards the steps alone. She took a ball of ivory-white substance from the pan she was holding and lunged at random members of the audience, pushing the proffered food into their mouths.

As she approached us, I saw that what she had in the pan looked very much like the kind of fat that clings to bodies when they drown. I have been squeamish about food since I was a child. If someone were to say, for instance, 'Eat this bowl of tripe or I will shoot you,' I would prefer them to pull the trigger than have to eat the tripe. I have personal issues with anything that comes from the inside of an animal. That night, I had issues with whatever was in the patient's dish; and I had never felt so grateful for being an *akunha* and thereby the outsider who would not merit having the drowned fat shoved into her mouth. Sofia, who is black and Mozambican and therefore much less of an out-

sider, was looking distinctly worried. She was staring point-
edly away from the approaching patient in the way that
lobsters in a restaurant's fish tank do when a potential client
approaches to choose one.

Despite her best efforts not to be noticed, Sofia got singled out for the honour of having a blob of the fatty thing
shoved into her mouth. As it passed her lips, I saw her eyes
bulge and water and her throat heave, but she kept whatever it was that had been put in her mouth in there.

I was just wondering how I could have managed not to
throw up if the honour had been mine, when a thumb and
forefinger thrust some of the yellowing substance into my
mouth.

Much as I wanted to, I knew I could not spit it out.
Equally, with my gorge already rising, I knew I could not
swallow it without throwing up. I noticed a mischievous
glee in Sofia's eyes as she continued to struggle to keep her
own mouthful down. I felt a hundred eyes upon me as I battled with the waves of nausea that followed on from
discovering how strange the texture was of what I had
thought to be fat. It was harder than fat and rubbery and it
had a *very* strange and unpleasant taste.

When we were little children, my sister, Lali, developed
the knack of keeping food in her mouth for hours on end.
She used to pouch all the vegetables in her food in one
cheek and keep it there in a pellet until she could spit it out
on our afternoon walk. Following suit, I pouched whatever
it was that I had in my mouth. However, after about half an
hour, I noticed that Sofia had stopped regurgitating hers,
and the presence of whatever it was we had been given to
eat was so unpleasant in my mouth that I decided to
swallow it whole and be done with it.

Having achieved this after a few abortive goes, it sat like
a large nugget of lead in my stomach for the next several

days. Long after the actual 'I swallowed a stone' sensation
faded, the sense of weight lingered for weeks. Sofia complained equally of the leaden feeling; and both of us tried
quizzing Adamji as to what it was. Either he didn't know or
didn't want to say because he just kept repeating that it was
'food from the *curandeiros*'.

After the drowned fat episode, neither I nor Sofia could
really concentrate properly on the rest of the ceremony and
we were both worried about what else in the edible department might get shared around. So we waited until the
curandeiros had taken their conga line back into the changing room and made our excuses and left.

It was a completely moonless night and the hurricane
lamp Adamji thoughtfully lent us on our way out was extin-
guished within seconds of joining the path along the edge of
the mangrove. As we bumped into each other and into
bushes and trees and the step of the governor's palace, Sofia
announced that compared to the mayhem of Maputo, the
Macua festival had been very civilized. From then on, she
revised her opinion of the state of savagery of the villagers,
whom she could not help but view, through the lens of the
Roman Catholicism that was the backbone of her own
belief, as hapless heathens. During the months after the ceremony we had witnessed, she went out into the village
more than ever, less afraid of the unknown and more at
home with the local *tradição*. Side by side with this new ease
was the lingering question: 'What was it we ate?' And also,
'Would the indigestion ever go away?'

Two days later, Adamji returned the Petromax lamp and
resumed his duties as college guard. He was so tired that he
kept breaking out into a cold sweat and keeling over at his
post by the gate. He was sent home to sleep for a night and
returned the following evening full of himself and sporting
an enormous red and gold cap, which he had bought in

Nampula the year before in a moment of weakness. Whenever he wore this cap, it was a sign that all was well *chez* Adamji's wives.

For several weeks after the healing ceremony, he mused over the various aspects of the event, checking details with me to highlight the enormous extravagance of such a visit to the village. By the end of the month, though, when his ex-wife relapsed back into a precarious state of health and took to her bed again, whenever he ran over the list of food and the costs of transport, it was with a hint of regret that he had footed so much of the bill on a micro credit against his future salary, thereby making the distance between him and his longed-for 'rooky tooky' much further away.

The latest assurance is that the college will have electricity by the end of 2007. There are 10-metre-long eucalyptus poles marching along the edge of the dunes en route to Varanda and new tri-phase wires have been installed between Chocas and Mossuril. From such movement, I can deduce that there will indeed be electricity from the national grid here in the near future. What I cannot say, and nor apparently can anyone else (including the installers), is how near that future is.

Meanwhile, big and small generators of varying capacity are ferried into the college to throb and vibrate in the narrow generator room until the inevitable day when they either stall or explode, hurling bits of Taiwanese steel into the coral-rock walls and plunging the college complex back into darkness. It is hard not to take the delinquent behaviour of the various generators personally because, almost out of spite, each time one dies it takes with it whatever it can. So with monotonous regularity, CD players and mobile phones, computers, regulators, DVD players, transformers and charges burn out with the offending engine.

There is no such thing as a buyer's warranty in Mozambique. What you see is what you get and what you buy is always at your own risk. Things look nice: they are bright and shiny and proudly bear brand names of world-wide renown, but alas they are almost all made in China and Taiwan and even the brand names are fake. The recycled iron and steel is the bane of every Mozambican who tries to rise up the economic ladder. Save up and buy whatever machine you can think of and the one thing you can be sure of is that it will break down. And once it is broken, it will prove impossible to buy 90 per cent of the spare parts you need. Add to this the fact that all machines cost more here than they do elsewhere and the mystery of why backyards and front rooms have house shrines of metal junk is solved. So much money goes into each purchase that even after the piece in question has irreversibly broken down, no one can bear to throw it away. We are now on our sixth generator and we too have a generator graveyard. It is a room of modern sculpture filling up with old engines, ghetto-blasters and the like. Covered with the blood, sweat and tears of Tigo and every mechanic within a radius of 100 kilometres, each derelict piece seems too precious to throw away despite the certain knowledge that it will never again be of any use to us or anyone else.

XIX

Mossuril and Fabulous Chocas-Mar

As OF A FEW YEARS AGO, passenger planes can land in Nampula. Before that, it took five days of driving day and night on pitted roads from Maputo to reach the capital of the north. Because Africa was colonized as a commodity, goods were supposed to travel to the ports to be shipped back to Europe. So railways and roads run from east to west across the continent, but rarely from north to south. Mozambique is no exception.

When I first arrived in Nampula, there was a tarmac road to the coast for 200 kilometres with craters in it so large Mees's Land Rover could have fallen right in one and we would not have been able to see over the edge. Our first several trips were accordingly nerve-racking and we both arrived half-broken from the bone-shaking we took en route. Two years ago, this road to Ilha was both widened and resurfaced. It is now a very reasonable highway.

Before reaching the road bridge to Ilha, there is a turn-off on the right to a red-dust road at a place called Naguema. A small signpost provides this information. Here I might pause, beckoned to the house of the *regulo* (the hereditary chief and heir to the title of 'King of Naguema').

Everyone else in Naguema lives in a simple mud hut, but there are three houses in the *regulo*'s compound, as befitting a king. All three wings of his mud-hut palace are stacked from floor to corrugated-iron ceiling with an eclectic array of products ranging from boxes of condoms to teacups, crates of insecticide to crates of Coca-Cola, engine oil and washing-up liquid, and sacks of seed corn. Like a conjuror, he pulls out rolls of animal skins from the dark recesses of his stores, and instructs me to give them to Mestre Canira (master carpenter of the Cabaceiras, drum-maker and a village leader).

Forty minutes of driving along the dust road from Naguema will bring you to Mossuril. Despite (with a fair wind) it being only thirty-five minutes by sailing dhow from Ilha, Mossuril is the start of another world: a lost world. It runs parallel to 'out there'.

Mossuril town is an ancient place and a sleepy testament to the grandeur of the Portuguese colonization. The town is known locally as a *sede*: the 'seat' of power and administration. Once it was a town, now it is a ruined village with an enclave of partially restored buildings around a square overlooking a spectacular bay. Beyond this square, most of the buildings are derelict or semi-derelict and many are piles of historic rubble.

The police station functions with great formality and the chief of police comes to work each morning with an immaculately laundered uniform to sit in an office so dilapidated it looks more like a carefully arranged film set than a scene from real life. Doors and windows, door frames and part of the roof are all missing and the walls themselves are coming away in chunks. Across the road, some of the villas that flaunt memories of better times are even worse off than the police station. Where once the Portuguese lived and worked in grandeur, there are now gutted shells, fallen pillars and roofless ruins, being slowly but surely reclaimed by tropical vegetation.

But Mossuril has electricity (when there isn't a power cut) and fixed landlines for telephones (when the line is working) and internet service (theoretically, but we have never managed to log on to it). And it has a public notary and a courthouse. It boasts a proper primary school, and a secondary school is finally being built there. In Mossuril Sede there are government officials from various sectors ranging from agriculture to health, education and culture. Work in such local offices is an uphill struggle to get any money to trickle down from the national and provincial budgets.

Thanks to vast amounts of foreign aid, there is money available to Mozambique, but very little of it reaches outposts like Mossuril. There are also hundreds of non-governmental organizations (NGOs) working in the country, but most of their lines of operation stop short of Mossuril. The NGOs or charities that do include this once important town tend to go no further. A couple of years ago, UNICEF gave every child in Mossuril District a school bag, but they didn't keep going to help provide schools.

On the edge of the sea, beyond the neatly laid-out central square, is a fortified church with an outside cellar in which the Portuguese conquistadores used to hide when under attack. It was here that they landed and dug in during the early to mid-sixteenth century. It was from here that they rode out and conquered the coast, seizing Macua village after village from their African and/or Arab overlords.

Having 'settled' the coast and built their palaces and villas, the Portuguese centred their attention on raw commerce, with Ilha at its hub. So, gradually, places like Mossuril and the Cabaceiras were left to their own devices and the tenuous hold of their colonizers disappeared, leaving little trace beyond their abandoned buildings. In a game of cat and mouse, sporadic efforts were made to tame and reclaim the wayward coastal villages and towns. Punitive missions were sent to collect taxes and subdue the coastal population. The Mediterranean overlords could kill the local population, enslave, forcibly convert and punish all the ones they could catch, but as soon as the overlords' backs were turned, the local Macua population escaped their control again.

This was a pattern often repeated across the entire country, not least because the Portuguese government was so overtly interested in financial gain from its colonies that it hardly even pretended to govern them. So long as the ivory, gold and slaves kept arriving on Ilha, what happened in the rest of the country was of little interest. Within this policy of laissez-faire, many inland areas had an easier time of it than the coast. Mossuril and Lumbo, Naguema and the Cabaceiras, on the other hand, were right under the Portuguese noses and thereby suffered more interference in their tribal affairs. For centuries, there were frequent native rebellions. In fact, it wasn't until 7 May 1897 that the last armed resistance to Portuguese rule was quashed. At the beginning, history brought Vasco da Gama to Mossuril District, and at the end it was also here that Mossuril's own King Mucutu-Munu made a last heroic stand against the Portuguese. With an army of Macua warriors, the native African defenders braved a battalion of the occupying army and were beaten under a rain of gunfire. King Mucutu-Munu was captured and held as a prisoner on Ilha. He died nailed to the wall of one of the grand palaces of Ilha.

Since Mossuril is so imbued with history, maybe it is not entirely by chance that it also played an important role during the 'civil war' that tore Mozambique apart for seventeen years after its hard-won independence from the

Portuguese. One of the 'Twelve Men of Mozambique', who swore to fight to the death to protect their country from the ravages of neighbouring South Africa, was from Mossuril.

Having finally forced the Portuguese colonizers out in 1975, Mozambicans embraced their fledgling independence by turning their country from a place of brutal injustice to a welfare state, and from a place of native despair to a place full of hope. It was, for many, a time of euphoria, a golden age. But it was a golden age run by a professed communist (Samora Machel), and although most of his fellow country-men were not communists, with the 'Reds under the Bed' phobia of Big Brother in Washington, there was no way such a government (freely elected or not) was going to be allowed to stay in place without a fight. So, with America's blessing, together with sore losers from the former Portuguese colonizers, elements of the reactionary South African Police Force invaded Mozambique to terrorize its citizens and destabilize its socialist government.

Under the charismatic leadership of Samora Machel, Mozambique struggled to ward off these illegal incursions. Long before 9/11 and the focus of Western attention on ending terrorism, the civilian population of this huge, back-ward country in East Africa was under almost constant terrorist attack. While the rest of the world either pretended not to notice or refused to help, twelve patriots gathered and swore to protect Mozambique's freedom with their lives. As they solemnly swore this oath, each of the twelve men cut off a joint of one of his own fingers. Since each would go on to fight, I have often wondered why they muti-lated themselves; but they did, and the gesture had a tremendous rallying effect on the new nation. Maybe, in a country where kings can get nailed to walls, and terrorists were running amok, and where, for years, the Portuguese secret police, the dreaded PIDE, had been chopping off people's fingers as blithely as trimming flower stalks, you had to do something dramatic to grab people's attention back then.

I was in a bar once in Chocas-Mar splashing out on fizzy orange Fantas with Morripa when one of these Twelve Men of Mozambique came in with an entourage. Everyone present stopped talking and stared in awe. Afterwards, Morripa explained to me that this man from Mossuril was a national hero.

One of the most powerful and richest Mozambicans of all time, the industrialist and entrepreneur João Ferreira dos Santos was also a Mossurilian. His company's logo JFS can be seen all over Mozambique. As an old man he used to return regularly to the place of his birth and be carried to the beach between Chocas and Varanda to bathe. That too is in the grand old past now because João Ferreira dos Santos has been dead for years. Mossuril's glory days are over and it is far away from any action. The only excitement it seems to have had in the last year is the occasional sighting of a big cobra in the undergrowth by the church. Big cobras are unusual in the area but Mees and Ramon had (unintentionally) been so close to it they almost tripped over its back. Mees took me back to the exact spot where he had seen it to ask if it was poisonous.

'Oh, yes,' a local boy informed me.

'Are you sure? How do you know?'

Since it was the first big snake any of us had seen in 'our' area, it seemed important to know. The boy shrugged and signalled towards an old man resting by a half sack of manioc under an African almond tree.

'Ask him if you don't believe me.'

I went up to the old man and greeted him, '*Mascamolo, babu.*' Then, having exhausted my Macua, I slipped into Portuguese to ask whether the cobra was poisonous.

'Without a doubt,' he assured me. 'You see, there is a *kha-pulu* [a lizard with giant scales] living in that pile of rubble and the *khapulu* is *amai-a-inowa* [the mother of all cobras]. It has poisonous saliva,' he told me, touching his mouth to convey the idea of dribble. 'They all go to the *khapulu* to get their venom. So the cobra must have been poisonous.'

I could not argue with such impeccable logic. When I checked the story of these *khapulu* with some of the workers, they confirmed that this lizard was indeed '*amai-a-inowa*'. Later on, I also asked some of the older students about it: 'I have heard that the Khapulu is the mother of all snakes. Does that mean that the two-headed blind snake also gets its poison from there?'

It was unanimously agreed to be the case. We never saw the giant poisonous cobra again, nor have we ever seen the dribbling *khapulu*, but others have, and in these parts, knowing someone who knows someone who has seen something turns that something into a fact.

Beyond the town/village, the ghostly and still graceful ruins of a pillared building perch on a hill overlooking a wide swathe of ivory sand and stunted marram grass, which is both a beach and a lagoon depending on how much of the sea has seeped over the mangroves. The pitted, dusty road up to this ruin is like a local Calvary because this war-damaged shell is what remains of Mossuril's former hospital. Like so many other medical facilities and schools, it was singled out for destruction. Now, in a newer wing behind, a cottage hospital does its humble best to operate as such despite having no doctor at all. It is run entirely by veteran nurses. The same war that wrecked it, crash-trained these nurses on its battlefields.

Headed by Said, a squat and unflappable male nurse, with a gentle smile and a grip like a vice, the medical team treats all ailments from major to minor. With insufficient medicines

and almost non-existent equipment, theirs is often a thankless task. But the steady flow of dead and dying who are
carried away downhill are the victims of a wider neglect
beyond the skeleton nursing team's control. No one locally
has a bad word to say about Said or his colleagues, who try
to make up in compassion what they lack in materials.

Front and back, the hospital grounds look like a refugee
camp. Here women squat and wait, squat and cook. One
piece of equipment this hospital does have is a malaria-
testing kit. So it is to here that people flock to discover how
many crosses of malaria they have. From the Cabaceiras, as
from many other villages, there is no transport; so a sick
person has to walk to Chocas and then hope for a communal taxi (*chapas*). The fare to Mossuril from Chocas is one
dollar. For those who don't have that money (and most
people do not) it is a nine-kilometre walk each way to get
malaria tested. Weakened by fever, this walk in the burning
sun is often the killing factor. But Mossuril has more and
better medicines than the local health posts, and malaria is
a killer. Unless a patient is unconscious, they will tend not
to be hospitalized for malaria. There aren't enough beds for
the hundreds of cases. Yet blood tests are taken one day and
the results delivered the next, so the journey has to be made
twice before treatment is given. This gap is too much for
many malaria victims. When the treatment is prescribed, the
hospital pharmacy does not always have the necessary medicine. The nearest pharmacies are on Ilha or in Monapo.
Both are far away. And when the treatment is taken, it is
often only to find that the malaria is a drug-resistant strain.

As a result, no matter what family you pick in this area,
at least one, if not many, members of it will have died from
this checkable but still unchecked disease. At any given
time, in any local village, there will be malaria victims fighting their fevers on the floor of a mud hut. Sometimes we see

such victims wrapped completely in a *capulana*, so that it covers their heads from the further ravages of mosquitoes, lying in the dust outside their huts.

After the darkness of all the local roads, the way to the hospital shines like a beacon across the salt flats. A line of street lamps brighter than any other lamps in the district light up the road from the hospital to the town it serves.

After Mossuril Sede, the dust road gets bumpier on its way to the former seaside playground town of Chocas-Mar. Halfway between the two small towns an enterprising family sells paraffin, petrol and diesel in beer bottles. This is the only refuelling place after Naguema. Mossuril Sede has a derelict petrol station which now sells cold drinks and crisps, thereby providing the only local bar facility. Chocas-Mar also has an abandoned filling station, but it doesn't sell drinks, hot or cold.

Chocas has a different sort of derelict building: its ruins are more 1930s domestic and less historic and monumental. It was and still is a seaside destination. It used to be a thriving resort, whereas now it is more of a ghost village overlooking a beautiful beach. Once the rich and powerful came here from Nampula city to take the waters, but seventeen years of war put an end to such frivolity and Chocas-Mar decayed into three streets of abandoned seaside cottages and small holiday villas with the odd tenacious local householder, and a handful of Indian businessmen holding on in the face of neglect.

Vakháni vakháni, Chocas is clawing its way back onto the tourist map as stragglers from Ilha drift across the channel to lunch in what used to be the only restaurant in Mossuril District but is now one of three. Each month sees new holiday homes being built on the shore, and gutted shells that had stood empty for nearly twenty years are gradually being restored. There is even talk of a hotel to come and a pizzeria, and there is also talk of a South African jam factory and a bio-diesel plant. In small towns there is always a lot of talk, but now it seems that something is really about to happen in Chocas. There are even piles of building sand and gravel being moved to the abandoned shell of a former restaurant overlooking the bay where word would have it there is to be a hotel.

Even Dona Ancha, who is virtually the unofficial queen of Chocas, says there is a hotel coming soon. Dona Ancha and her Portuguese husband, Senhor Falcão, run the local shop which extends into a bar tended mostly by their children. It is here that people come from far and wide to buy cold drinks, ice, coffee, candles, razors, tomato paste, sardines and a good twenty other products, none of which are available elsewhere for a wide radius.

Meanwhile, every day, under a spreading ficus tree, a gaggle of fifty women with jerry cans queue for water, while local boys wander up and down the main street selling lemons, mangoes, fish, squid, lobster and crabs.

For travellers arriving from Nampula, Chocas-Mar might look like a one-horse town, but coming from the Cabaceiras it is almost a metropolis. It has cars and TVs, ice and electricity. People have motorbikes and dune quads, shoes and proper clothes. Houses have floors and running water. Just four kilometres away by dirt road from Cabaceira Grande and eight from Cabaceira Pequena, a time warp occurs. As the dunes and bush unfold away from Chocas, the houses stop abruptly. There is an expanse of bush and then the mud huts begin with their palm-thatch roofs.

For volunteer staff at the college and for me and Mees, and for Lolly and Jason, it became known as 'Fabulous Chocas-Mar'. It is fabulous, if only for its ice. In the heat, hour after hour one begins to fantasize about cold drinks. With no electricity, fantasize is about all one can do unless

by walking, cycling or driving one can get to Chocas. A bar
doesn't have to give you much in the tropics if it can supply
an iced drink.

This was actually a problem for a while because Chocas's
one and only restaurant (o Compleixo) used to peak early:
it reached that heady cold-drink point and then stopped. So
you could get an iced coke or a cold beer but little else
besides. The simplest meals were taking several hours to
materialize. Such is the movement being whipped into the
area that the Compleixo is now under new management,
which serves fresh butter with the bread and proper meals
on clean cloths, the food arrives within the hour and the
kitchen even rises to puddings. Whatever next?

The physical distance isn't far, but the economic and
mental leap is enormous between Chocas and Cabaceira
Grande. Hundreds of older people in the Cabaceiras have
never been to Chocas, let alone to Mossuril or beyond.
There is no proper road and no transport. It is a long hot
walk. In a village so poor it merely subsists, there is nothing to sell. With nothing to sell and no money to spend, and
with every ounce of energy needed to keep up at home,
there is no point in wasting that energy on alien soil. From
time to time, someone takes the leap and travels out to
Mossuril for documents or to Monapo or Nampula to buy
nails or wire, a bicycle or cotton. For the very poor, there
is little joy in travelling with up to fifty people in the back
of a truck or squeezed into a minibus with thirty fellow passengers.

Travelling beyond the village means venturing into the
unknown. With the rapid changes of our digital, technolog-
ical world, a Cabaceirian elder is at a huge disadvantage 'out
there'. The position of power and respect he or she holds
within his or her own community and the back-up of the
tradição are all lost once the invisible frontier from the bush

to Chocas is crossed. The rest of the world moved on without them. Even the super-cool young men who hang around the market baskets in the Cabaceiras are mere country bumpkins outside their community. They are all targets to be duped and dumped. They are figures of fun in Nampula, to be treated with disdain in shops and ignored by even the lowest shop assistants. Even someone like Morripa, who has travelled the communist world from Cuba to Russia to China and who is a project manager, will get neither service nor respect in the cities, where the shops and emporiums are mostly owned by Indian merchants, most of whom have no time for local citizens who make good.

Twice a day, while the relentless tides cut off the Cabaceiras and the mangroves are claimed back by the sea, the educational, cultural and social divide deepens, cutting off the villagers from the country's stride into the twenty-first century. After centuries of mistreatment by slavers and colonizers, not many rural Mozambicans will stand up for their rights. After centuries of isolation, not many rural Mozambicans know what those rights are; and if they do, they have a sneaking suspicion that such rights are for everyone else but somehow not for them.

The pride of the Macua, so evident within the villages, is lost once they leave that magic circle round their home. As things stand, to make good, a local person *has* to leave home. Cabaceirians can subsist unless disaster strikes. But disaster does strike all too often, be it in the form of an illness or a death in the family, a fine, a capsized boat, or just the need for a new macuti roof. Emigration to Ilha, Nampula, Nacala or beyond is the only way to get past fourth-year primary school or to get a job. And Ilha is already overcrowded, its schools are overcrowded, and it has massive unemployment problems of its own.

Less than one per cent of the Cabaceirians have a job

with a salary. Approximately four hundred men (out of a total of twelve hundred fishermen) go out to fish each day, unless the wind or the tide is wrong for them, in which case none of the fishermen can go out to fish. There are many hungry days. When there is no fish, there is no food that day.

Some of the local men and women earn twenty dollar-cents a shift carrying salt in the salt flats. Each family plants approximately fifty square metres of manioc. When the manioc fails, as it often does through exhaustion of the soil and manioc diseases, villagers starve. For eight months of the year there is no fresh fruit or vegetables; for four months of the year, people can buy tomatoes, onions, pota-toes and mangoes. With most families (of five people) managing on under forty dollar-cents a day per family, there is no money for such purchases.

So the Cabaceirians make do with what they have and some of them dream of better times. Most men and women dream of better times for their children. Most parents have to see some, at least, of their children die before them. The tide steals children, as do malaria, chest infections and diar-rhoea. Women die in childbirth, men die at sea. On land, men tend to die from ruptured hernias, which they get from lifting weights far beyond their strength. And throughout the year, men, women and children die of malaria. On the whole, no one comes to help, so no help is expected. The people help each other. In twin villages of seven thousand souls, there are no visible orphans and no glaring signs of poverty. Almost everyone suffers from sub-nutrition but there are no starving people lying in the gutter.

Calamity comes time and again and takes its toll, but the villagers absorb the shock and lend each other a hand. When a mud hut burns down, friends and neighbours help rebuild it. When someone is sick, small rations of food get smaller. When someone dies, a winding sheet will always be provided to wrap the body in before laying a dead person in a box in the ground. The few chickens and goats wander freely between the huts. There are no locks on doors: sometimes there are no doors. It is not only the police who rarely come as far as here, the villages sit at the end of a dead-end track and no one comes. Actually, no one came until 2006, but now there is a trickle of visitors who know we have ice in the bush. But the villagers continue to take care of and to police themselves with their *tradição*. And the fear of shame and banishment continue to be stronger than any written law. And the traces of what the Portuguese did and what they left must make the wandering spirit of King Mucutu-Munu proud because, despite 450 years of Portugal trying to suppress the Macua, history has proven how dismally it failed.

As I write, Mees has been travelling backwards and forwards to Amsterdam for fifteen months now, juggling between keeping his investors happy and getting on with things here. Every time he goes away, it feels as though a neap tide has drained me. And every time he comes back my life leaps to new heights. Trying to be together has proven harder than trying to lift this little bit of the world to face the future from a better angle.

In terms of separation, 2006 has been our worst year yet. Spending five months apart didn't damage our relationship, but it made a tough time tougher. We didn't plan it that way, it just happened, and it made us both sad enough to not ever let it happen again.

Being without him after years of round-the-clock contact has given me many hundreds more hours on my hands than I would have chosen to have. Sifting through them I found time to study again. Or, to be precise, I found the desire to study plus the time to go with it. As a result, I can now write in Portuguese (something the college really needed because my former illiterate notes to very formal officials were a little too funky for a hierarchical society like this). And I am making enough headway with Macua to see that if I keep it up for several more years I may be able to write the history of its culture that I feel is missing. And last, but not least, I have been able to learn a lot more about medicinal plants. Mees will be back soon and here to stay; but the system of study that I dredged out of my loneliness in his absence is also here to stay.

When I was a child, I wanted to traipse around the tropics finding and drawing plants like Marianne Evans. I have often wondered what I would do in my old age and now I know. I will go full circle and gather the medicinal plants of the mangrove; and I will draw and chart them and gradually compile a botanical reference book.

The past year has also been a year of mourning for the death (from cancer) first of my sister Lali, followed by that of my older sister, Gillie. Grief, loss and missing someone are very different emotions, but they are related and overlap.

I moved here to be with Mees and although we have ended up so often with an ocean between us, I feel that in spirit he is here in this spiritual place. Everything and everywhere is imbued with his touch; so much so, that if I discover new wonders, I wait to savour them with him because to do so alone feels almost like treachery. I hoard troves of new beaches, new paths, 'new' ruins, new books and new projects for his return.

Because Lolly and I are living on the edge of the earth, some friends assume that we are in a place full of danger. They imagine our staying here to be a brave stance. But there is no daring involved. This is one of the safest places

I have ever known. At night, as we walk through the bush returning from Chocas or the mangrove, along footpaths so narrow they have to be known, past mud huts nestling beside cashew and mango trees, past salt flats and ruined palaces, our only fear is 'Will we know the way home?' I have never felt afraid of man or beast here. On the one hand, the local people are friendly, helpful, polite and amazingly tolerant. On the other hand, there are practically no beasts left bigger than a dog, or wilder than one.

Most days, vervet monkeys lope through the mangroves and sometimes whole families of them run along the sands. There are some small gazelles (fewer than there might be if the people of Naguema would stop spearing them to cover drums) and some giant iguanas. Some people say they have seen a panther on the dunes, but I find this unlikely. In the days of famine, some twenty years ago, the Mozambicans ate just about every wild animal in the country. Where the Big Five used to roam, hungry huntsmen rounded them up, down to the last lion casserole.

Further inland, where the Big Five migrate from the Niassa Game Reserve on the Tanzanian frontier, many of the animals have returned. In Mossuril District, this has not been the case. Last year Morripa's dogs and goats were attacked by hyenas. Nocturnal genets will kill any chicken not protected by a basket with a stone on top, but short of these, there are no predators by day or night, except for the Grim Reaper, who seems to work overtime here.

XX

The Remains of Slavery

MY ORIGINAL PLAN FOR THIS book was to write a diary to describe my time in north Mozambique in daily units. But time as I know it doesn't exist. The sensual cocoon which changes shape occasionally as things happen flows in an unpredictable pattern. There are currents, and whirlpools, and waves. The result on the page is more random than I intended, but it keeps pace with the place.

The coast of northern Mozambique has had a chequered history. For over a thousand years, ships came to find fresh water, to repair and renew their masts, and to trade. The forests of Lunga and Matibane were and are still a rich source of timber. Matibane is one of the few forests left of iron wood. It is no longer legal to export this dense timber, although I have heard that it trades on a black market. The forest is reserved for the restoration of monuments. In the past, ships were lured by Ilha's water reservoirs and the valuable iron wood it could muster. They also came to buy other timbers, spices, herbal remedies, gold, ivory and the seemingly endless supply of black gold: slaves.

Not far away, on Zanzibar, a similar history unfolded. But Ilha is further south on the circumnavigation from Europe.

Ilha has ingenious and vast water deposits and most of the houses still have flat roofs criss-crossed with rain-catching gullies to supply this otherwise arid island. For ships sailing up from the Horn of Africa, Ilha was a must. It took advantage of its strategic location and grew into one of the richest prizes in the Indian Ocean.

The Chinese were the first to discover its worth, then Indians, then Arabs, then the Portuguese. Twice the Dutch tried to seize it and twice they failed miserably. The second Dutch attempt to seize Ilha's fortress was made with the British Royal Navy. Their joint failure is entombed under sand banks on the seabed. Enterprising boys dive down and haul up fragments of treasure. Even more enterprising and controversial salvage teams, notably from Britain and the US, are salvaging the treasure on a more industrial scale. It is fairly hush-hush because the sunken ships lie well within Mozambique's territorial waters. But it is only fairly hush-hush because Ilha is a small island and the professional divers and their advisors tend to discuss their secrets in stage whispers that echo from pillar to post in the island's very few bars and restaurants. Also a website showing part of the treasure trove of the American millionaire who has backed some of the 'secret' missions advertises its origins to the four corners of the world.

In the centre of this Fortress of São Sebastião are two ancient Arabic cisterns. In 1558, the Portuguese conquerors started to construct the fort. It was finished sixty-two years later. From its parapets I can see across the channel to the Cabaceiras and its ruined palaces. From the Cabaceiras, the chunky grey fort is clearly visible weighing down one entire end of the island. In the two rainy seasons, the flat roofs become a rumpled green carpet with a lush pile, then a meadow of wild flowers, then an impenetrable tangle of overgrown grass, saplings and vetch. Reflecting the season, this yellows and dies, becomes a fire-hazard of dry straw and eventually blows into the sea leaving nothing but a mat of future mulch for the next rains.

In the olden days, these roofs would have been spick and span, gathering every available drop of rain for the waterless island. But the fortress has suffered the same fate as everything else and fallen prey to decay. Only nesting seabirds and occasional tourists disturb its long hibernation until the rare times when a dance festival or a concert jerks it awake. As a setting, it is magnificent. As a piece of architecture, it is astonishing; and as a place to wander around it has in its atmosphere a curious mix of the fine and the foul through which a paradoxically peaceful feeling pervades. The paradox lies in the horror of the tens of thousands of lost souls who have passed through its gates.

For many centuries this island was a hub of slavery. It is full of former slave warehouses, slave docks, and great and small slave markets. Incalculable numbers of slaves passed through this place landing on the stone steps by the fortress in blinding sunlight on their way to a life of darkness. Records show 90,000 slaves in one year, 58,000 in another, waning to 27,000 as the slave trade died elsewhere. There are steps worn down by the tread of slaves being taken out to waiting ships.

Being an inveterate fantasist, I like to imagine that my own slave ancestors also passed through here, or even came from here originally. The chances of this being the case are small, but having built my life on small chances, I like to persist in this fantasy and justify my new affinity and latest love as answering a call from my blood. I can never prove this to be the case, but nor can anyone else prove the contrary. My great-great-grandmother, Belle, was a slave from Benin sold in Belem, northern Brazil to my great-great-grandfather, a Sr Mendonça, who saw her in the slave

market of Belem and fell in love with her. Belle was six feet
tall and had royal blood (or so the story goes) and she
fetched a high price as my ancestor bid for the woman he
saw as his wife. To avoid the gossip, the couple moved
across the frontier to British Guiana where they bought land
and lived a grande passion, producing many children whom
they largely neglected, so enraptured were the parents in
each other.

My being here and conceivably hailing from here would
seem even more serendipitous were it not for my having
fallen in love with so many other places in the past and also
felt that I belonged there, wherever that particular 'there'
happened to be. My memory is full of places where on
arrival I felt the urge and even the need to stay. They were
always beautiful; and being there made me feel good.
Sometimes I have upped stakes and moved somewhere new
for six months or a couple of years; sometimes circumstances have detained me longer. When I travel, I carry a
mental notebook in which I jot down the desire to spend a
month, six months or a year in any given place. If, as when
I moved to Umbria, for example, I decide to drop anchor
and make a base, it is with the certain knowledge that I will
keep travelling away and coming back to it. The difference
between everywhere else I have seen or known and
Mossuril District is that when I first set foot on Varanda and
looked out to Ilha and along the coast to the Cabaceiras, I
felt that I never wanted to leave: not then and not ever.

It is a paradox that in the Western world we have much
more knowledge of slavery than most people do here where
the drama was enacted. The lack of access to books, newspapers, TV, cinema, the internet and even basic education
has blocked out great chunks of history. So Lolly, my
teenage daughter who was born in Italy, knows more about
the East African slave trade than the descendants of its

victims and perpetrators here. Wherever there have been slave markets, there must also be the descendants of Arab and local native Africans alike who whipped the 'black gold' across the land and onto the ships. Popular myth would have all Africans be direct victims. To some extent, all Africans are, because the devastation slavery caused within the continent is such that all suffered from its aftermath. What many descendants of slaves in the diaspora find unthinkable is the part some black Africans played in the sale of their brothers and sisters.

Within the chapter of history entitled 'The Slave Trade', the buyers and sellers will always be tarnished by their inhumanity. What is often forgotten is that a black skin does not in itself make any African brother to another. What used to be called 'tribes' and are now called 'ethnic groups' are what define who gets allegiance, help, respect and even the right to live from whom.

The word 'slave' is known: *escravo* is the Portuguese term, but what the slave trade was and what it did is yet another mystery here. Visitors arrive and talk about slaves and slavery. They say that hundreds of thousands of men and women were brought to Ilha. If asked about it, most locals will smile and nod because it is an *Akunha* asking, or at best a city man distanced from them by wealth. So locals smile and nod and agree to something they cannot believe. Some extra delving brings up such arguments against it as: '*Epa!* Think about it, not a single person lands on Ilha without many others knowing about it. So how could tens of thousands of strangers have landed and none of us have seen them?'

This is followed by a grin and a slight grimace of regret for the outsider, who must inevitably feel foolish in the face of such a truth. Losing face is almost the worst thing that can happen socially. It is almost as bad as shame. Shame cements the villages together. Shame is the local police force and judiciary rolled into one. Shame nurtures honesty and kindness. Avoiding shame is essential in a place where your village is not just the home you come from, but also the home you aspire to stay in till the day you die, and the home your spirit will rest in after you die. Someone's community is his or her way of life and religion; it is the recipient of their love and loyalty, their law, and the only resting place of their ancestors without whom none can thrive.

To try and explain that the slave trade happened long ago doesn't usually help.

'Long ago when?' People ask and then shake their heads before there is a chance to reply. Older brothers or parents, aunts or uncles would certainly have mentioned such an event if it had taken place.

'Tens of thousands of men and women, you say? *Eeh! Nada!*'

And that is the end of the discussion. The notion of tens of thousands is graspable in a country where, until the currency changed in January 2007, a bread roll costs a thousand meticals and a day's unskilled labour was worth between 15,000 and 30,000 meticals.

'During the war, more than ten thousand people came but there is a misunderstanding because most of them walked over the bridge from Lumbo and no more than fifty landed on the fortress steps as you say. We don't call them slaves though: they were *refugiados* [refugees].'

To try and define slavery doesn't help clarify the concept either. There were people under Portuguese rule only thirty years ago whose condition was little different from that of a slave, except that the colonial subject didn't have to be purchased in the first place so their life was cheaper.

There are still people here in almost the same boat.

There are estimated to be over two million actual slaves worldwide as of 2007; among the many countries accused of harbouring slaves are Britain, the Netherlands and the USA. Here in Mozambique, drudgery has replaced slavery, but there are still many workers who work for their food only and receive no wage. They sleep on the bare ground and eat fish heads and manioc flour. Their 'masters' assure me that 'this is what they like'. Out of hunger, most people will eat scraps, but not out of preference. It is true that fish heads are always eaten by choice, but given the chance, most workers would also like to eat the rest of the fish.

In theory, there is a minimum wage; in practice, with over half the population unemployed, and less than 10 per cent of Mozambicans having a regular salary, hundreds of thousands of men, women and children are reduced to serfdom.

When Lolly arrived in the summer of 2005, she taught the students to sing Bob Marley's 'Redemption Song'. It caught on and the lyrics finally provoked some emotion and the emotion provoked discussion. An idea of what slavery might have been like began to grow. The idea that there are millions of people beyond Mossuril descended from slaves began to sink in. *Vakháni vakháni*, the concept of what goes on 'out there' is starting to take shape.

Unlike, say, in the Caribbean where many men still aspire to 'marry light' as a way of climbing up the strictly colour-regulated class system imposed by the British, the light skin of a mestizo has no intrinsic cachet in Mozambique. There have been centuries of racial mixing, particularly with the former Arab rulers. The deep colour prejudice of, say, the Ashanti, where a mixed race child is virtually outcast, does not exist here. But the Macua seem proud and happy to be who they are. None of the skin whiteners so popular in the West Indies are in the shops. When a local woman whitens her face it is with a mussiro

bark mask. This is Mozambique (pronounced 'Mossambeaky'
by all and sundry), and almost no one knows or really cares
what goes on elsewhere.

Morripa is very good at talking in local metaphors. For
people who don't really grasp what Mozambique is, or
Africa, or that there are other continents such as Europe and
America, everything has to be brought down to simple
descriptions and then enlarged gradually. Many of the students and workers are very bright, a few exceptionally so,
but their isolation has been almost complete. Morripa is a
mine of local history, which he is gathering for a book of his
own. When the Portuguese arrived on Ilha in 1498, the
sultan was Musa Malik, or some say Musa Mbiki. The name
'Moçambique' is believed to be derived from his name. This
is one of the few things I can corroborate from a book.

There seem to be only two English language guidebooks
on Mozambique: the Lonely Planet for East Africa and the
Bradt guides. Even though both have minimal coverage of
this part of the north, they are all there is and tourists on
Ilha travel armed with one or the other. Morripa quickly
surpassed both guidebooks. We barter information: tales from
my country in return for tales from his. It is too confusing to
explain that I don't have a country as such, that I have many
and none. The idea of having no village to call home is so
disturbing a concept here that having once ventured down
the road of trying to explain it, I now keep it as a shameful
secret. It stays in the small bag of shameful secrets that are
my legacy. If Bob Dylan was right when he sang 'there is no
success like failure' then I could be cooking with gas.

One thing that failure does bring is a better understanding of others who, for whatever reason, have also failed. By
the same token, anyone who has been broke can sympathize
more easily with the vast majority of the world's population
who still are. Comfort can become a cocoon and wealth a

blindfold. Any past other than the ancestral past of this area is irrelevant here. In one way or another, everyone is starting from scratch. In a curious way, I, too, am starting my life again, building from zero with the guidance of my own ancestors both known and unknown.

On Ilha, where many of the grand palaces were built from slavery (as indeed were many of the grand country houses of England, France, Portugal, Spain and the United States), there was to be a museum of slavery in what used to be the police barracks. It is a fine derelict mansion. When restoration began, though, in early 2005, all mention of the museum of slavery vanished. Instead, it seems, there will be a conference facility, and a fancy restaurant.

Slavery and the notorious Middle Passage may have little place as points of interest in the popular culture, but Hollywood has. So when Danny Glover declared he would make a movie about slavery on Ilha with Halle Berry as the star, there was much excitement here. (Had it been a Bollywood movie, there would have been even more excitement.) As a result of the movie news, at the end of 2005 the island was a hive of gossip and speculation, if not activity.

Visits were made from LA and black Americans were sighted. A black American arriving on the island is as foreign to the local people as an Englishman. It is not skin colour that divides people here: it is ethnicity and wealth. The latter is the real divider. All foreigners are wealthy by comparison to a local person and our habits are as mysterious to local residents as theirs are to us. Just as the movie speculation peaked, Ilha was cancelled as a location and gossip shifted from stars and dates to the reasons why the deal slipped through Ilha's net. On such a small island, even non-events provide months of table talk.

XXI

Ilha

THIS PARTICULAR ISLAND IN the sun is somewhere to either love or hate. It is a place where all passion has been spent, languishing in the aftermath of an exciting and violent history. You cannot take a step here without being confronted by elements of the past, yet nor can you take a step without being struck by its extraordinary, somnolent calm.

By night, approaching it by sea, it has a fairytale quality. Parts of the island are beautiful almost beyond description, parts are magnificent, parts are gracefully decayed, and half the island is a very large African village under what looks from above like one enormous undulating macuti roof.

Coral stone to build the palaces on the north end of the island was dug by slaves from the south end of the island. As a result, there is a difference in height of about two metres. Inside this pit, for hundreds of years, Ilha's native population have built their huts. Roof touches roof for shade, creating a rabbit-warren effect underneath the gigantic palm-leaf canopy of what is called the Macuti City.

Beyond the Stone City where intrepid tourists stay and the local grandees and officials have their rambling offices, there is virtually no indoor plumbing and there are no sewers. It would take a Mahatma Gandhi to sort out the sewage here. It is a problem many have studied and all have abandoned. Meanwhile, thousands of Omuhipitians use the biggest self-cleaning toilet in the world and life goes on regardless.

Uninvited or unescorted visitors are not really welcome in the Macuti City where people spill into the narrow lanes to wash, cook and chat. Tourists who wander in are invading the little privacy there is there. Elsewhere, few tourists would barge into someone's house uninvited and observe or photograph strangers in their bedrooms and bathrooms. Because Ilha is seriously overcrowded and hundreds of people sleep in the lanes and conduct their lives on their doorsteps, to wander through it lacks respect. Several visitors of mine who spent a few days on Ilha before joining us at the college have told me they felt unwelcome when they strolled through the macuti warren and took against the island as a result. We are visitors, our money is needed and our presence is desired, but not to observe the sanctuary of the Macuti City, which belongs to the Omuhipitians and not to us. It is home to 14,000 people, not a zoo. The Stone City is and always was the domain of foreigners.

If Ilha were the heroine of a fairytale, a Sleeping Beauty, then one could say that she pricked her finger in 1898 when the Powers-that-be decided that Mozambique should have a capital nearer to its South African neighbour's. At that time, hundreds of thousands of Mozambicans were crossing the border to work in the South African gold and diamond mines. Although Portugal failed to provide sufficient funds to develop the new capital, the city grew. By the 1940s, with a boom in the 1950s and 1960s, thousands of white South Africans were using the beach city of Lourenço Marques as their playground and trading post. Access by air and overland was relatively easy there, whereas access to Ilha de Moçambique, the former capital city far to the north, was difficult and costly.

Mozambique Island had made sense as a capital city in the days when trade was by sea. With railways and roads taking over as the main means of transport, the absence of any rail link from north to south or of a proper road from South Africa, plus territorial threats from the British in Natal, doomed the island to be demoted. The stroke of a pen had decreed that the new capital would be Lourenço Marques, but as with other new capitals designated by politicians in other countries, it takes more than a piece of paper to make one.

In the case of Ilha, the seat of government moved, but the island's social supremacy continued for several decades. From 1507 when the first Portuguese settlement was established there to the turn of the twentieth century, wealthy and important families had lived and traded there. The politicians might move south, but the happy few did not follow them. While the beach resorts along the southern coast grew up, Ilha's own resort – Lumbo, known as the St Tropez of East Africa – continued to flourish.

With the 1930s rail link to Nampula, Cuamba and Entre Lagos on the Malawian frontier en route to Blantyre, and the 1940s rail link to the Port of Nacala, Ilha held its own and continued to thrive. However, the lack of government money began to take its toll and the Stone City began imperceptibly to deteriorate. Fewer new businesses came, fewer contracts arrived, fewer kickbacks trickled down, and there was less new blood. Those who would enter government and attain power no longer needed to lobby on the island or network the glamorous bars at Lumbo. Thus Ilha stopped luring the intelligentsia and that sector of society full of energy and ambition.

For the fairytale princess, a potent sedative was beginning to course through her veins. Across the channel, Lumbo continued as a favourite beach haven for wealthy Nampulese and as a hideaway for nostalgic international tourists. Lumbo was the chosen holiday resort for many of the colonizers and hosted a steady stream of other Portuguese visitors. In the 1930s it was at the Hotel do Lumbo that the Aga Khan had his famous love affair with Hollywood's Ava Gardner. The Hotel do Lumbo is now no more than a ruin in a ruined town cradled by a ruined railway terminal beside a disused airport. But enough villas remain on the former esplanade and enough jacaranda trees and sculpted pillars for the imagination to see how lovely it must once have been.

Between them, Lumbo and Ilha limped along as the abandoned dowager and her attractive daughter. Lumbo Airport was the second to open in Mozambique and had regular weekend traffic of light planes ferrying in the rich and famous. LAM, the national airline, also ran a passenger service there.

The passenger terminal remains intact and is one of the prettiest airport buildings I have ever flown to. For a few heady months in 2004, LAM reopened a service from Nampula to Lumbo, but there were not enough passengers to keep it open. However, in the future, Lumbo will open again. Its runway is big enough to take a 747 jet. Mees landed there with the Presidential Jet when he first toured the country. When Lumbo Airport does eventually open, presumably in time for Coral Lodge's guests, the Cabaceiras will benefit enormously.

In June 1975, when the first president of the still ruling Frelimo Party issued the 48/5 decree (whereby all of the Portuguese colonizers had forty-eight hours to leave the country and each could take only five pieces of luggage with them), panic reigned and the Portuguese fled.

Mees told me that he first knew of this exodus from the other side. A Dutch TV network sent him to Portugal to film extensively the fleeing refugees, or *ritornados* as they came to be called. Tens of thousands of distressed refugees were taken in by their fellow countrymen. Mees interviewed dozens of them for the documentary he filmed. Their stories were of grief and loss: they had been cruelly thrown out of the country they loved and had helped to build; they had lost everything from houses to businesses, farms to shops, books to children's toys. Their distress was genuine and heart-wrenching. Many were penniless and unemployable. Many were just old and homeless. Some had been born in Mozambique, some had merely lived there. Some families had been there for many generations. Mees told me, 'It was a shocking sight. There were so many of them. I remember wondering at the time what sort of people would be so cruel.'

It was the people whose liberation leader, Eduardo Mondlane (who had studied in the USA and worked at the UN with Kofi Annan), had been killed by a Portuguese letter bomb while in exile in Dar es Salaam. People who had fought a long slow war of independence and had had to reclaim their land by fighting for every inch of it. It was the millions of people who were sick of being marginalized and punished by a minority of foreigners.

In the wake of centuries of harsh and unjust treatment: of slavery followed by virtual serfdom, of extreme physical abuse, imprisonment and torture, disappearances, theft and rape, sending the perpetrators out of the country with forty-eight hours' notice doesn't seem so cruel any more. In fact, it shows a degree of tolerance. In many other countries, thousands of the former oppressors would have been shot.

Evidence of the former Portuguese oppression is abundant. Even the beautiful groves of cashew trees that are spread across Nampula Province and beyond have a history of cruelty behind them. Martin Mason, an agricultural consultant working with the US government, told me that under Portuguese rule, every time a worker had a new child, twenty-five cashew or mango trees had to be planted by him and his family. If any of these twenty-five trees died, the worker in question was flogged as an example to his colleagues.

The countryside is full of cashew trees, huge, wonderful oases of shade. I had often wondered how they got there: who had planted, watered and nursed them in this arid climate? Because this is not a place where a man can just plant a tree; after planting, that tree needs coaxing and tending like a sick child. Cashew trees grow to be enormously top heavy and then they tend to topple over. Unlike most other trees, this partial uprooting does not signal their demise. The roots run very deep into the ground. Once a cashew tree collapses sideways, it continues to grow, making new roots to join its forefathers and often sprouting a second head. In every village there are these fallen but still growing trees. In some villages, they have become the communal meeting place, providing ample sitting space for an entire committee.

After her crown and sceptre were rudely snatched away by the southern rival, Ilha was never going to regain her former glory, but economically she had a chance. That is, until 1975 when the 48/5 decree rid Mozambique of its former Portuguese masters. Arguably, no other city took such a body blow as Ilha. Elsewhere, houses were vacated and businesses abandoned, and then, over the years, the same buildings were swallowed up by Indian merchants and shopkeepers and by government offices and by the few local people who made good. But Ilha didn't have houses as such: it had hundreds of palaces, enormous, stately, costly, ghostly buildings far too big for an average family of shopkeepers to slip into and convert to a holiday home.

Elsewhere, the Portuguese colonizers' houses and warehouses were mostly left empty for years. 'What if they came back?' the local black Mozambicans asked themselves. 'What if the white masters came back and found their guards and servants living in their houses and sleeping in their beds?' It didn't bear thinking about. The Portuguese had beaten and abused their local staff when they had done nothing wrong; they would probably kill them if they took over their houses. It was one thing for a liberated Mozambican to step into his or her former master's shoes: but step into his bed? No way. As the years passed, though, ways were found; people started living in a bit of a house and then edging in a bit further. When it became clear that the Portuguese masters were not coming back, door and windows, tiles and furniture, buckets and tools began to disappear discreetly.

On Ilha, there was nothing discreet about the magnificent abandoned palaces, nothing discreet about the monumental doors. The last violence Ilha saw was after the country's liberation and immediately after the Portuguese fled. In Perugia, Italy, the local Umbrians tore down the vast Rocca Paolina, symbol of papal rule in that former Vatican State after the papal forces were beaten and Perugia regained its freedom. So on Ilha, after the Portuguese exodus the Omuhipitians attacked and vandalized some of the palaces that most symbolized their vanquished masters. The islanders had borne their oppression patiently, but as soon as they were free, groups of them took to the streets, forced open some houses and smashed up what they could.

Like the fortress, houses on Ilha are built of huge coral rocks. They were built to last. Their beams are made of almost indestructible ironwood, their doors are six inches thick, their stairs are massive and their arches structural.

The 'tearing down' of the Stone City was more a gesture than a fact. It would have taken dozens of bulldozers, wrecking balls and cranes or a great quantity of explosives to raze the Stone City. Undoubtedly some damage was done, but how much, thirty years on, it is hard to tell.

Ilha is a small island: 350 metres wide, 2.5 kilometres long. The Macuti City has always been overcrowded; the Stone City was always serviced by hundreds of servants from the Macuti City. There cannot have been many secrets kept there. During the final, brutal years of Portuguese rule, when opposition was rampant, Ilha was a seat of oppression. It may be forgotten now, but it was not forgotten then. In Lourenço Marques, police and army chiefs remembered the great fortress of São Sebastião. Far in the north, away from the prying eyes of foreigners, journalists and relatives, prisoners could be kept and tortured there and their bodies could be disposed of without any fuss or publicity. Some of the worst atrocities of the outbound government are said to have taken place on Ilha in the thousand-year-old dungeons of São Sebastião.

The muezzin calling to prayer from the seaweed-green mosque that towers over the northern shore can be heard all over the island. A cry in the night from any of the stone or mud buildings echoes through the streets. Only from within the massive walls of the lonely fortress of São Sebastião could the cries of the prisoners being interrogated be hidden from the rest of the island. But colonies, by their nature, use and abuse the native people. And being waited on hand and foot becomes so addictive that not even a state of national emergency could make Portuguese soldiers and officers and their civilian counterparts clean out their own latrines or wash the bloodstains off their office walls. The secrets leaked out via the local servants, who whispered them on.

In Maputo, as Lourenço Marques is now called, people remember with a shudder family members being sent to Ilha. Someone whose family suffered during the final years of Portuguese rule told me, 'For a prisoner to be sent to Ilha was a death sentence: too far away for anyone to visit or help. And even if anyone did manage to get there, no visitors were allowed into the fortress.'

Over the years, in the Macuti City, local islanders must have heard sad and shocking tales from prisoners' relatives. Through them, and the things they themselves saw, heard and overheard, they must have pieced together a grim picture.

Wandering through the island now, seeing beautiful buildings choked by their own rubble where the annual rains have eventually brought down a floor or a wall, it seems like wanton vandalism when one first hears how the islanders tried to destroy their own city. But vandalism is a phenomenon of the Western world. This is an ordered society where people do things for a reason. We come to admire the city and gaze at the architecture and find it a shame that it is so decayed without considering the shame of past atrocities. The beauty that remains is impregnated with passion and violence. It has stayed in the stones. In most cities, elements of such violence are at large in the streets. But Ilha is a soporific place where tranquil domesticity spills into its unpaved streets and grandiose civic buildings are the camping grounds of hundreds of families.

From the dhows being hand-carved on the seashore by a chapel to nets being mended on a green-slimed beach, from fruit and bread being sold on an esplanade to fishing dhows sailing into port by the collapsed jetty in front of the vermilion museum, there is no hurry, no rush and no aggression. Even the market seems to have been sprinkled with sleepy dust. With few cars passing between the tree-lined streets, the noise is that of children playing, women chatting and the few pedestrians in the Stone City greeting each other with the formal effusive greeting of the Macua.

The Macuti City is the part of Ilha that is full of life. In the Stone City, day and night, silence reigns despite the many squatters in among the ruins and the wealthy residents of the restored stately villas and the handful of relatively new hotels. Its name is apt because the stones overshadow the people who inhabit them.

Each year, more ruins are restored. The difference is noticeable and entire streets are beginning to look quite smart as more and more people discover this architectural treasure. It will take many years, probably decades before Ilha is fully restored. Maybe it never will be; maybe there will always be ruins and rubble between the pristine walls of this or that palace.

Whatever the future is for many of her derelict buildings, the Sleeping Beauty of Ilha has woken up. Unlike the fairytale princess, she was not woken by the kiss of a lovelorn prince. Ilha was woken by the various kisses of intrepid foreign tourists who found their way here and discovered the sleeping dowager of the Indian Ocean. Despite the efforts of UNICEF and its declaration that the entire island be a World Heritage site, and despite the efforts of aid organizations – predominantly from Scandinavia – it is the arrival of tourism that is breathing life into Ilha's economy. It is tourists in ever-increasing numbers who are generating the restoration of the Stone City and providing income to the Macuti City dwellers.

After the waking kiss, the Sleeping Beauty proved not to be immune to age. The passing centuries had left warps and wrinkles and her once immaculate stone gown had decayed in places. But hers is still a real and ancient beauty. As work progresses on her coral vestments, it is not the superficial work of cosmetic surgery. Description and photographs can never capture all the pleats and folds, her marine hems or her concealed charms.

Now that Ilha has been discovered and made its mark on the tourist map, foreign visitors will continue to come. New accommodation is under way to receive them. The pioneer hotel, the four-star Omuhipiti, stands out as the only modern building on the island. It used also to stand out as the one and only hotel, but now it has competition from the likes of Hotel Escondidinho, and Pensão Casa Branca. An Italian architect, Gabriele, has a delightful *pensão* opposite the mosque. Open the door and you are confronted by a courtyard shaded by a large palm, follow through and climb the stairs to the typical flat rain-catching roof and look out across the whole island or watch the stars. More can be learned of the goings-on of Ilha from an afternoon spent on Gabriele's roof terrace overlooking the main mosque and its fishing beach than on several days of extensive touring. And given the heat on Ilha and its magnified glare from acres of white and pastel walls, chilled drinks and real Italian cappuccino sipped in shade are an added bonus.

Another long-term resident, Jorge, has built the simulacrum of a Portuguese village by the sea. Leading straight onto a small beach, Jorge's *pensão* (which is beside the BIM Bank's palace, which is on a corner of the square by the market square) has rows of cottage-type rooms overlooking a long garden with a wall of blue at the end that merges visually with the sea beyond. The back part of his *pensão* is a traditional Ilhan palace housing restaurant, bar and rooms galore. Though, like much of the island, this *pensão* still has work in progress. Many of the rooms are finished and the garden is a delight. When the need to get away and write somewhere with the luxury of hot showers, electric light and a fan arises, I sail to Ilha and stay in one of Jorge's pretty cottages, undisturbed by any sound except the wind rustling palm leaves and the sea lapping at the private dock.

Slowly but surely a number of local householders are also doing up and opening rooms for tourists. In the long run, this will help solve the inevitable accommodation congestion that Ilha will have. Even though it is not necessarily a holiday destination where tourists will stay for weeks at a time, it will get more tourists than it can cater for and I think it will get them very soon.

Once Ilha is up and running with more tourist infrastructure, she has one rival in the Indian Ocean: Zanzibar. Where Ilha can beat this rival is if the island manages to remain a safe haven for tourists. Being able to wander around the streets, being able to admire the city, the luxury of being truly welcome are great attractions. This is a predominantly Muslim stronghold without any religious tension. The local people are far from any undertow of fundamentalism. Ilha is not lobbying for independence and it is not lobbying for Shiite rule; in fact, it is not lobbying for anything other than a good wind for its fishermen, a good meal at night and a good feeling for all and sundry, be they visitors or natives. Maintaining this easy-going feeling as waves of foreigners invade its shores and unintentionally upset the status quo will not be easy, but I think it is and always will be a priority for tourists.

Ilha is a bazaar of bright sun glittering on splintered blue and peeling pastels against the horizon. It is a job lot of sand roads and fragmented pavements, avenues of fat trees bulging into the roads, fragments of old stone, rusty cannon balls, pieces of anchors and massive beams chewed by time. Ilha is a kaleidoscope of shreds of beige and ochre sprinkled with astonishingly bright colours. Women in vivid yellow, green, red, pink and orange *capulanas* stroll through the streets or sit in doorways.

PART FOUR

XXII

Morripa, the Local Hero

ABDALA MORRIPA IS THE hardest of all the local people to describe because he is an enigma. His knowledge is deep rooted in the mangroves but has been fed by the twelve years he has spent abroad. To see him in his compound (known affectionately not as Morripa's house but as Morripa's village because of its size and the size of his immediate family), is to see a powerful, authoritarian 47-year-old man who has made good despite almost impossible odds. Part of the great esteem he is held in is because he has visibly 'made it'. He lives at a markedly different economic level from his immediate peers. One possible exception is his brother, who is a step ahead with a 4x4 truck to Morripa's Honda motorbike. Discussion of Morripa's well-being is a favourite topic. His staunchest fans maintain that Morripa could have a 4x4 if he so desired and that he doesn't have one because he doesn't want one.

This could be true. I remember him explaining to me on one of our many walks that he was bound by an oath to his father never to drive. 'My father was a driver, a chauffeur by profession. I was still a boy when he made me take the oath never to drive. My father has been dead for years but I made him a promise and I cannot break it.'

Much of Morripa's life is governed by promises. He is the most dedicated motivator of the twin Cabaceiras and determined to set them on the path of economic development within his own lifetime. To this end, long before I, or Mees, or the former Dutch owners ever came here, he has been educating himself the better to help his people and organizing them into self-help groups.

Another, equally important promise is to his family. He has vowed to put food on their plates every day and to send all his children to school. This is no easy task for any father in the Cabaceiras, but for one like Morripa who has twenty-eight children, only the quartermaster skills he gleaned from his long military service have enabled him to honour it.

Morripa is an entrepreneur: he builds holiday homes for the Indian community in Chocas-Mar. He keeps sheep and grows mulberry trees in his garden. He is always building. Behind the split-bamboo fence of his compound he does actually own a small village. Every time I go away for more than a few months, another traditionally built bamboo-frame mud hut springs up among his fruit trees like an adobe mushroom.

Replete with mobile phone, generator, refrigerator, TV, video player and stately furniture, it is his home that supplies the chairs carried to the college whenever special guests are coming.

When the first fourteen staff members were camping and squatting in his houses and grounds, I was not surprised that they were reluctant to leave. Compared to the college, Morripa has all mod cons. Daily the order to strike camp and move into the *palaceu* was skilfully ignored until it was pointed out that while seven of the fourteen had beds and rooms there, where did they think Morripa's enormous family was sleeping? Generous to a fault, Morripa hosted all the first staff for ten days without once drawing their attention to the fact that their occupation had rendered his children homeless.

As a result of his hospitality, there was no excitement about moving into the college by anyone except Ellie and Ramon. Most of the others saw it as an enforced downgrade and failed to see any potential for rendering the numerous bare rooms more comfortable or turning any of the intrinsically beautiful building into a semblance of home.

I remember the first time I visited Morripa in his compound. In those days, he had a pergola in his garden with tables and chairs where we sat and talked. Thanks to the many years he spent living in Cuba as a military instructor, his Spanish is fluent. But for this, we would not have been able to communicate beyond the boundaries of my then very limited Portuguese.

When he is relaxed, Morripa describes his world and the way he sees its future in the most lyrical terms. He is a natural poet who speaks in metaphors. Sometimes, to this day, I have to ask him to say things again because he loses me in his leaps of imagination. On the first day I visited him, he decreed that I accept and eat a boiled egg. It was an incredibly hot mid-afternoon and a boiled egg was the last thing I wanted. I demurred politely but he would have none of it.

'You have to eat it, it is from Peru,' he told me, and went out to give instructions to one of his numerous daughters.

A boiled egg in the tropics is a dodgy thing. Once in a while a little cooked embryo lurks inside the shell. I am a squeamish eater and not fond of finding surprises in my food. Only a few days before when making an omelette at Varanda, I had cracked open a blob of putrid green slime with a glutinous lump inside it. The smell was strong enough to linger in the little storeroom kitchen for several days. As a result, I was off eggs.

The thought of an egg imported from Peru was scary. It still took five days by road to get to Maputo. I didn't imagine eggs were being airlifted into Mozambique from South America along with essential medical supplies and tractor parts. Ellie came from Peru originally and I had travelled there: an egg had not much chance of being fresh even before it started its descent from the Andes.

I looked around the pergola for somewhere to hide the egg when it came and began to think of ways to distract my host while I disposed of the Peruvian offering. As luck would have it, I had no handbag and my thin dress had no pockets. Through the still skimpy bougainvillea I could see two teenage girls laying and then lighting a small charcoal fire. A battered aluminium pan was filled with water and a very large egg was put to boil.

It was a slow process and the longer it took, the more I determined, in this place of no doctors, not to eat the imported egg no matter how prized a possession it might be. I broached the subject as tactfully as I could.

'How does a Peruvian egg get transported?'

Morripa looked at me quizzically and smiled.

'I mean, how can you get an egg from Peru here in this isolated village?'

Morripa looked at me, clearly proudly aware that it was indeed no small feat. I was not to be daunted and kept going.

'Don't eggs have to be fresh? Do you just have the one or has anyone here eaten one?'

I didn't add, 'and lived', but I was thinking it. Morripa looked worried. Up at Varanda we had talked a lot and he had high hopes of what a future alliance might bring. We had already solemnly pledged to join forces on some matters. I could see him wondering if that had been such a good idea after all. He changed the subject but I pushed it back to the Andean egg. Eventually he told me that he had personally eaten several of them.

At that point, the offending delicacy arrived hot from the pan and was placed in my lap. Morripa nodded to me to crack it open and set to. Nothing happened and he ordered salt and piri-piri pepper to be brought. Both arrived and I continued to look at the egg in my lap and Morripa continued to encourage me to eat it.

Finally, crestfallen, he asked me, 'Don't you like eggs from Peru?'

I wrinkled my nose. 'It's not the egg: it's the Peru bit. Peru is so far away ...'

He looked at me and then stood up. 'Come with me,' he said, leading me out of the pergola to a small yard beside the outside kitchen. Pointing to a large bush, he said, 'That is a Peru.'

A very stately and very ugly turkey emerged from the shade and gobbled its way towards us.

If all our linguistic misunderstandings were as easily solved, both he and I would have an easier time of it. Since then I have worked hard at my Portuguese and he has done the same with English. Our lingua franca is now Portuguese and the times when Mees asks me to translate something and I have to admit that I can't because I have no idea what Morripa has just said are getting fewer. Each time a muddle is clarified, he laughs like a child with his perfect alabaster teeth gleefully displayed.

Deep down, there is a well of sadness which his eyes occasionally reflect. Sometimes, when I observe him off his guard, I see a man carrying an enormous burden and worrying if he will have the strength to take it to its destination. When provoked, he is the most diplomatic person in the world. When truly angry – a formidable sight – he clams up completely and the anger flashes in his eyes. Jealously protective, anyone who damages or disrespects me or Mees, Varanda, or the college, or any of his own, incurs his seething wrath.

Despite the power and authority he exudes, he is physically weakened by serious asthma. He is prone to bronchitis and pneumonia. But he is a workaholic, punctual to the minute and entirely reliable.

Before he joined Varanda as its local manager, he was a government tax inspector. Before that, for fifteen years he was a military hostage negotiator. Before that, for two years, he was a volunteer soldier in Frelimo's army defending his country against a vicious outside attack. Twice he was one of only two in an entire battalion to survive a battle. He has lived extensively in Russia, China and Cuba, and has travelled to many of Mozambique's neighbouring states.

He works five full days and one half day every week for Varanda. He is also the director of the college; he builds houses and farms manioc, pumpkins, tomatoes and sheep. He breeds poultry. He is writing a memoir. He studies. He is an active member of the village committee. He is starting a prawn farm with sixty-three local villagers. He has a wife on Ilha and a large family there and common-law wives in Cabaceira Grande, Cabaceira Pequena and Nampula. He has twenty-seven children, each of whom he cares about deeply, helps bring up and educate; I have tested him and I know that he not only remembers each and every name but also each and every birthday.

Given all the above, a great mystery is how does he find the time to go courting? Yet Morripa is a tremendous flirt and the best 'catch' in the village. It is believed that no female can ride on the back of his scarlet Honda without getting pregnant. I have personally ridden many times and disproved this theory, but each time we twist and turn through the dirt tracks of our and other villages, there are screams of lewd anticipation from the men and women we pass.

Several of our students are his children and one of our students has a three-year-old child by him. For some Western men, there is something almost threatening about Morripa's prowess both as a local motivator and sexual mover.

How he came to be what he is and to achieve what he has must be told by him to do it full justice. His story combines that of hundreds of thousands of other northern Mozambicans. It is as though in one immensely vibrant body the essence of all his fellow men has been combined.

Tall, ebony-skinned, gleaming and dressed to kill, he is the closest friend I have here. As each old pleat of his densely packed life unfolds, I realize that our relationship is more intuitive than anything else. It will take many years to really know him. It took only a few hours to really appreciate him. Every day, across the whole of Mossuril District from Naguema to Cabaceira Pequena, he is my calling card, my reference. It is not he who works with me but I who work with him.

His is a name to conjure with and a face to count on. A walk down any street, be it a red dirt road in the bush or the stony streets of Ilha is a slow process. Every few metres we must stop and greet as Morripa is hailed like the local hero he is.

XXIII

The Staff and Students

WE HAVE A PHOTOGRAPH, TAKEN just before the Minister of Tourism arrived, of all twenty-one of the first students standing on the portico steps in their new uniforms of tartan *capulanas* or trousers and beige shirts. I bought the shirts in the Waterlooplein market in Amsterdam as an ex-army bargain: one hundred, for one hundred Euros. The *capulana* cloth came from a little shop in the bush up a dust track behind Morripa's house. We bought four rolls and the local dressmaker sewed all twenty-one outfits overnight. The photograph is full of expectation and was taken on a wave of euphoria. Since then, there have been almost daily dips and highs. Now, no new group of students will probably ever look so excited because no new class will ever be venturing quite as far into the unknown.

When the college opened with its twenty-one students, the head boy was Morripa. I pointed out that since he was also a director of the college it was a bit bizarre for him to be a student as well. He pointed out that it wouldn't do for his peers and juniors to know things he didn't.

'Imagine if my own children can speak English and I can't. I want to learn everything there is to learn. You cannot imagine how hungry we are here to learn things. I am not embarrassed to go to school at my age. I went to secondary school on Ilha when I was thirty-nine. I sat in a little desk with twelve-year-olds either side of me. They laughed the way people always laugh at Cabaceirians. We are the idiots, the backward ones. Well, I went every day with Marufo from Cabaceira Pequena. We went by boat at dawn, and when there was no wind, we rowed. When we could not return, we slept over on Ilha, and when the sea did not let us go we made up the work the next day.

'Here in the village everyone laughed as well. Why was an old man like me going to school? Well, I got my tenth grade and I got a job as a tax inspector and now I am the local manager of Varanda and a director of this college. They don't laugh any more. I have a motorbike and mobile, my house has beds and tables. My children eat well and wear shoes. I know that knowledge is the key to everything. As a friend, teach me all you know.'

Muanema, the oldest of the students, is fifty. I discovered later that she had been tagged onto the student list by the community elders because her husband had an accident and was paralysed from the waist down and the two of them were virtually starving. By joining the first class, Muanema got a subsidy which keeps them going. To her great credit, she tries very hard to keep up, but with zero schooling and limited Portuguese, language and learning just don't sink in any more. I know the feeling; I got too old to just 'pick up' Dutch. After four years of living in Holland my Dutch is about as shaky as Muanema's English. But she is stubborn and loyal and not just here for her subsidy. She cares about the college and is proud to be part of it. As a compromise, she found her way to the outside kitchen and bonded with Atija and her team; Muanema now spends most of her lesson time there.

Cooking for thirty workers a day and also for the students and staff, Atija's crew are already under pressure. Just as Atija used to be a student who is now in a job, so Muanema has found her own job within the college and will spend the rest of her working days there. Now that she doesn't have to pretend to want to learn English, she is actually picking up more of it than she ever did in class.

To start with, 'tourism' is an alien concept. The first lesson at the College of Tourism – *o colégio* – is to try and explain what a tourist is. For people who leave their village only because they are forced to by fear or famine or the need to survive, the idea of *choosing* to leave your home and then squandering vast amounts of money abroad is more than just bizarre: it is madness.

'Who in their right mind would willingly go to where they have no family?'

'Who would choose to eat strange food and sleep under a strange roof?'

'What sort of human pigs piss – and more – inside a house?'

'How disgusting is that, when there is all the bush and the mangrove to do your business in!'

And when someone can afford to rest, they trudge around under a burning sun staring at and photographing the sea and the sand, the mangroves and ruins. Why?

It is puzzling enough to the historically cosmopolitan islanders on Ilha, but in the Cabaceiras, where tourists have yet to arrive, it is harder still to explain. Most of the local people have never seen a tourist so they have no idea what one is. *Turísmo* is a meaningless word much vaunted and desired without most people grasping what it entails. There is a rumour that when tourists come they will bring wealth and economic development, but few people grasp how that will happen. So few visitors come to the Cabaceiras that whenever someone from the college goes into the village, children run and hide and shout '*Akunha!*' as they might once have shouted 'Pirates!' in the olden days.

As a way of bridging the gap between the college and the village, we have taken to hiring 'Dr' Rocha's stereo system once a week and running local music on it via our generator. Between two hundred and three hundred young people and children come to the college's cultural centre to dance and drink lurid vermilion Jolly Jus and eat bread rolls. It has been a good way to recruit new, younger students. For people who barely speak Portuguese, have only three or four years of very basic primary school, who don't know what a tourist is and have never seen a farm, a College of Tourism and Agriculture on their doorstep can be a little bit too strange to join.

Even when Morripa and the current students try to explain that the college exists to train people so that they can have good jobs, not many people comprehend, because there *are* no jobs here beyond those supplied by the college itself and Varanda. The average Cabaceirian family of five, with two adults bringing in money from fishing, shell-gathering, peddling matches, Jolly Jus and torch batteries, and whatever else can produce an income, live on between forty and eighty dollar-cents a day. The higher rate is only sixteen dollar-cents per day per person. The concept of a regular salary at a living wage is beyond the dreams of most of the villagers, including our students. We explain it over and over again, but the women, in particular, don't get it. There are no jobs for women within their experience so how can someone suddenly give them money? We explain that the money is for work, but that doesn't sink in because life is one long task from 4am, when they go to fetch water, until dusk when they finish planting, weeding, harvesting or grinding their manioc, and no one ever paid them for it.

One day, news of a spate of robberies in Nacala drifted into the village and aroused sensations of outrage and shame. Ibraimo shook his head and wondered what the country was coming to. 'Such things could only happen in Mozambique,' he said. 'What must such reports make you think of us all?'

I told him that theft was international and universal. In fact, there had just been a particularly bad robbery at my office in Amsterdam. Ibraimo, the mangrove guide and deputy foreman of Varanda, stopped me short and, wide-eyed, asked me to repeat the story. After hearing the details, he was amazed.

'Are you saying there are thieves beyond Nampula?'

When I reiterated that there were thieves everywhere, he was speechless. He went off shaking his head. I could hear him in the carpentry workshop telling Mestre Canira and some other workers in Macua that there were thieves in 'Dona Lisa's and o Mesi's village'. During the day, everyone pondered this and came back to it, almost visibly shifting their entire perception of foreigners and 'out there'.

The more time I spend here, the farther away 'out there' seems to be. After so much success and so many failures, I have stepped out of whatever race it was I used to want to win. Now I want to be the one who stands by and cheers when Morripa and Ibraimo, Mestre Canira, Sergio and Marufo, Vulai and Momade, Sumaila and Victorino, Ancha, Amina, Atija and Sheik Namana lead their people out of the economic slavery they live and die in.

Being their cheerleader started as a hobby and then, as hobbies will, it began to take over my life. Like a brightly coloured *capulana*, I try to wrap it round my life. When it comes untied, I rearrange it. It comes untied a lot as we find our way and discover who our friends and allies are and who they are not.

In Cabaceira Grande, where once a complicated system of wells and irrigation channels watered market gardens and palm and cashew plantations, there is now such a water shortage that women sometimes walk for hours with a 20-litre yellow plastic jerry can on their heads to bring back the bare necessities. Were it not for the ruins, it would be hard to imagine such a poor and backward place could ever have been a centre of thriving enterprise and home to foreign dignitaries, let alone that this was the case until only thirty years ago.

The set has been here for centuries. The scenery is of fallen splendour gathering dust: from the former Governor General's summer palace to the ancient parador wrapped mysteriously in a high wall. The former is home to dozens of bush squirrels with striped tails who dislodge the last of the roof tiles.

XXIV

Vakháni Vakháni

AFTER THE CONFUSION AND culture shock of the first group of volunteers, we have changed the criteria of what a volunteer needs to come here. The first group was very carefully sifted and selected; each had a special development qualification or at least some aspect of their CV that would make them of particular use out here. One was an HIV prevention specialist, another had quartermaster's skills, others came from a background of educational development, and so on. When it came to the crunch, though, none of these skills were put into action and many of the basic requirements needed to manage here were missing.

Like everything else, recruiting has followed a giant learning curve. What we look for now are willing hands, with an emphasis on the *willing*. People have to want to help the local community. Volunteers have to have a sense of humour, they have to have initiative and common sense and they need to have travelled before. On arrival, the culture shock is enormous.

I can only blame myself for not personally testing the first group of volunteers to arrive. The almost immediate breakdown of their group leader was something that neither he nor I could have foreseen, but a leaderless, uncohesive group, dropped into the chaotic start-up phase, was a recipe for disaster.

Some of the first group would probably have been pretty good if they had arrived even a few weeks later, or if they had believed that the college would work. Some of the group rose above the bickering and were fantastic. Most notable of these was Mauro Annacarato, who stayed for six months; long enough for the villagers to keep asking when he is coming back.

The stars of the staff group were Ramon and Ellie, who travelled out from London via Zimbabwe and endured a baptism of fire on their journey only to be greeted by a second trial when they arrived to find a new but disintegrating team to work with.

There was a lack of faith from some of the volunteers and their own group leaders, but the project was also a new concept and hard to believe in. It had never been done quite like this before. To start something up requires a lot of patience, stamina, initiative and faith. For young people coming straight out of the comfort zone, the poor conditions (and they were very poor) of the college itself were enough to dash all their hopes. With a leader and rallier they believed in, I think most of the group could have pulled through; without that guidance, it was too tough a task. But no matter what some of them felt at the time, their presence did 'make a difference here', as the Minister of Tourism predicted it would when he visited the college on its first day, and by having had the guts to come here in the first place, they did allow the college to start.

It was a rocky start and I don't think anyone much enjoyed it, not least the sixty-three local workers who had worked so hard to get it ready and habitable in time.

No matter what occurred during the first ten weeks, the

fact remains that the first group of volunteers started the college. That most of them refused to believe it would work is now irrelevant, it has worked and it is working. Local villagers who only spoke Macua can now communicate in basic English and a first group of them could find and hold good jobs within the tourist industry. It still remains to be seen what overall percentage of the students will get their diploma, but there is every reason to believe that most of them will succeed.

On 10 December 2004, the first term came to an end. Eleven of the first fourteen volunteers and staff had left either of their own volition or mine or through sickness. That left Ellie and Ramon, Mauro and the new team chosen to come out and help. This new team was chosen by the new criteria. First and foremost, they had to care. Secondly, they had to have a good sense of humour. Thirdly, they had to have initiative and/or experience roughing it. In real terms, the latter meant that they had, at least, to have been camping.

For our new start, it was the family from Maputo who stepped into the breach: Sofia (she of the kitchen), Isabel and Tigo (he of the dreadlocks and incredibly long legs). This team comprising a mother, daughter and son are the family of Neco, a musician friend in the Netherlands. Beyond the border of isolation in which Mossuril lies, across the length and breadth of most of the rest of Mozambique, Neco is a household name as one of the country's most famous musical stars. Born in Maputo into a musical family of eight brothers and sisters, Neco showed an early and remarkable talent. While still a boy, he toured in the family band and then went to Johannesburg with two of his brothers to make his name abroad. The African fusion music he plays, sings and writes is now making him a name in Europe, but he is also a virtuoso classical guitarist and an operatic tenor. For some years he has studied at the Rotterdam Music Conservatory while playing gigs on the side.

When Don Mattera, the South African gangster-cum-saintly-popular-hero, visited Amsterdam, a group of his admirers decided to throw a party for him, to which all the Dutch people who helped end apartheid would be invited. It quickly turned into a grand affair begging for some live music. Esther, one of the organizers and a close friend of Don's, also had links to the music world. It was she who introduced me to Neco.

Although there are thousands of young people who would like to come out and help in Africa, it is both hard for them to know where to go, and even harder for projects like ours to get hold of the potential pool of willing and expert hands. So far, most of our international volunteers have come via friends. Tigo & Co arrived by sheer chance via Neco.

On the night of our Dutch–South African party, Neco turned up and gave a performance which earned him both a standing ovation and the chance to dance the tribal celebration of the Zulu with Don Mattera himself. From then on, whenever Mees and I held a Mozambican evening in Amsterdam, Neco was invited to play. At a subsequent investors' meeting, a short film was shown of the Cabaceiras, Varanda, the college and the villages. When all the guests had gone and Neco was packing up his guitar, he asked if Mozambicans as well as foreigners could volunteer as staff for the college. I explained that this was Morripa's and my dream, but the conditions were still too harsh to host his average compatriot. What to a foreigner could seem like an adventure, to a national could seem like hell.

'I think my family would like to go and help,' he told me. 'Let me call them and explain.'

I gave him some brochures and as much information as I could; and thought it a long shot, to say the least.

But ten days later, Neco came back and told me that three of his family were willing to go out to the Cabaceiras to help. The only thing stopping them was money. If airfares to Nampula could be found and a few hundred dollars a month, then Sofia, his mother, Isabel, his sister, and Castigo (Tigo) his brother were ready to take up community service.

Ever since they arrived, they have been the backbone of the college. Sofia is a professional cook, Isabel is a professional singer and dancer, and Tigo has found his niche teaching English and Portuguese and also gradually rewiring the entire building. Far away and long ago, Tigo was an electrician in Maputo.

Despite being Mozambicans, their culture shock was nearly as great as the international team's. They had no idea that such poverty existed in their own land. Their ethnic group and language is Shona. Once they settled in, not speaking Macua was their biggest problem. The monotonous diet of rice, fish and beans was a hot second. As a close-knit family, they brought stability and a determination to help. They have made an enormous difference to the project and in return have grown fond of the area. Between them, they have bought a little house and some land in Chocas-Mar, and at weekends Sofia takes pleasure in fixing the place up for future family visits and planting a garden.

Isabel arrived full of ideas and suggestions, including the starting up of a Cultural Centre (*Casa Cultural*) for the village. Sadly, she was knocked down by severe malaria and had to fly back to Maputo for emergency treatment. Just as Isabel was about to return from Maputo, Neco made a breakthrough in the Netherlands and was offered a proper concert at Rotterdam's prestigious Doelen, the biggest Dutch concert hall. He wanted Isabel and another of their sisters to back the band. Isabel flew to Holland and thereby missed the opening of the Cultural Centre she was supposed to run.

Meanwhile, a food-distribution programme in Mossuril town had just come to an end and Jorge, who had been working on it briefly, was at a loose end so, introduced by Ramon, who had met him over a beer in Chocas, he joined the college staff. Jorge comes from Nacala and is Macua. Within days of arriving, he began to work as head of orientation. He could unravel mysteries to new students where others can't. He and Tigo became very close friends and spent much of their spare time together. Both were close to 'Dr' Roche. When Jorge's interest in the college flagged and he eventually left, we were all happy that Tigo chose to stay. After eighteen months of living in the Cabaceiras, Tigo's network within the village is extensive.

In January 2006, a charismatic young man called Tauacal Victorino came to see me. He told me (in fluent English) that he was born and brought up in Cabaceira Grande, where he attended school until fourth-year primary. After that, he walked to Chocas every day for his fifth year. After that, he walked to Mossuril every day to get to seventh-year primary. There is nowhere else to walk to school after Mossuril. The next stop is Monapo, nearly 100 kilometres away. So Tauacal's parents sent him to school in Nampula, where he survived on a diet of learning and semi-starvation. Each year his parents scraped the money together until he passed his tenth grade.

'Now I want to get ten A and ten B and train to be a teacher, but my parents are reduced to nothing: there is no way they can help me even to enrol. So I want to help here at the college and save up enough to pay my own way. I can motivate students from here because they all know me.'

He started on his month's trial and proved to be a star. All new students now get eight weeks of 'Professor' Tauacal's orientation course and make very rapid progress. The years of hunger have taken their toll on their new teacher, giving him an almost insatiable appetite. The extra food is a small price to pay for his constant good will and dedication and his innate gifts as a teacher. Luckily for the college, from joining for one year, Tauacal has decided to stay for three.

One of the things that any project needs is enormous amounts of positive energy. Tauacal exudes it. He has a ready grin and a quick mind brimful of new ideas, and because he is a local boy who has made good, he is the perfect example of what others here can do. Having struggled to learn English in Nampula, he knows exactly which are the difficult words and concepts, and he cajoles the students over their language hurdles with such compassion and skill that he is a pleasure to work with. He is the first to pounce on any new books that arrive via our post box and he has such a hunger for knowledge that he stays up most of each night reading in his mud hut.

Whereas so many of his compatriots lack confidence, Tauacal is brimful of it. He tends to refer to himself as Tauacal, and relates episodes of his life in the third person. Perhaps the most remarkable thing about him is that he has one foot firmly planted in the past and the other as firmly in the future, and having mastered this conjuring trick he is determined to show every member of the village he loves how to hold the same stance.

A few months after Tauacal's arrival, Sofia left us to nurse her sick mother in Maputo, thereby leaving not only a serious gap in the kitchen, but also a social void. This was filled by Ana Cristina from Monapo. Many of the steps forward the college takes occur by chance, and it was a chance meeting that brought Ana Cristina our way. I have been into Monapo town (*sede*) only about three times in four years because it is several kilometres off the main road. However, limited as Monapo's resources may be, I learned from our new driver/mechanic (who went to school there) that it has a bank and an ATM machine. This might not sound remarkable, but here in north Mozambique it is. Furthermore, whereas in Nampula one can stand for up to two hours in an ATM machine queue waiting to draw cash, in Monapo there is hardly any queue for the same service.

Therefore, one day just after the training restaurant opened, on a beer run to Nampula, we detoured to Monapo to visit this ATM machine. As luck would have it, there was a small queue. I took my place and waited while a girl at the head stuck her card in the machine and typed in her password. Only she typed in the wrong password three times in a row and jammed the machine. It took forty minutes to start the cash point up again. Meanwhile, I noticed a young mixed-race woman beside me and felt a sudden urge to speak to her. This in itself surprised me because I am shy and usually neither speak to strangers nor feel the urge to. But my intuition told me to speak to this one, who turned out to be Ana Cristina, a professional but unemployed chef in search of a job.

Within a week, Ana Cristina had moved into the college and was galvanizing the cooking teams with her professionalism and her way with pastry. Within three weeks, her six-year-old daughter, Vivi, had joined her.

Uphill as the teaching challenge is, the college now has a team. It is joined by visiting volunteers and the departure of each is a wrench for the ones who stay. Volunteering for short or long stints is not for the faint-hearted: it is tough and endlessly frustrating. But for those who care, the lack of money is compensated for by the rewards of seeing positive results. We are lucky to have our core staff, but we have also been lucky with many of our short-term international volunteers.

There isn't space to mention all of them here, but that doesn't mean that the college and I thank them any the less for having joined us. The first of many after our new start arrived within weeks of Dona Sofia and her children in January 2005. Marna van Hal is a Dutch graduate who found me in Amsterdam (via a friend in Nampula). I was apprehensive about sending out any more foreign volunteers until the new national staff had had a chance to settle in. Rather than encourage Marna, an enormously enthusiastic girl, I did my utmost to discourage her; but she kept coming back to my office and asking to be given a chance. Once it was really clear to her that working in the Cabaceiras was a tough assignment, and the loos needed buckets of water to flush them, and the food was monotonous, and the village was about as isolated as could be, and the beaches were a hot walk away, Marna signed on for three months.

She was an instant success, and it is pages from her diary that are given to new would-be volunteers to show what it is like on the edge of the world.

Danny and Ulla, from England and Finland respectively, also fitted into the project from the start. Danny had contracted a truly disgusting skin disease while travelling up through Southern Africa and much of his visit was marred by the state of his feet. Despite this handicap, both of them made a difference and, like Marna and Mauro, their exploits entered the village myths. The workers still talk about Ulla's extraordinary energy and strength as she installed the new Moments of Joy storeroom.

After endless lessons in which students pretended to mix drinks and serve food, and pretended to pass each other kitchen utensils, laboriously learning the names of each in English, a qualified chef was anxiously awaited. There is only so much of holding up a whisk and asking, 'What is this?', and the class chanting back, 'That is a whisk,' that can be borne.

'Where is the whisk?'

'The whisk is in the big plastic jug.'

'What is this?'

'That is a saucepan lid.'

'Where is the saucepan lid?'

'The saucepan lid is in the rack,' or 'In your left hand,' or, 'On the saucepan.'

By September 2005, all the whisks and lids and pans were in place and all that was missing was a chef to start teaching what to do with them all beyond the daily rice and fish and beans, matapa, basic salads, grilled chicken and some delicious fried biscuits that came under Dona Sofia's domain. Sofia had made it clear she did not want to enforce any rules or methods in the kitchen. She cooked and students could watch and help, but Sofia did not want to actively teach. There had been talk of this and that chef coming out but when it came down to making the arrangements, other things kept coming up and all three candidates rain-checked.

Then Michelle arrived. I had met her very briefly at a literary festival in the Lake District (to which, I subsequently learned, she had been reluctantly dragged by her mother). I have taken to giving the Cabaceirians a plug wherever and whenever I can, and the Lake District was no exception. Michelle came up to me in the bar after my reading and asked me more about the college. She told me she was a chef. Since chefs, waiters and barmen are the people we most need in the tourism sector, I gave her as much information as I could.

It turned out that a close friend of hers had helped set up a community lodge project near Lichinga, in the far north-west of Mozambique, and Michelle was intrigued by the idea of following in her footsteps and going out to do her bit. We corresponded fairly irregularly for over six months and then at the beginning of October 2005, armed with a striped butcher's apron and an extremely valuable carving knife, she arrived in Nampula.

On her first day of teaching, she was very nervous and so was I. Apart from the five starfish hooked onto nails over the front door to denote the five stars we aspire to, Michelle was the first five-star anyone to come our way. If she succeeded in teaching any of the first class how to cook anything other than the fish, beans and rice to a five-star way, then I knew we would be able to keep going until enough of the students were similarly trained and the tourist classes could serve their purpose.

If, however, her trying to teach a local group proved absolutely impossible, we as a college would have to lower our sights, albeit temporarily. Because the only available jobs we could guarantee were to be for the two barefoot luxury lodges coming to the area, we needed to get the students up to that level. A failure to do so would result in a failure to secure over a hundred jobs for them.

The evening before, a flagon of wine had circulated freely on the veranda and, between other talk, Michelle and I had discussed kitchen strategy.

By 9.50am and Jolly Jus break-time, without a word of Portuguese and with conditions entirely unsuited to her elevated status as 'chef to the stars', Michelle Oldroyd was turning the battle her way. By the end of the day, a class of four students – Ancha, Anifa, Victorino and Sumaila – could chop and peel like restaurant kitchen pros. Over the next four weeks, Michelle taught the same and three other groups how to make Spanish omelette, a tuna salad that looked like something out of a foodie magazine, banoffee pie, Thai pumpkin soup and numerous other recipes.

Although her contribution was fantastic, the giving of it was taking its toll on her. There had been no time to adjust to the culture shock, no time to find the rhythm of the village, no time to get her bearings and find a way to deal with domestic ties back in Europe in this unnaturally faraway place. As though to mock her attempts to settle in, she became *the* victim of random drop in all its manifestations. Her emails disappeared into cyber space in Nampula, her phone calls were truncated and her mobile got caught on the sing-song loop of '*Liga mais tarde*'.

I think the thing that really freaked her out was something she saw after distributing the Thai pumpkin soup to all her students to take home with them. She had a star pupil: someone she told me was truly gifted and could go far. She also had some cookery duds whom she recommended be barred from the kitchen thereafter. Her star pupil was a great satisfaction to her, so it was doubly disturbing when she saw her tipping half a litre of used cooking oil all over her delicately flavoured soup before taking it home.

Michelle was appalled. 'How could she do that? She's ruined the whole dish!'

Reflecting on this, her set of perceptions and values shifted. This teaching wasn't about cooking gorgeous little nibbly things: this was about people who were actually starving. This incident took the wind out of Michelle's sails and, coinciding with domestic hiccups, she cut her tour short by a month and set off to do some travelling.

The first to do anything has the hardest time. No one understood what to expect of Michelle until she arrived. Any other chef has had his or her way paved now. Starting with students who have some concept of basic kitchen skills and ingredients, recipes and cuisine is easier by far than what Michelle pioneered.

She stayed long enough to prove that the cookery side of things *is* possible. Yet she probably left too soon to have really enjoyed her stay. In a give and take, she gave an enormous amount and, I suspect, got back little more than a sensory overload exacerbated by two incredibly stressful trips to Nampula within her four-week span.

Future specialists, if they can, should come for a minimum of eight weeks and take several days to acclimatize before even attempting to start. Despite that, the results Professora Michelle produced in under four weeks have become legendary in the neighbourhood. In the end, her efforts to buy and donate a gas cooker to the college proved her undoing. Trying to buy *anything* in Nampula is a nightmare. It was her dream to teach the students to bake and make cakes. It proved quite impossible to buy a cooker on both attempts and the disappointment was huge.

Ironically, after she left, while discussing what to make for the college Christmas party, Atija and Ancha suggested cakes.

'How? We are still waiting for a door for the new charcoal oven.'

'No problem, we can make an oven out of a big pot – we do it all the time,' Atija said.

True to their word, they rigged up burning embers under a giant pot and covered the lid with embers, hot ash and stones, and baked three perfect sponges.

I felt incredibly stupid: it had never occurred to me to ask if they knew how to bake. None of them had the money to pay for the ingredients for a cake so I just assumed they didn't know how to make one. Yet long ago, in Fabulous Chocas-Mar, someone had taught them. And *voilà!* We had two chocolate and one plain sponges, each light as a feather and absolutely delicious. Cut into ninety pieces, there was a mere wedge for each of us, but it wasn't a fluke. They have now baked cakes again and again, cracking each egg into a separate bowl in case a little, fetid chick plops into the mix.

XXV

Pacino, the Enraged Baboon

JUST BEFORE CHRISTMAS 2005, Lolly went to Nampula to see her new boyfriend and came back with a baby. This was not in the brochure for her weekend off. She called me on her mobile from Naguema to warn me that she and the driver, Mussagy, were not returning alone. There was also a three- or four-day-old baby baboon which had jumped off someone's shoulder onto her arm and clung to her for dear life, refusing to let go. Any attempt to remove the tiny monkey resulted in screams and even tighter clinging. She continued to forewarn me: 'There were twenty people there at the market, but he chose me. So we have to look after him.'

An hour later, Lolly arrived back with the newly christened Al Pacino in her arms. He was small enough to fit into the palm of my hand. He was almost dehydrated with his pink skin sagging on his bare shoulders. His face was disconcertingly humanoid and his bum was a disconcerting shiny red. From time to time he pursed his lips and made a low, aggrieved call. Pacino's forlorn 'Ooh' sounds very like Robbie Coltrane playing Hagrid in the Harry Potter films when Hagrid says, 'Ooh. I shouldn't have said that, should

I?' Only Pacino's forlorn little cry has an extra note of recrimination, as though after his 'Ooh' there is an implied '*You* shouldn't have done that, should you?'

He was practically hairless and all skin and bones. Mussagy reported that it seemed the mother had met with an accident, but such was the reticence of the market group at Naguema that the 'accident' was quite likely that of having been killed and eaten by the same person telling the tale. All game is fair game to the hungry and 'bush beef' is not an unknown meat around Naguema. The infant baboon had wandered into a mud hut alone and no one knew quite what to do with it. Only the rich buy milk for their children; no one rich or poor would squander money on milk for a monkey.

We gave him some watered-down condensed milk in a syringe and he guzzled it. After which, every hour or so, we gave him a little more. He was sweet and cuddly, clingy, and traumatized. At a certain point, Lolly put him on the ground and the baby primate transformed into what looked like an enraged, hairy tarantula, screaming and shrieking. Every time he was held, he was a surrogate dozy baby. But every time he was put down, he went berserk. Suffering the indignity of being peed and shat on by a monkey, Lolly kept him with her all night. By morning, he had gained enough strength to sit up more and pay attention, but he still did not have the strength to climb. By the afternoon, Pacino had recovered enough to be convinced that he had the strength to climb at least around Lolly's torso. As a result, he kept falling, and catching him became quite tricky. At one point we both missed and he fell on the floor and knocked his head. A large bump formed and turned blue.

As the days passed, the joys of motherhood began to pall and Lolly decided she could not have him running around her bed from four every morning, jumping on her neck and face and clawing at her hair in his efforts to master climbing. For daytime, we concocted a sling, and for night-time we rigged him up a big basket with a lid. As the early riser, it fell to me to rescue Pacino from the basket each morning at around 4.30 and feed him.

Having first imprinted on Lolly and persuaded himself that *she* was his mother and protector, Pacino made a fickle switch and began to attach himself to me. Time-consuming as he was, I found his company charming, that is, when he was neither incontinent nor enraged.

Gradually, he began to venture a few metres away from me to play and explore, always rushing back to grab my leg and cling on if he encountered anything unforeseen or if anyone else approached.

I managed to get a baby's bottle in Nampula and he calmed down a lot after that, drinking three or four ounces of milk and ground peanuts and then sucking the empty bottle in his sleep. When the bottle broke – almost everything breaks sooner than it would elsewhere because almost everything available is a cheap and poor-quality Taiwanese or Chinese replica of something else – we found an empty quarter-litre Travel Gin bottle, which Pacino clutches like a little drunkard. The teat is rock hard and broken so that milk and peanut splash out and half choke him. He has found a way round this by lying down with one cheek on the ground with the bottle flat beside him and thereby pacing his drinking.

Fond as I am of this baby baboon, he was a lot sweeter when he was tiny and afraid, and sleeping for most of the day. Now that he has plumped out and rehydrated, grown muscles and developed all sorts of climbing and jumping skills, he has become the college delinquent. Morripa and the guards tell me that when fully grown – to a height of over one metre – he will be a formidable bodyguard.

Meanwhile, he is a miniature simian Dennis the Menace and is both too young to know what he is doing and too young to leave on his own for any length of time.

When not swinging and leaping from pillar to post with varying degrees of success, or stealing bulbs, spoons, lids, pens and anything else he can scamper away with, he spends a great deal of time either clinging to my right calf or clawing his way up and down my clothes, rendering them filthy in the process. He insists on keeping me, his surrogate mother, in his sight.

Apart from his attempts to eat broken glass, wet cement, stones, matches, paint, nails and almost everything he sees, I find his most disconcerting habit is his attempts at affection. Several times a day he goes for what I suppose in monkey terms is a big kiss. For this, Pacino leaps, mouth wide open, up to my face. Each time he goes for the running kiss I have visions of him as a fully grown baboon with a mouth that could pretty much bite my head off, and I cannot receive his endearment in the spirit in which I know it is given. So he leaps and I catch his small body in my fist.

While looking forward to the day when he grasps that it is not a good idea to try and jump out of a moving car's window or jump off a three-metre-high veranda or down an eight-metre-deep well, or bite Smokey's (the guard dog's) nose, or chase chicks when their ferocious hen mother is nearby, or grab scalding hot coffee, we still have our bonding moments at dawn and dusk. As the sun rises, Pacino is so pleased to see me and be released from his monkey house and given his first bottle of the day that he clings happily to the crook of my arm for a quarter of an hour or so.

After that, he lives on adrenalin and circus tricks, which he teaches himself and then shows off. At night, after a frenzied neo-clockwork run around, he always stops abruptly and without any warning falls asleep. One minute he is

clambering, slithering and somersaulting over me, and the
next he is almost completely limp, just holding on to my
shirt with his long delicate fingers, but not holding on
enough not to fall off. For these times, I have a *capulana*
sling, which I tie round my waist. Transferring him to his
own box bed varies: sometimes he hardly stirs in his sleep;
at others he transforms back into the enraged tarantula leaping up and down and screaming in shrill outrage.

The first time I took him to Varanda, he had a fine time
playing in the dunes and climbing in bushes until he half
leapt, half flew into a thorn tree and got all clingy for the
rest of the afternoon. Since I wanted to swim, I dumped him
on the beach and ran into the lagoon. He shrieked and ran
after me, leaping into the sea. Although he could swim, he
did so while crying and swallowed a lot of seawater.
Choking and slowly sinking, he had almost reached me
when I rescued him. He was more afraid of being abandoned again than he was of drowning.

The next time I went to the beach, I thought he would
hate the water after his first experience with it, but he
merely clung tightly to me and stayed very still. The lagoon
water is tepid and has a gentle current. He closed his eyes
and nestled before falling asleep on my shoulder mid-
lagoon. We stayed in the water for half an hour and he
didn't stir once. I kept his mouth and nose above the water
as I lay on a submerged sandbank, and we spent the quietest
time we've had together in over a month.

Now, once or twice a week I take him up for a submer-
sion. He gets thoroughly clean and rested and I get the time
to remember that he is my dear little friend and not the
pain in the neck he keeps trying to be. Morripa assures me
he will get easier when he is older. Alas, that will not be for
nearly two years. Meanwhile, a year into our partnership,
my future bodyguard and I are learning each other's ways.

The workers assure me that one can learn a lot from a monkey. 'For instance, anything a monkey eats, we can.'

But obviously not yet, because broken glass, wet cement, stones, nails, earth, paint, Coca-Cola lids, all have to be removed from his mouth because Pacino tries to eat anything.

He is going through what Henry James might call his 'awkward age'. His enormous agility is marred by clumsiness. He shows off and grabs at Atija's ankles. He knows Atija hates it, and he kept running up to Dona Sofia, full knowing that Sofia hated him.

Bringing up Pacino often overlapped with Mees being away and my feeling lonely. In the evenings, when everyone else has gone to bed, I spend several hours with Pacino, who is less delinquent in the dark. Intuitively, he is afraid of it, stays close to me and manages to resist the temptation to wreck everything in my room. Sometimes I catch myself talking to him as though he could actually understand. Unlike chimpanzees, baboons don't understand very much human speech. Pacino has managed to grasp his name more, I think, by tone than actual word recognition; he knows when he has gone too far and when I am really cross with him. He never shows any repentance for his acts, but he doesn't like my being cross with him or rejecting him. Thus when he ate my USP stick and my camera card, stole and chewed my mobile, favourite sunglasses, etc., he was not sorry, just sad.

He has become my companion and I find myself missing my little friend when I am away for anything more than a day. When out for walks, as he runs away and back, students warn me that he might run away and then I would be sorry. I have grown so fond of Pacino that I hope one day he does run back to the wild, but I fear it is unlikely because he was so new born when he came and there are no bare-bummed orange baboons in the Cabaceiras. The local black-faced vervet monkeys are unlikely to break a life-time's habit and accept a giant ginger stranger into their tribe.

When he is older, maybe I shall consult with the *regulo* of Naguema to see if he has any magical suggestions as to what should be done. The *regulo* is a wise man, and when not farming he solves the problems and settles the disputes of several thousand subjects. On the other hand, maybe putting Pacino's fate back into the hands of the people of Naguema is not such a good idea, given the local penchant for bush beef.

The college baboon may not be the most intelligent of creatures, and he certainly is not the best behaved, but he does have a little fan club. Foremost among his fans is Jacobo, who came to visit from England and half adopted Pacino. Rather as one would be with a difficult child, I feel grateful to anyone who takes a shine to my little malad-justed friend and can discern his sweet nature under his troublesome acts. Such was Jacobo's affection for the baby ape that he is formally Pacino's co-guardian. I like to think that Pacino is aware of this, but (to Lolly's consternation) I like to think he is aware of many things.

Adamji (another member of Pacino's fan club) says when Pacino is older he will teach him to be a guard. During his current delinquent phase, I feel there is more chance of teaching me to carry a fifty-kilogram sack of manioc on my head than teaching Pacino to do anything. Watching him day by day, though, it is interesting to see what he can teach himself. For instance, he has now learnt to lift his Travel Gin bottle up and drink it while standing. He can perform somersaults from one branch to another. His learn-ing curve on this one was quite painful to watch as time after time he smashed to the ground until he perfected the action. And he can unlock the door of his monkey house.

He is also extremely telepathic. If I stub my toe or get stung by a wasp, Pacino screams and cowers. What he won't seem to learn is to walk more by himself, so a lot of our walks through bush, sand and gardens are conducted with Pacino clinging to my right ankle and resting on my foot like a prisoner's shackle. For the time being it just looks very silly and slows down my pace. If he keeps it up, he will become too heavy for me. When I take him off my foot he does that local thing of transforming: in his case back into an enraged hairy spider, leaping and levitating in a monkey tantrum.

XXVI

Nampula, Capital of the North

THE FIRST TIME I VISITED Nampula, I couldn't wait to leave. After Maputo, with its stately avenues and Portuguese colonial grandeur, its bars and shops and numerous explorable streets, its bay and its undeniable, if rather sleepy, buzz, Nampula was a big disappointment. Back in 2003, though, it was the only access airport for Ilha and the coast, so the only way to Mossuril was via that characterless, littered, colourful, frantic sprawl of a place. I felt cheated. I had arrived predisposed to like at least some aspects of everywhere I went. And I am a travel writer specializing in the 'hello birds, hello trees', experience. I can find a rubbish tip beautiful if I set my mind to it, so why was whatever hidden charm Nampula had eluding me? I was location-scouting and needed to find 'filmic' places. I think I have always been harder on Nampula than I probably should be because it disappointed me so greatly at first sight.

That was some years ago. Since then, that first sight has had a serious makeover, together with much of the city centre. It will never be a beauty, but the handful of fine buildings it does have now stand out, and some serious and mostly successful inroads have been made into the litter.

There is even a shopping centre now with luxury shops and 3 new four-star hotels.

Over many later visits, I have become quite fond of the city. Sometimes I find this alarming and ask myself what next? If I stay here for another five years, will I develop a taste for chemical Jolly Jus, or start thinking that it is fun to travel on the back of a *chapas* pick-up truck in the burning sun with thirty other passengers and their luggage?

Am I deluding myself, or have I really found things I like about Nampula? Objectively, I know that no future tourists are likely to ask themselves: 'Where shall I go for my summer holiday this year? Shall I go to Bali, Capri or Goa, Capetown, Mombassa or Maputo, or shall I go back to Nampula?'

It doesn't have tourist charm, but it does have some hidden charms and it is interesting for short spells of time. For people living in its province, it has the obvious attraction of being the place where you can buy things, and do things not to be bought or done anywhere else for a very wide radius. Living in Mossuril District, I have to go to Nampula sometimes, whether I like it or not. It is where the airport and airline office is, and the car hire, and the train station. It is where there are actual doctors and a proper hospital. It is where chemists' shops have a choice of pharmaceuticals. All government offices are there, from the car registry to the immigration office. All the provincial heads of department are there: from culture to health, education to environment. Most of the banks are there and the money-changers. All the hardware stores are there, and the food stores, the proper markets and shops.

We can buy so little locally that it would be impossible, say, to restore a building without importing materials from Nampula. Now that we have our market garden, we can manage to eat reasonably well by shopping in Mossuril District and Ilha and using our own produce. Before we had the garden, though, the food situation was bleak and we had to top up at least once a fortnight in Nampula.

All the basic urban amenities Nampula has I find useful but I don't consider them reasons to like or dislike a city. We don't like Jaguars or Audis or Ferraris because they have wheels: they are cars, cars are meant to have wheels, so any car judgement has to start after standard criteria have been fulfilled. It is the same with cities: they can't get on the Beauty Map or even on the Towns of Interest list by having shops and banks, filling stations and medical facilities. The bottom line is that they are there making the place a city in the first place. Otherwise, like Pompeii, it would be on the Map of Ruins.

When it comes to cities, my standards are high – no doubt from having lived in Italy for twenty years. For me, it is Ilha that has beauty, not Nampula; but I know people who hate Ilha and think it a dirty dump and who find Nampula aesthetically pleasing. I am giving my impressions here; on matters of taste, they cannot be judgements. Architecturally, Nampula has its vermilion Museum of Ethnicity, an externally pleasing cathedral, a Government House and a street of pretty, faded villas on the Station Road. The rest is not really to my taste. I find Florence more attractive than Milton Keynes, but if others don't, *vive la différence*!

Nampula does have one selling point over and above the call of duty as an urban centre and capital of the north; and it is a selling point. It has a huge local market that people flock to from a radius of 200 kilometres. On Saturdays and Sundays all roads to Nampula are full of mostly barefoot people trudging along with vast bundles on their heads: baskets, rush mats, wooden furniture, wooden planks, doors, cooking pots, water holders, jerry cans, *capulanas* and dozens of mysterious bundles the contents of which will only be revealed at the fair (*feira*).

On Sundays, starting very early in the morning, this *feira* is a fabulous, colourful and chaotic market. I mostly come to Nampula on weekdays to shop and to visit government offices, so I am hardly ever there on a Sunday. But the market is exciting and full of things I want, rather than need, to buy; so I try and manipulate trips and even flights into Nampula to include being able to attend this pooling of local energy and cottage industry. The few times I have been, I have shopped till I dropped there. The first couple of times I was also robbed. This is standard procedure for locals and foreigners alike.

The market is packed and the lanes between stalls are labyrinthine. Foreigners attract a crowd which quickly turns into a mob. The best way to negotiate it is with a local guide. There are numerous homeless boys in the town centre and it is easy to take a couple with you as guides and negotiators. This is a paid job, but the 20 to 50 dollar-cents it costs you will probably earn back on your first purchase. The locals know the real prices. The goods on sale seem so cheap to a Westerner that it is hard to know when they have been doubled and tripled for the *Akunha*.

Once you have been thoroughly pickpocketed there and realize that if you take a handbag or wallet with you, you will be again, and once you have a local guide trotting along beside you like a small protective knight, you can wander freely past the hundreds of stalls of local crafts. What's so nice about the Sunday market is that it isn't for tourists, it's for local people to buy what they need and rural sellers to sell what they can. The mat-weavers and basket-makers, the carvers and metal-workers, broom-makers and rope-makers are all there. In fact, there are thousands of local people with their entire families there, buying, selling, cruising, touting, bartering, stealing, gossiping, meeting cousins from out of town and exchanging news.

Sometimes, new staff members want to go to Nampula so as not to go stir-crazy in the bush. They plan a night out, an evening of fun, and a day of luxuries. It is new staff who do this because anyone who has been there regularly knows that it is a pretty dead city with less lively discos than the local ones; shopping is deeply frustrating and often unfruitful and the general stress-factor tends to knock out its visitors rather than filling them with fun.

But, to be fair, when visits to Nampula are paced and a few hours are dedicated to shopping, after which the shopping list is abandoned, the city does have some places where a visitor can spend a lazy day, such as sipping drinks on the terrace of the Hotel Tropical or by the bamboos of the Italian-owned Copacabana opposite it.

The trick is in the pace. Nampula is frantic: there are vendors all over the sprawling streets. Every shop has a queue and the service is painfully slow. The idea that shops should be attractive to the consumer hasn't really caught on yet, so the existing ones are designed more on the warehouse principle. Some even have metal grids over their counters to keep the customers back. You can rarely see what you want to buy and you can rarely buy what you see.

When Michelle, our visiting chef, tried to buy a gas cooker to donate to the college, she could hardly believe how hard it was. It took two abortive trips to *not* buy one. It took hours and hours of stress and frustration. Newly arrived, she and Lolly set out for a girls'-night-out trip to the city. They talked about it for days before, and plans were made, and shopping lists compiled. They set off from the sticks full of enthusiasm and came back two days later looking older and wiser.

Phone calls home fell prey to random drop. Long emails full of first impressions disappeared off the screen before they could be sent. Most of what was on the shopping list was out of stock, or never had been in stock, or might be back in stock next month but don't hold your breath. And the tiny part of the shopping that Michelle had been able to get had taken the best part of the day to purchase.

This is how you buy, for example, a nail or a broom, a door hinge or a pot of paint, a screwdriver, screws or just about any other item of hardware. First you park your car and offer to pay a small boy to protect it from thieves. Know your small boy, though, or he might be one of the thieves. If you are on foot, then God help you because it is very hot and dusty, and the sparse traffic includes gleaming new 4x4s driven by their wealthy owners up and down the main streets at perilous speeds. So, on entering a shop:

1. Join the queue and wait to be served and be ready to be ignored.
2. Ask for what you want, such as some 4-inch nails, and be ready for the super-bored shop assistant to tell you the size you want are not in stock before you have even managed to specify it.
3. Suggest there might be some four-inch nails in stock and ask the assistant to find out.
4. Wait while one assistant grudgingly asks another. Use the spare time to start getting used to the stifling, toxic atmosphere.
5. Wait a very long time for either a) To be told they are in stock, or b) To be told they aren't in stock.
6. If what you have asked for is in stock, wait a very long time while the price of your nails is written out very slowly, then wait again for the chit to be handed to you.
7. Either queue at the cash booth or try to get the attention of a very bored cashier.

8. Pay for your nails.

9. Wait while your money is counted three times.

10. Wait while your change is counted equally slowly.

11. Wait to receive the change and receipt.

12. If you need an official receipt, it is not the same as the one you have just been given, so ask for an official one and be prepared to wait up to forty minutes longer to get it.

13. Take the cash receipt back to the shop assistant.

14. Wait while the shop assistant hands it to a stock assistant and the latter disappears with your nails.

15. Resist the temptation to grab your purchase and run: it isn't yours yet.

16. Yet another bored assistant will hand your purchase to the despatch counter.

17. Show your cash receipt to the despatch assistant.

18. Wait while he verifies your receipt price against the price on his stock list. This can take long enough for you to pop out for a cold drink and return, but if you are unlucky and miss your moment, the process goes back to step one again.

19. Receive your purchase.

20. Get stopped by a guard at the door who will check your purchase against the receipt you had better still have in your hand.

21. Go and buy something else but bear in mind all shops close at noon and will not open again until two. And don't forget that most government offices do not open in the afternoon. Look at your watch and discover that you just spent two to three hours buying some four-inch nails.

The whole process can be multiplied by the number of things you need to buy. On a building site, that is a lot.

Some days I get so tired of the endless procedure that I do leave the hardware store mid-purchase, have a drink, take a few deep breaths and go back in with a bit less consumer rage. The whole process is so absurd and the people involved in many of its steps are so obviously trying to waste time and alienate their customers that I have taken to observing the farce with the eye of an amateur social anthropologist to see what lies behind it all.

I often shop in Nampula with Morripa, who seems to be almost immune to the frustration of having entire mornings wasted. Despite being a more patient victim of it, he has also analysed the process. He reckons it is the poor man's revenge.

'Most of the shops in the province are owned by Indians. They were the traders with money under the Portuguese. When we got independence, the Portuguese were given forty-eight hours to get out of the country and they were only allowed to take five pieces of luggage each. That was the 48/5 degree you may have heard mentioned before.

'Since the Portuguese owned more or less everything and they left it overnight, the one class who could step in and buy them out were the Indians. We black Mozambicans couldn't: we didn't have any money. So that left the Indians even richer.

'There had never been much respect or kindness from Indians to blacks, and with the Indians' sudden rise to extra wealth and power, they took to despising their black workers more and more. Of course, we don't have their education, and as you can see in the shops, there is no way anyone can learn to run a shop or set up a rival one because all the work is divided. No one person knows what there is or how to sell it.

'The shop assistants are not bad people, but some of them have been working in there for thirty years, day after day, and they hate it. They can't steal from the shop because every screw is counted, and they never even get to smell any money, and yet everything is designed to humiliate them and treat them like potential thieves.

'No matter how far down you push a man, he can always fight back somehow. One of the few ways left to the Mozambican worker is sabotage. You see, it isn't *his* shop. He doesn't lose money if the owner does. The assistant doesn't lose a client if a client gets really cross and leaves. It is the owner who will suffer. That's the point, you see: get at the owner, lose him his clients, have people curse his name. It's a small victory, but at the end of the day it is theirs, the shop assistants'.

'It is sad for our future and for the economic development of our country because such sabotage is widespread.'

Over the last couple of years I have tried to make friends, bit by bit, with some of the saboteurs. It took surprisingly little to break through the sullen barrier to a few at least of them. As soon as they see a glimmer of interest, to a man, they try to jump the counter and offer their services to work at the college. In one hardware shop there are two assistants so insistent that I save them from their horrible jobs that I have had to stop going because the Indian floor manager has become suspicious and spies on us, and I am sure if he were to hear how they plead to be taken away from their semi-serfdom, they would lose their meagre employment. Nampula is full of people who would jump to replace them, who would ignore the insults from the management and the scorn of the cashiers to be able to take home a salary.

Baboons obviously have more clout than *Akunhas*, because when I take Pacino shopping with me, we get a lot better service than when I go on my own.

Shopping in Nampula often includes buying more yellow

ochre pigment to keep painting the college's outside walls as yet another of them gets re-plastered and ready to paint. Because the building is enormous, it drinks up hundreds of gallons of paint. We mix the colour ourselves by adding the yellow ochre powder to lime and water. But we used so much that we bought up the entire stock available in Nampula Province. After the main stores had sold out, we scoured other ones. For some reason, though, I had missed a very big store, called Armazenes Ganil; I was told that they had yellow ochre in stock.

Sure enough, they had one 25-kilogram sack left. While buying it – at treble the speed of anywhere else, thereby suggesting a marked reduction in sales sabotage, and therefore a much worker-friendlier boss – I saw the shop had lots of hardware supplies that we were in the habit of buying elsewhere.

I started looking around and a lugubrious, rather elegant Indian gentleman asked me in perfect English if I needed any help. I was doubly surprised because unsolicited help is the last thing I had come to expect in a Nampulese hardware store, and few foreigners speak such excellent English as this man did. I complimented him on it.

'I lived in Leicester,' he told me with the same deadpan expression. 'I went there for a holiday and stayed for fifteen years. But it was cold there. Very cold, so I came back.'

I told him that I had a sister who had lived in Leicestershire and that I knew the city well. We reminisced about the Phoenix Theatre there, and the Odeon Cinema, this bread shop, that café, the public libraries.

On the strength of our British Midlands connection, his charming manners and his efficient staff, I switched my not inconsiderable custom to this shop, of which he is the owner. I look forward to our brief conversations. When

Lolly and I were contemplating a visit to Lichinga, he even offered to arrange for us to stay with his sister there. *Vakhâni vakhâni*, I find little islands of calm within the urban frenzy. Sr Ganil has an aura of extraordinary calm, of the long-suffering, almost saintly variety.

Thus, on the upside so far, Nampula has two bar terraces and Sr Ganil. And, if I stop trying to give it marks out of ten as a holiday resort, it also has a large museum worth visiting, with a small, not-to-be-missed craft centre behind it where Macua wood-carvers and gold- and silversmiths make traditional craftwork. I should really go back to the top and say that Nampula has very nice filigree silver worked into bracelets, necklaces, chains and earrings.

When city trips come up there are usually several village people or college staff who need to go to town. Some need to renew a visa, to see a doctor, to apply for a document, to visit family or to shop. The local sporadic transport is by *chapas*: a truck or minibus packed with travellers, each of whom pays a fare. It is four US dollars each way from Chocas to Nampula, eight dollars return. The minimum wage is just under two dollars a day. Only the happy few earn minimum wage; most workers get less than half, some less than a quarter in a full-time job, such as a guard or porter. For local people not attached to the college and Varanda projects, the eight-dollar return fare (200 meticals) is out of the question. For those on our payroll, it is still a huge bite out of their monthly budget. Being offered a lift is probably one of the biggest ways local people can be helped in the short run.

There are a handful of villagers who left and returned and have made good. Two of them have made good enough to buy trucks, and another couple have motorbikes. Beyond the village, in Fabulous Chocas-Mar, there are dozens of people, mostly Indian, who have 4x4 trucks and Land

Cruisers which regularly make the run to Nampula and back. Chocas has become a beacon as constant to NGOs and their consultants as the lighthouse of Ilha de Goa is to ships. Whereas the lighthouse blinks in vain on what used to be the trade route to Goa, Chocas's beacon, in the guise of the Compleixo Turístico (complete with a fish menu and cold beers), lures a steady trickle of new cars to its terrace tables. These cars also rattle and race up and down the dirt road to Naguema.

Therefore, one might think, there would be enough lifts to ferry at least the most needy local people to Naguema (where regular transport starts) or even to Nampula. This is not the case. Lifts are not given and most locals don't even bother to try hailing one: they know there is no point. They know that they are beneath consideration 'out there', and that 'out there' starts where their own village ends. Even locals who have made good tend to extort ridiculously high transport costs from their fellow villagers. In the middle of the night, if a child is dying in the Cabaceiras and a life could be saved by getting that child to the cottage hospital in Mossuril, parents and family have to start running around to find a car and driver. The nearest place is Chocas, so several family members will run several kilometres there to start asking. If they are lucky, a car owner will get out of bed and drive on to Mossuril; meanwhile, the sick child has been carried the four to six kilometres to Chocas (depending along which track and from which part of the village the walk starts). The driver will then ask for anything up to twenty dollars to make the run. The child is dying, time is short and every minute counts. No local can pay twenty dollars so time is lost in negotiation to reach the bottom-line price of 150 meticals (six dollars, or between six and fifteen days of the entire family's income). A few families have been able to borrow it. There are no lifts on credit;

locals have to pay up front. If there is no money, there is no lift.

The child is dying, dehydrating, and there is under an hour to jog to Mossuril. It is another four kilometres to the hospital. The family set off carrying the child. Mostly, the sick die en route; the family walk all the way back with another small corpse to bury under the frangipani trees.

'Dr' Rocha is the village nurse and he runs a health post which is open six days a week. But there is no doctor and no electricity and therefore no refrigerator for all those medicines that have to be refrigerated. So there are very few medicines and no way to deal with serious cases here. If 'Dr' Rocha is not in the village, there is no one to help. If the case is serious, Dr Rocha will send them on to Mossuril anyway.

For those villagers who fall sick during the day, the same transport nightmare is involved, but it is easier to get a driver when he is up than to persuade one to get out of bed. Assuming a patient can get to Mossuril, on arrival at the cottage hospital there will be beds, nurses, medicines and saline drips, though no analysis can be done after dark. Without a doctor, the cottage hospital is not able to treat the serious cases. So these are sent on to Monapo (on the way to Nampula), where there is a proper hospital with doctors. But Monapo's is a small hospital and it serves an enormous area. Understaffed and understocked, it, in turn, has to send serious cases on to Nampula.

Like it or not, all roads lead to Nampula. Actually, there is only the one main road in and out, just as there is only one railway line. Each cuts through the city, not making that metropolis any calmer.

XXVII

In Search of Our Lady of the Cures

THE LOCAL CHURCH, THE beautiful, battered Church of Our Lady of the Cures (Nossa Senhora de Remedios, 1549), sits with its back to the sea. Its latticed portico stares into a palm grove and the mangroves on the salt flats wherein no souls live. The church is as solidly built as a fortress and exudes a curious aura of resignation, as though by some foreknowledge it knew it was doomed to languish without priest or congregation.

Once a week (or two weeks, or three) a travelling priest comes from Monapo, and once a week, up to thirty-nine tenacious local Catholics gather to pray in Macua. The average Sunday attendance is fifteen, but at Easter, Whitsun, Christmas and on certain saints' days, there are more. Sometimes the faithful arrive but the priest can't get there, in which case Victorino unlocks the church and the flock holds its own service. I imagine that once, long ago, this important historic church was packed. Even now, with a village priest, the flock would stand a better chance of thriving.

The thrice-daily planes from Maputo to Nampula always carry several missionaries and nuns, which begs the question why none of them come here to what is arguably the most important church in Mozambique. When I put on my tourist developer hat, I see this as a place for pilgrims. The church is said to be the oldest in the southern hemisphere that was built as such. Earlier churches were converted (usually from mosques).

The roof is leaking, the walls are covered in green slime and the ceiling is starting to rot. For once, it is not for the government to deal with a case of neglect, it is for that far richer body, the Vatican. Probably unbeknown to anyone in those Roman corridors of power, a jewel in the Indian Ocean has been thrown away. Elsewhere, worldwide, Roman Catholics are losing their faith, while here, a tiny hub of the faithful are struggling unaided to keep theirs. It seems as though Our Lady of the Cures has forgotten this village and taken her miraculous cures away with her.

In the absence of miracles and holy balm, and where the local *curandeiros* fail, all cures are in the hands of the medical authorities. In a tropical country like Mozambique, children sicken and die in the arc of a day unless they receive emergency treatment; Nampula is just too far away. For the adult sick, it is even more difficult to get out of the village because carrying a grown man to Chocas is difficult and transportation thereafter is unviable.

A simple solution for many local health problems would be to lure a doctor to Cabaceira Grande, upgrade the health post there, and ask him or her to care for both the villages. One of the reasons why there is no doctor is, I think, because the Albert Schweitzers of this world are few and far between, and few fully qualified doctors can survive in the bush. Where would they live? What would they eat? In the days of missionaries, medical teams went out and battled with disease in the most isolated places. Today, some back-up is both needed and wanted.

For the past thirty years, a doctor in the village might have found it very hard to stay, whereas now the college can provide accommodation, three meals a day, laundry facilities and, maybe as importantly, some kind of social back-up. Due to the lack of facilities, there are no teachers living in the village. The teachers stay in Chocas and walk in through the bush every day to teach. Most teachers don't want to come to the Cabaceiras either. Having struggled to get an education to grade ten B and paid to qualify as a teacher, nurse, doctor, social worker, health worker or whatever else, the last thing most people want is to be relegated to a backwater with no running water, no electricity, no transport, no proper back-up, an almost total lack of materials to work with and to be forced to live in a mud hut.

It will be hard for a Mozambican doctor to take up the Cabaceira challenge. Mozambican doctors are in very short supply and most have just emerged from their own poverty and are supporting extended families on their meagre incomes. Nor have I come across the foreign doctor who will rally to the cause, but I feel sure he or she is out there. The experience would be invaluable for any graduate of tropical medicine. Furthermore, as the fight against AIDS/ HIV has become a worldwide campaign, these villages offer a unique opportunity for research.

To date, statistics of HIV-positive cases have been based on limited tests. Certain fairly small groups of people are tested, such as mothers who give birth in particular clinics, prisoners, selected groups of schoolchildren, workers from a given factory. The final statistics tend to be based on non-representative or incomplete groups. To find out how many people are really infected, entire villages need to be tested. In the Cabaceiras, there are two entire villages willing to co-operate with such a survey. Over seven thousand people are here waiting to help.

There is more, and this second point is one I have tried in vain to bring to the attention of aid workers. The presence of HIV/AIDS infection seems to be substantially lower in the Cabaceiras than elsewhere, not just in Mozambique, but in Africa. The local communities are willing to help combat this disease, which has only just begun to show itself here. Because of its extreme isolation, hardly anyone has come in or gone out of this area. Tests that could have been done earlier elsewhere to establish base lines weren't done because nobody knew then how serious the AIDS epidemic would become. Here in this forgotten village there is a chance to step back in time and establish base lines from which the spread of the disease can be studied.

On the one hand, we want a doctor and AIDS researchers to come to the village. On the other hand, those researchers should come. They should be here in force. A unique opportunity is being missed. With millions of dollars a year being spent to combat AIDS, a tiny part of it would be better spent here than maybe anywhere else in the continent. So far, the HIV present would appear to be imported from villagers who left to live and work in Nacala and Nampula and who came home, terminally ill, to die in one or other of the Cabaceiras.

Last, but not least, there is malaria. On a World Health Organization map, Mossuril District, which includes the twin villages, is shaded as a 'low-to-no malaria' zone. By so doing, it has condemned the local people to receive 'low to no help' with what is an ongoing plague. Malaria-prevention methods have not been explained here. No one told the villagers that puddles and pools and uncovered wells help spread the disease. No one explained the importance of mosquito nets and of covering up at night. No one has come to teach local families how to recognize the early symptoms. The villagers did not know they had to rush for treatment, nor how to nurse malaria patients at home. A recent report showed that of a US government fund of 95 million dollars given to eradicate malaria, 90 million dollars was spent on consultants. The retail cost of a mosquito net is four dollars. Approximately four children can sleep under one single net.

The seven-thousand-plus villagers are scattered over as many kilometres. We do what we can, but we need help. The local health centres do what they can, but they need help. The district health authorities do what they can, but they need help. Each entity is struggling to keep up with its own overload. There is no time, money or personnel to tackle this extra problem. The organizations that help elsewhere draw a line before the Cabaceiras. It is an invisible line, but none cross it.

Just as Rabobank Foundation has stepped in to help the community to farm (of which, more later), so others could follow suit and step in to help combat malaria and monitor and prevent the spread of AIDS.

The *tradição*, so effective in many fields with its medicinal herbs administered by *curandeiros*, is ineffectual against malaria. The *tradição* treats local illnesses with local remedies. To date, most ailments that occur in any given area will also have a natural cure available within that same area. Knowledge of what that cure is and how to prepare and use it has been the business of witches and witchdoctors since time immemorial. Plants that can cure can often kill so it takes great skill to work with them. The local *curandeiros* are mystified as to why their indubitable powers and expertise fail so miserably to combat malaria.

With the morass of mysteries that come from the village to me, this is one mystery that a little-known theory can explain. There is evidence of malaria in Europe for two thousand years, but there is no evidence for it having existed in Africa prior to the arrival of Europeans. Thus, the theory claims, malaria is not a local disease – not here, not in Mozambique and not in Africa. It has long been the bane of the continent and it decimates the population, but it didn't originate here: it was imported from Europe. The *tradição* is handed down from generation to generation and adheres to the knowledge of ancestors from the time when the Macua settled here. That was over a thousand years ago. Malaria was imported here after Vasco da Gama by the Conquistadores. It was imported from Europe, where, until Columbus took it to South America, and the British to Asia, it was an exclusively European disease. In England, it was finally eradicated from the Norfolk Fens as late as the 1930s. In Italy, it weakened the entire Roman Empire.

For centuries after unwittingly exporting malaria, European colonizers then suffered its scourge. The tropical climate was a paradise to anopheles mosquitoes, they were in mosquito paradise. Unchecked by European winters, they multiplied and spread. The reason why there are no traditional cures to be found locally is because there is nothing traditional about the mosquito.

Malaria killed more soldiers and sailors in military campaigns than the enemy did. Africa, in particular, came to be known as the White Man's Cemetery. The one and only cure that emerged was quinine, and the one and only place it was found was in the bark of the cinchona tree in Peru. For the British, the fact that Peru was Catholic made quinine seem like a Jesuitical anathema. It was called the Devil's Bark and the average upstanding Englishman stubbornly preferred to die than to take it. The average poor British soldier would most likely have preferred to risk eternal hellfire and have taken the cure, but it was very expensive and not made available to him.

In the past, beating malaria meant making money. Beating malaria meant being able to colonize and rape more tropical countries. It is both the good fortune and the misfortune of several large ethnic groups in West Africa to be genetically immune to malaria. While they remained safe from the disease, they became the perfect slaves for the colonizers. West Africans could be sent with impunity to the Americas and work the ever-expanding sugar plantations without succumbing to the fever that killed off everyone else.

Meanwhile, malaria spread, and wherever else it spread to, it was no respecter of persons. It is still killing millions of people a year. And in the summer of 2005, malaria cut a swathe through the village. Master plasterer Mestre Tauacal was one of those who died. His fellow workers grieved doubly for him. They grieved because his time had come in his prime and because he died before he could see the better life his children will have. He died before the college project was completed, even though every wall of the *palaceu* bears his mark.

Day by day during this crisis, people queued outside the college gates for anti-malaria pills. I use the term 'college gates' as though there were such a thing, but we have no gates. We have a gateway, where long ago there must have been gates. For us, to begin with, the courtyard was entered via a gaping hole where several metres of wall and one of the gateposts had fallen down. In those early days, people came to a pile of rubble and called for a guard. Then Ramon and the workers mended the wall and built a new gatepost. After that, a sisal rope with a small stop sign was slung across the opening. Now Adamji has built a bamboo bar, which he and his fellow guard Daniel take great plea-sure in letting rise and fall.

I always used to travel to Mozambique with a stock of Malarone, a relatively new anti-malarial drug which does not have the harsh side effects of others on the market, such as Lariam and Chloroquine. Everyone coming out took Malarone and it seemed to work very well. The drawback is the price: each pill costs over one dollar. We took them as malaria prevention. We handed them out as an actual treatment: at the rate of four pills a day per person. It was hard not to keep doing this; people died without them. Yet there came a time when neither we, nor friends of the college, could afford to keep up with the demand.

In the summer of 2005 there was a health crisis in the whole of Mossuril. The drugs that the district urgently needed were not being supplied. Health centres like the ones in the Cabaceiras had no malaria treatment. In the case of Cabaceira Pequena, nor did it have even basic supplies to treat such problems as wounds and eye infections.

The summer of 2005 was the first time I had spent more than a few weeks in the village. It was my first opportunity to really see how dire the healthcare situation was. Back in the Venezuelan Andes, we didn't have much healthcare either. During the years I spent there, I became reasonably expert as the district nurse. So I knew how to treat wounds and lower fevers, to treat vomiting and diarrhoea, bronchitis, ringworm, scabies, conjunctivitis and some other basic tropical maladies. In the Andes, with a similar scarcity of pharmaceuticals, I learnt many herbal remedies.

From May to July, it was these herbal cures, my Dutch-stocked medical bag and *Malarone* that were called upon daily to assist the villagers. 'Dr' Rocha still had some medicines at his health post and he was treating Cabaceira Grande's wounded beyond the college gates. But Cabaceira Pequena is the cut-off place. The tide keeps it to itself. When the tide is low, you can walk to it in an hour across the sandy mangrove fields from the college. When the tide is rising, that walk becomes a two-hour wade. When the tide is high, it is out of bounds and anyone attempting to cross will drown.

The college has no car, no 4x4, no truck or lorry. It has a recalcitrant motorbike which guzzles spare parts and dumps its driver in the bush with monotonous regularity. During the summer, the motorbike spent most of its time out of action and leaning against a tree. So our means of transport were the *chapas* (squeezed in with between twenty and once a record of thirty-five other passengers), the dhows, bicycles and on foot.

It was Marufo, one of the first and best students, who asked me to go with him to Cabaceira Pequena to help the sick. Because Marufo was captain of the Varanda football team, I had more to do with him than some of the other students. He is also the one who speaks the best English and the one who borrows books to read.

He is twenty-two, strong and handsome, with the proud bearing of the Macua. He had spiked his foot on a cone shell while commuting to the college and had a major infection which he asked me to treat. A week later, cured, he asked if I could treat some of his village. 'There are no medicines at the post. There is a wounded boy. We have no dressings. The tide is still out; if I guide you there and back, can you come after school?'

That was the first of what became a daily visit to his village. Each day, more people came to be treated. Deep cuts tied up with dirty rags were presented to me for treatment. Some of them were truly disgusting. None of them had had the benefit of either disinfectant or clean dressings. The concept of the latter was so obviously a novelty that it brought home how deep the lack of basic education ran there. Every day, the local people walk in the sea. Every day, saltwater acted as a natural disinfectant. When a fisherman cut himself, the sea washed and cleaned his cut. If it was a bad one, it was tied up with a strip of old *capulana*. Beyond that, no medical knowledge had seeped in.

In the planning stage, the college project aimed to send its volunteers out into the villages to teach basic healthcare and to gather data on local maladies. Some of the volunteers were chosen for their experience in these fields. This part of the plan didn't happen. The qualified volunteers who were there lacked guidance; and in the absence of it, they also lacked the initiative to teach even basic hygiene. So no one knew about cleaning wounds or covering them with boiled cloths, no one knew they were supposed to wash their hands. As to disinfectant: what was that?

At the end of every visit, a queue formed for anti-malaria pills. Within a fortnight, I had run out. Ilha had none. In fact, Ilha had no malaria treatment at all in its one pharmacy. I took the three *chapas* to Nampula, setting off at 3.30am and reaching the city just before noon (just before the shops closed). I caught the main chemist and bought up his stock of Malarone. I asked when more would be becoming in. The chemist raised his eyebrows and shrugged: probably not for a few months.

Those were early days and I had not learned not to rush around in Nampula, so I rushed, trying to do and buy dozens of things and got hot, tired and frustrated.

Back in the village, I reassessed what we were doing and, realistically, how much more we could do. Alone, on the health front, I was trying to plough the sea. We needed help, we needed a lot of volunteers to come and help but we also needed a powerful partner with qualified medical personnel.

Meanwhile, Marufo and I kept commuting to Cabaceira Pequena and with my limited knowledge and expertise I was able to help a bit. I also took medical supplies to the health post there and spoke at length to the forlorn lone male nurse. I explained that more help would be on its way but it would take time. I promised to bring a few more supplies myself when I next visited Holland, including a medical chart to adorn his bare walls. He perked up a lot, then he showed me a few things that would make an immediate improvement and we made a list. They were embarrassing things he asked for, like a bucket for water and a plastic cup, some mosquito netting for the window and a rush mat to lay across the bare iron grid of the bed on which local women gave birth. The total value of these things that made such a difference to his work was five dollars.

We are not supposed to donate things to the health centres. They are supposed to run on government money. The nurse should be paid by the government and all supplies are supposed to be sent to him on request. That is the theory. I had been warned by the previous owners of Varanda not to interfere with this system as to do so would relegate the new health post to governmental neglect. Yet when a nurse has no water container and no cup for patients to take the pills he prescribes, and when, as he rightly pointed out, so many of his patients don't know how to take pills because they have never had to before, and when the government doesn't even send down the pills, small necessities have to come from somewhere.

Being the official nurse in Cabaceira Pequena is a pretty thankless task. The pay is non-existent, the facilities are almost permanently undersupplied; there is nothing to do for an outsider and nowhere decent to live. Having received a modicum of attention, he took the initiative of walking to Mossuril to draw attention in person to the fact that Cabaceira Pequena had no medical supplies. I went on the back of Morripa's motorbike to Mossuril to inform the District Administrator of the health crisis in the Cabaceiras. It was he who informed me of the much bigger scale of the problem, that the whole of Mossuril was lacking supplies, that every health post in his district was being run by nurses.

'We don't have a single doctor. The nurses are brilliant and I don't know how they manage as well as they do, but some of their formal qualifications are only to trainee status. Schools, health and banks – you name it, this is a forgotten zone. Our one hope of getting out of this mess is to develop international tourism.'

What began as a mission of mercy became a daily pleasure. The more I commuted, the stronger I became and the less arduous the miles of walking. I made friends with Marufo and learnt a lot about his family. He and his brother were two of the few villagers to get away and get an education. Marufo had been to secondary school on Ilha (with Morripa). He had commuted by boat, missing endless days when the sea forbade the crossing. By lamplight, he had made up his lost lessons and passed his exams. His brother before him had also got himself through school.

'My brother and I were very close. We both loved our village and we both decided to do something to make it better. We saw that some of the others couldn't see a future because they couldn't see past all the obstacles, but we could. I know that if we can unite and do things together, we can make this a much better place.'

He told me that his brother had gone to Nampula and got a good job as a government driver. Drivers earn three times the minimum wage and thereby have the opportunity to pull their entire families out of the poverty trap. In the first week of May, the week I arrived at the college, his brother was killed in a car crash. A speeding *chapas* had smashed into his car.

'Now it's just me left to do the things we planned.'

Marufo lives with his mother, grandmother, aunts and his adorable baby daughter, Fifi. Aged twenty, he married for love and Fifi is the fruit of that marriage. When his daughter was eight months old, his wife ran away to Nampula, leaving Marufo to bring up Fifi. He is a doting parent. On days when he cannot leave her, he carries his pretty little daughter on his shoulder across the mangrove to school. She is shy and clings to him, but plays happily with Bia and the handful of other toddlers in the college crèche. When we eventually get a proper kindergarten going, Fifi will be one of the star pupils.

Meanwhile, a chance photo of this charming toddler caught the attention of a friend of the college in the Netherlands. Fifi will now receive forty euros per month until she is eighteen. In real terms, the equivalent of a Mozambican worker's minimum wage (as paid to that lucky 7 per cent of the population) will enter Fifi's household for many years to come. Little Fifi will have better food, a mosquito net, medicines, clothes, shoes, school books and many other things besides. For Nicolette, her Dutch sponsor, there is not only the satisfaction of helping a poor family have a better standard of living with the certainty that her money goes directly to help a child in need, she will also have a personal connection and regular reports and photos of 'her' child. One day, hopefully, they will meet. When they do, Nicolette will be more than a tourist visiting the village. She will be a welcome and long-standing friend.

I learned more on my walks through the mangrove in the two summer months of 2005 than I had in all my time before. Marufo's brother had just died and he was quietly grieving. My own sister, Lali, had also died the previous February, and I too was quietly grieving. Lali was the sister closest to me in age. Less than two years apart, we grew up together with a special closeness. The circumstances of our lives conspired to keep us physically much farther apart than we wanted to be and as we grew older, we shared a dream of one day living together, she, I and Anna (the next sister up from her) with our partners and children somewhere warm and beautiful. In our shared dream, we three sisters would sit in our old age on rocking chairs on a long sunny veranda.

Night by night as I sat and stared up at the canopy of stars on the long veranda at the college, I thought of Lali. It seemed ironic to be out here alone. Of all the family, she was the person with the most generous and purest heart. The need to remember her and talk about her was great. This was something I could do with Ellie, Lali's and my niece. Ellie was grieving without closure for the aunt she had virtually grown up with. After a long battle with cancer which she seemed to be winning, her death had come too suddenly for Ellie to make the long trek back either to see her or attend her Spanish funeral.

When the classes were over and the oil lamps lit, when the vegetables were watered and the wells closed, when the was supper was served and the kitchen cleaned, when the chickens were locked away from marauding genets and the goat was tethered, when the guards had changed shift and all was quiet except for the distant drums, Ellie and I could share memories of Lali.

Because Marufo was similarly bereaved, when we walked back and forth through the mangroves, we swapped stories of our lost brother and sister. He also shared a love of medicinal plants and taught me to recognize many local varieties, describing their preparation and uses. I saw the flora and fauna of the sand flats in more detail than I ever had before. Each day, I looked forward to the quiet beauty of the inland sea.

I was getting to feel more and more what it was like to be a Cabaceirian. I was following their footsteps along paths trodden through the centuries. One afternoon, we were delayed in the village. Just as we were about to leave, Marufo told me that his grandmother was dying. She had been treated for malaria at the hospital in Monapo and not responded to the treatment. She was semi-comatose in their house. And it was a house rather than a mud hut. It was a semi-restored ruin overlooking Ilha from the days when Cabaceira was a trading port.

Marufo asked me to treat her with Malarone and led me to her. 'She says her time has come and she has said good-bye to all of us, but before this fever she was strong. I would like you to try.'

We could have gone there first, but it was typical of Marufo not to ask for anything for himself. He always makes it very clear that the extra time and energy he gives to the college are his contribution to the community. Inside the house, in a back room, the stick-thin old lady was curled up on a mat on a bed. Beside her, a huddle of other women, some of them almost equally old, were sitting sorrowfully watching the sick grandmother.

Marufo spoke in Macua and all the nurses and watchers looked up. One came forward and was introduced as his mother. None spoke any Portuguese. Via Marufo, I described how they should take the Malarone and I left chemical tissue salts to be administered with water. By the next day, the grandmother had rallied and changed her mind. She wasn't going to die after all. Instead she was being spoon-fed some rice soup and via Marufo she thanked me for the pills.

It cost 12 dollars to save the old lady's life. That isn't a lot, but multiplied by the number of villagers who would also need it, it was too much for me. Mees was in Holland and is an inveterate surfer of the net. He sits for hours sometimes in the early morning randomly discovering new things. I told him that we had a malaria crisis and what he thought we should do. He chanced on a report from Washington about breakthrough results treating malaria with artemisia-based pills. The Chinese have been using artemisia for 2,000 years. During the Vietnam War, the Viet Cong were losing so many men and women to malaria in the damp network of tunnels they built and lived in that they begged the Chinese to help. The People's Republic of

China duly supplied hundreds of thousands of artemisia tablets, to great and immediate effect.

Artemisia absinthium is better known in Europe as the base of absinthe, the liquor that sent so many poets and painters mad and blind. When not fermented and when not heated, this age-old cure was also widely used in Europe as a purge. Better known as wormwood, the bitter substance repels larvae, and was once used to cure intestinal worms. After some further research and a little experimentation, Mees and I came up with a herbal recipe that looks like the herbal remedy to tackle the local malaria. We made ourselves the guinea pigs and stopped taking Malarone or any other preventative. Local people who take the *Artemisia absinthium*-based cure do so at their own risk and of their own volition. Many of the cases we have treated are returnees from other malaria treatments at the local health centres or the hospitals.

So far, in fifteen months, 207 people have taken the remedy and so far, 203 have been cured. These include Ramon, me (thrice cured), Lolly (twice cured and once not responding), Dona Sofia, Tigo, Adamji and 'Dr' Roche himself, who called just before midnight one night to say he was very sick and could he have some of 'that powder'. The guards and I take turns grinding the herbal mix in a Lebanese coffee grinder we brought out for the purpose. With a pharmaceutical scales and empty capsules, we have what we need. When we run out of capsules, we wrap the powder in aluminium foil squares and twist them up. Hopefully, a qualified medical researcher will come out and monitor this. Meanwhile, a cheap and simple treatment is keeping the death rate down.

Ironically, the mystery of why there was no known cure growing in the vicinity of this fatal illness in Europe has been solved: there was. Wormwood grows wild there. The problem was that no one made the connection. Perhaps if fewer witches had been burned in earlier centuries, one of them could have handed the knowledge down.

Bodily resistance to all the known patented anti-malarial drugs is growing worldwide. Just as quinine, the Devil's Bark, was once scorned by Protestants for being tainted by Papism, so has artemisia been sadly ignored by the capitalist West for being tainted with Communism.

We are not the first Westerners to dabble in wormwood. A Belgian pharmaceutical company announced a breakthrough with another variety of artemisia at the Artemisia Seminar in Gabon at the end of 2005. There is also an artemisia-planting experiment in Tanzania. The Chinese were even selling test artemisia tablets to Mozambique in the 1990s. But those tablets were prohibitively expensive and the experiment was dropped. Such tablets don't have or need to be expensive. Artemisia is a weed with abundant foliage. Artemisia Ariva has become a mainstay of malaria treatment and Artemisia Combined Treatments (ACT) are the goal of the World Health Organization. But, Artemisia Absinthium is still being ignored.

If we can lure some medical researcher here, the coming years could also bring a small pill factory to the village to bring out dirt-cheap antimalaria tablets to sell farther afield.

Out of the many drum beats, the ones that have become recognizable are the drumming for the sick and the drumming for the dead. The *tradição* demands that the immediate family of the deceased gather for ten nights under the same roof. For each child stolen by the sea and each person seized by disease and poverty, the drums beat relentlessly. Those are the ones I don't want to have to keep hearing, night after night.

XXVIII

Momade and the Farm

WHEN MOMADE STARTED AT the college as a student in September 2004, he hardly spoke or understood a word of Portuguese. He was also shy and kept himself to himself. He did not join in much with the joking and camaraderie of the two cliques of other students. He wore a pair of super-baggy long shorts which he subconsciously stroked from time to time, thereby drawing attention to the fact they were his pride and joy. He struggled to keep up during lessons and his reports showed that he was embarrassed by his ignorance to the point where he rarely answered questions in class. I met him briefly when he enrolled and again during the opening days and then I didn't meet him again until May. By that time, he had learnt a lot of Portuguese and a smattering of English.

He is small and nimble. His lack of height seems to be from malnutrition if his prodigious appetite is anything to go by. All the students and workers have a camel-like ability to store food. They can eat quantities that I, with a naturally big appetite, just could not swallow. It is as though each knows that food is scarce and real nourishment scarcer. When presented with the opportunity of consuming nutritious substances, they stockpile for the lean future.

Food is so limited here that no one has eaten or ever tried to eat most of the things others see as normal everyday fare. Some of the students, particularly under Michelle Oldroyd's breakthrough guidance, are prepared to try new things. Not so Momade, who absolutely refuses to be steered towards anything that hints of what is foreign or new.

At break-time and at the weekly dances and occasional parties, all the students and workers drink a beaker of Jolly Jus. Each sachet of artificially flavoured and coloured powder concentrate is diluted with two litres of water. Sachets cost a few cents each and are sold on almost every market stall and basket across the length and breadth of Mozambique. Jolly Jus comes in four flavours: raspberry, pineapple, orange and cola. The powder stains hands and tongues. Each 'flavour' is drowned by the chemical taste of whatever colourants and toxins lie therein. It is made in South Africa and has Arabic script and English on the packet. On the front, it claims to be a fruit-flavoured drink with vitamin C. On the back, in several languages, it claims to contain approved flavouring agents and approved colourants as well as phenylalanine. Other than this, it does not say which colourants or flavourings it contains or by whom they are approved.

Such a glut of E colourants is anathema to a Western mother, and as part of a project designed to raise the local nutritional standards, this so-called juice should be at the top of the list for elimination. But the villagers love it. They drink it at home. They grew up on it and I have a sneaking suspicion that it is powerful enough to kill the bacteria in their drinking water. On my secret agenda, known only to myself, Morripa and a couple of other personnel, the replacement of chemical 'juice' with fresh fruit juice is a priority.

Elsewhere this could be easily done, but in northern Mozambique there is virtually no fresh fruit beyond the seasonal mangoes and the cashew fruits. Thus for at least eight months of the year there is nothing to make fresh juice with. On Ilha and in Nampula, in Monapo and Nacala, when anyone asks for a fresh juice in a bar or restaurant, that juice comes fresh from a Parmalat packet. If one insists on asking for some other juice, then sometimes a waiter can dig out a rival make, but the concept of fresh fruit juice, smoothies and all the joys of vitamins fresh from the skin has yet to arrive.

Meanwhile, in an attempt to rectify the fruit shortage long term, we are planting numerous trees and dozens of passionfruit vines. Once in a while, I manage to get enough limes from Nampula, or passionfruit from an old lady who lives far beyond Mossuril town, or oranges from Nacala, to provide freshly squeezed juice for all the students and workers. This expensive novelty is not met with universal joy. Most of them prefer the chemical stainer but they will, somewhat grudgingly, drink the day's proffered nectar. That is, all except for Momade, who will have nothing to do with any juice that is not proper juice and proper juice comes out of a packet and stains your tongue.

On Ilha, the Hotel Escondidinho has a new French couple running their kitchen with delightful results. Breakfasts include eggs and bacon (there isn't a lot of bacon around in a predominantly Muslim town) and home-made jam, invariably fresh butter and espresso coffee. It also includes fresh fruit salad and juice. For months last summer the juice was usually cashew, which can have an interesting and quite pleasant flavour, but can also be bitter, and on a bad day, while still being fresh, can have an undertow flavour of vomit. For a couple of weeks, though, there was mandarin juice, which was such a treat the day I had it that I sailed back the next day for more.

Fresh fruit and vegetables on Ilha for all the hotels, bars and restaurants – now numbering about a dozen – come from Nampula (200 kilometres) or Nacala (140 kilometres). An abundant supply virtually on their doorstep would not be unwelcome. For a few weeks, Vulai, one of the senior students, was taking lettuces, tomatoes and beetroots to sell to the hotels on Ilha, but until we get a regular supply, it messes up our local stocks to do this and we stopped selling after giving an initial taste of some of what could be available in the future. The lady at Escondidinho has a way with salads. A salad in Mozambique tends to be a couple of slices of green tomato with a lot of sliced raw onion round it. This may or may not lie on two or three very small lettuce leaves, which may or may not (subject to availability) have sliced cucumber with them.

At the Compleixo Turístico in Chocas-Mar, the owners have a pipeline out there somewhere bringing white cabbages to their kitchen. It seems to arrive at the end of the week and last until about Tuesday. Finely sliced and served generously, it used to be the salad king of the neighbourhood. Now, on Ilha, a French lady makes real French salads worth crossing the water for.

When the college opened, it was always the intention to use its very large walled garden to grow salads and vegetables. These were to start enriching the college food, then to increase to upgrade the local diet and then for excess products to be sold to boost the college kitty.

We had the land, we had the tools, we had the workers and we had the seeds. The latter are like gold dust and cannot be obtained even in Nampula for love or money. Local people grow manioc. Local farmers wait for the rains and then grow tomatoes, onions, garlic, lettuces and hot piri-piri peppers. No other seeds are available, no other vegetables are eaten and few other vegetables are known.

I very much wanted to start the vegetable garden myself but the final rush to get ready for the official delegation, to get the roof finished and the façade painted, to get the uniforms made and the party arrangements ready, to get the volunteers settled and sort out their (largely imaginary) health problems, rushing them to and from the hospital in Nampula just in case, took up the few days I had in Mossuril. So the tools and the seeds remained after I left, and no garden was started, so none could grow.

Meanwhile, the volunteers and staff in particular were stuck with a diet consisting almost exclusively of fish, rice and beans. Delicious as each of these can be, without the benefit of herbs, spices, flavourings and accompanying vegetables and salads, they can become horribly monotonous. Letters of complaint about the food were emailed back to Holland in a steady stream, and replies urging for the seed to go into the ground were returned. From October to March, nothing happened. Not a stalk of parsley or a head of lettuce found its way to germination.

Attempts were made to clear the rubble from the naturally stony ground. Complicated plans were drawn up, discussions took place and votes were taken about who should do what, but no action was taken beyond shifting a few stones. The walled garden contains almost a hectare of land and the task seemed too huge for anyone to deal with it. At a distance, by email and mobile text messages, I tried to explain that all that was needed were a few square metres of soil for the seeds to be planted and watered and fresh food would be on the table within four weeks.

For a gardener, it was a simple task; for people with no experience of growing anything, and as luck would have it none of the sixteen staff seemed to know anything about gardening, the instruction seemed like yet another impossible task set from afar.

Then in February 2005 Mees went out to Mossuril and helped to organize the staff, students and workers into teams. By April, when he left, the first seeds were up and growing in their various beds. By early May, when I arrived, there were lettuce and tomatoes, cabbages, carrots and onions, radishes, peppers and chillies growing in lush abundance. And it was Momade who was making them grow. Ellie, who is a vegetarian, was finally eating something other than rice and beans, and everyone else had enough fresh food to stay healthy. Ironically, Momade had been there all along, but none of the staff or volunteers had thought to ask the students if any of them knew how to make things grow. Of all the class, it was only Momade who had the knowledge.

In my first weeks at the college, visiting with Lolly and able for the first time to carry out so many of the plans I had for it, I expanded the vegetable garden to include parsley, dill and sage, basil and coriander, beetroot, celery, rocket, borage, courgettes, aubergines, spinach, green beans, melons and watermelons, a passionfruit nursery, a lime tree nursery and a papaya nursery. Then I left these to grow under Momade's care while Lolly and I and some of the students made a flower garden in the courtyard, digging and planting round piles of rubble.

Sumaila, a lead student from the group with an extraordinary baritone voice, turned into a star gardener with a feeling not only for flowers but also design. By August, Sumaila was our first student success in the tourism class. Had there been a gardener's job anywhere in Mossuril, he could have filled it. When such jobs come up in Mees's lodge, Sumaila can be sure to get one of them. Were it not for his green fingers, he could just as easily get a job in any local restaurant kitchen. He is a natural decorator and designer with a real flare for composition. His hidden innate skills emerged, surprising everyone including himself. He is one of the few villagers to have travelled. During the civil war, he spent three years as a soldier in Beira in the centre of Mozambique. He then spent another three years demo-bilizing there.

'Imagine my surprise,' he told me, 'when one day, I saw this training instructor with a big group of soldiers around him. I went up closer to see what was so interesting, and guess who the instructor was? It was Morripa. From here: from home. I waited some months for him and then we travelled back together. I came back; but life was much easier there. I had a little house and some land and there was always work and the chance to put food in my family's bowls. Now, if I had a regular job, I would be very happy. And although this may be hard to believe, the gardens we make will be the prettiest in the whole of Mossuril.'

We set out to turn uneducated fishermen into qualified hotel industry staff, and Sumaila was the first proof that it could be done.

As the year progressed, other successes would follow with Atija, Ancha, Anifa and Victorino in the kitchen. These were the first students we could have let go with the certainty that each could hold down a qualified job. I had never really had any doubts that it would be possible to jump from Macua to English and slip some Portuguese in between while teaching various groups of students how to cook, clean, wait at table, garden and launder. What was always more of a challenge was how to make things grow in a village that fished rather than farmed.

Some agricultural experts declared (long distance) that if things could grow in the area then they would already be

growing there and that the absence of fresh food had to be
due to the inability of the local soil to sustain it. The biggest
gamble I took with the college was to defy such opinions
and back my own hunch (based on the trees and flowers
that did grow locally and stories of vegetables growing there
before the war) that it would be possible to successfully
market garden in the Cabaceiras. The sustainability of the
college depended on this being the case. Therefore, when
six months after the college opened there was still not a lettuce leaf in sight, I was very grateful when Momade
revealed his hidden talent as a market gardener.

Momade was born in Cabaceira Grande but taken as a
child to help his father grow tomatoes and onions in
Cuamba, in the far north-east of Mozambique. It is during
this early foray that Momade learnt his skills. When he
started the college garden, he planted strictly according to
the secret rules of the *tradiçao*. Other than occasionally finding a stalk of grass tied round a papaya trunk with a cowrie
shell attached to it, I don't know what traditional farming
involves. When plants come under attack, Momade jogs
away into the bush with a small yellow jerry can and comes
back about an hour later with a mysterious liquid called
wasi wasi. This he uses to spray against pests. I think *wasi
wasi* comes from a form of acacia mixed with neem, but the
variety, although once pointed out to me by Morripa, I
don't know.

Momade comes to the college at 4.30 every morning and
together with the students Dalaty and Vulai waters the
vegetables. We have a running battle, as yet unresolved, about
watering the plants he has grown and watering the varieties
that I add to the vegetable garden. Some of my plants he has
tasted or recognized and will water, regardless of whether I
check them or not. Others, he has doomed to die. Some, like
the spinach, finally gave up the ghost to dehydration, while

others, such as the rocket and herbs, he refuses to see as worthy of precious water and have survived only through intercession by me and Dalaty.

There is something more to Momade's resistance to certain plants than bolshiness or laziness. He is very proud of his vegetable garden and far from lazy. By June, given his hidden backlog of knowledge and experience, I shifted him away from the students and gave him a full-time job as head of the vegetable garden, or *machamba* as it is known locally. It is more that he is fighting his corner. He is a traditionalist who doesn't see certain things as right. He is too young to remember the days when Mossuril was like the Garden of Eden growing every kind of vegetable under the sun; he can barely read or write and can have learnt almost nothing in school because he couldn't then speak Portuguese, the language in which all schools teach.

Salads and herbs that I am sure he has secretly tasted and spat out he considers to be intruding on his space. They affront his rights as chief of the *machamba*. He listens politely to what I have to say and then goes his own way. As a result, several crops were lost and Momade and I have had long and sometimes frustrating talks, which often end in bringing Morripa in to intervene and insist that this or that crop is allowed to grow in our garden.

Because I am an early riser, I spend a lot of time each day between 4.30 and 6am with the guards and water carriers. We have taken to drinking tea together and eating a breakfast of bread and home-made jam on the well top after the watering is done. This group also includes the students Sumaila and Victorino who tend to the front and back flower and herb gardens.

The dawn talks have been an invaluable way of getting closer both to the students and the local folklore. From a mutually shy beginning, we now have long discussions over our tea. Individual and group grievances, doubts and questions surface, as do the dreams and ambitions of each of the students and guards. It is thanks to these early morning talks that I now know much more what each of the students aspires to, what they truly find hardest in their lives and what things big and small make a real improvement. Conversation is in Portuguese, with all difficult concepts, for example, about economics or nutrition, translated back into Macua for a better understanding by the group. After the translation process, there are often quite heated mini-discussions in Macua, which are very helpful for my own tenuous grasp of that language.

It is also in these talks, far from the formality of a classroom, that the students can learn more about 'out there'. In school, questions are still few and far between because the students lack confidence about what they know and understand and no one wants to look stupid. There is less restraint in our dawn sessions and questions abound about geography, history, health and economic development. Each waterer is keen to relay their new knowledge to their friends and family, thereby gradually filtering into the community a sense of what it can achieve, what each family can do and how to do it.

From October 2005 to February 2006, we were joined by Mussagy, who was both a student and the driver/mechanic. Mussagy grew up mostly on Ilha and in Nampula. He has studied to tenth-grade secondary and has a view of the world which far outstrips any of the other students'. He is often able to confirm as true things Momade and his fellow waterers perceive as outrageous nonsense. Mussagy's role is somewhere in the middle between the staff and the students. Like a coloured South African as described by Don Mattera, who is too white to be black and too black to be white, Mussagy is too citified, rich and educated to be one of the locals and yet too local to be one of the city folk. We hope that by returning to the Cabaceiras to work with the college, he has helped form an invaluable bridge between the two worlds of the village and 'out there'.

Momade aspires to owning a bed and a blanket, nice clothes for himself, his wife and two children, shoes on his feet, a bicycle and enough food on his table so as not to know hunger any more. He fears the outside world and does not want to travel even to Ilha for the sake of it, but when he saves enough money to buy things, he would like to go to Nampula under escort to buy from shops that have a selection. He was in Nampula in 1992 and he was robbed. He says (in Portuguese smattered with the odd English word for emphasis and to show off that he too was a student and has not forgotten what he learnt), 'Nampulese wait for the *chapas* from Mossuril to target the incoming passengers. They can spot us from a distance. Yes, they know we come from the coast. Yes, they know we are village people and not used to city ways. They follow us and pretend to show us the way but it is to steal the little money we have saved. It is very frightening to be in the city and not to even have the *chapas* fare back. I don't ever want to go back to visit. Even on Ilha, the shopkeepers and market people see us Cabaceirians and you can see them thinking: Aha. There goes an easy target. I will double the price for this country fool.

'*Epa!* It is like that for all of us. We know it is like that, but what can we do? Sr Morripa can find his way around. He can go wherever he likes on Ilha and no one will mess with him. He has respect.' Momade shrugs, challenging his companions to contradict him. 'Well, what do we have? All we have is our poverty: even when we have money in our pocket we are poor.'

Meanwhile, Mussagy aspires to buying a truck and one day to continue his studies. And one day, he would like to travel abroad.

Adamji, who is not only a guard but also a founder member of the Varanda team of workers, and whose two wives have divorced him, aspires to buying his own house and having his own bed and mat. He would like the house to have a proper door that can close. He would like to have a chair on the porch and a pot to cook water for tea. He would like to have a coconut palm and a papaya tree and a mango tree in his yard.

'In the evenings, when I am tired from work, I would like to sit back in a real chair and look at the stars with a cup of tea in my hands, sweetened with two sugars. When I feel like eating fruit or a coconut sometimes, I would like to be able to pluck them from my own trees and for people to say: "Adamji has a nice house and yard, look how much fruit he has on his trees." I would like to go home to somewhere I can call my own and be able to invite my children to come and stay with me.'

He is fifty-three years old and has worked all his life. When he is too old to work any more, he would like to be able to lay his head somewhere he can call his own. Meanwhile, he is the lodger in the house of one of his ex-wives.

Vulai would like to be able to put proper food on his table. 'Proper food,' he explains. 'You know: fish and beans sometimes and bread for the children, and even cartons of juice like Dona Ancha sells, and sugar. My mother and aunts live with me. Sometimes the food doesn't go round. I would like to *know* that I could work and have fifty meticals a day for us to live on. We could live well with that. *Epa!* Fifty meticals every day would make us rich.'

He pauses to think and does some mental calculations, which end in a broad grin. 'With fifty a day *every* day, my wife could have a lot of things and so could our children. Maybe I could even save up for a bicycle and save my leg.'

Fifty meticals is approximately two US dollars. Vulai Ossene is forty-one. He has had serious problems with nerve damage in both his legs. While accompanying him to hospital I have seen his eyes glaze over with the pain on the three-hour ride to Nampula. In the hospital, when a doctor roughly probed his leg, Vulai nearly passed out, but he did not complain. He has a student grant to study at the college: he receives 500 meticals per month (twenty dollars). This is roughly 16,000 meticals per day and is just under a third of what he needs to feel well off. He supports seven people on his student grant eked out with anything he can find to sell. His nightly meals consist mostly of manioc flour boiled in water.

On the days when I visited his house during the worst of his illness, the manioc flour was eaten on its own: there was no sauce or fish. Arriving at suppertime, Vulai immediately offered me his bowl of food (the manioc flour or 'chima'). Huddled onto a rush mat in one of the two small rooms inside his mud hut, Vulai's mother and aunts were also eating their supper. I was introduced to them and they tried to insist that Lolly and I sit and share their meal (of boiled chima). Unlike her son, the old lady and her sisters had three green mangoes between them. They absolutely insisted on giving one of these to me.

Vulai is still quite shy and retiring. When the market garden was very new, Momade went away for nearly a month without warning and the entire crop would have died unless it received its twice- or, at worst, once-daily ration of water. It was Vulai who stepped in during that summer holiday when the college was officially closed to help Ramon save the vegetable plots. Ramon told me Vulai had volunteered to do it. He was the only one who grasped how important it was to the college to make the vegetable garden work. He came one day and said to Ramon and

Ellie, 'I am too poor not to work: my family will starve unless I put chima on the table each day. I have to go to the salt flats and carry salt and then I have to go and gather fish to sell. If you buy me a sack of *farinha celeste* or manioc flour to make chima, my family can eat and I can come and work every day on the vegetable garden.'

After Momade returned, Ramon and Morripa made it clear that our *machamba* was not a cut-and-burn affair, not a let-it-grow-if-the-good-lord-wills-it-to-rain-and-die-if-not, but something that had to be watered every day without fail year round. Momade retained his supremacy in the *machamba* courtesy of his years of experience, and Vulai was appointed deputy head.

The students who prove themselves in various tasks get an extra subsidy. Vulai got his for saving the vegetable garden.

Momade's father died some time ago and his mother has no one but her son to support her. Last year, Momade also had two wives, one of whom was financially very demanding, and two babies. (Since few people have jobs in the area, a man with a job is a very good catch indeed.) Momade was always short of cash and was the most regular borrower of the entire workforce. Wife number two was rocking his boat pretty badly. When she ran away to Nampula late in the year, I think her abandoned husband was quite relieved. As we sat round the well he said as much, but he bemoaned the fact that his fleeing bride had taken him to the cleaners. When people own as little as the local ones do, to lose the family cooking pot and bucket, the one ladle and single knife is a disaster. Despite that, he seems much happier since she left and he claims that he doesn't care what other men say, one wife and family are all he needs.

Over a period of some months of observing Momade, I noticed that Vulai and Sumaila, Dalaty and Marufo and also many of the women were physically much stronger than him. After a couple of hours at his job, our head market gardener was slowing down far beyond the habitual slow pacing of his fellows. I had also noticed on two occasions that Momade would sometimes volunteer to help with the morning washing-up, take a pan through to his walled garden and then scrape out its contents and cram them ravenously into his mouth. Each time I caught him doing this he looked embarrassed.

After the second time, we began to cook up more supper so that a couple of platefuls would be left over in the morning. The watering crew and the guards divided these leftover meals up and devoured them. The more food left over, the more Momade worked, so I began to single him out for feeding up. Extra bread was bought for him and he was given his own pot of jam, a tea and sugar ration and a large cooked breakfast, albeit of whatever there had been for supper the night before. From being a rather silent member of the team, he transformed into a man of many opinions and he took to holding forth around the well during breaktimes, flaunting his jam and other treats, to the annoyance of Sofia, the head of the kitchen.

'He acts as though he owns the kitchen now,' she complained, 'and when he has scoffed his jam, he dips into ours as though it were his right to do so.'

'Luxury' food can be a bone of contention, because it is tightly rationed and tends to run out. Jam, tea, sugar, and margarine are not really luxuries but they count as such at the college. I don't like Sofia to be upset about things because hers is a difficult job and she works very hard at it. On the other hand, Momade is the only available local person apart from Morripa who knows which end of a tomato seedling goes in the ground, and who can consistently make a seed bed and get seeds to grow. By jealously guarding his knowledge and refusing to let students have proper access to the growing process, I see that Momade was merely trying to protect his job. I have tried to explain that the whole point of expansion is to get bigger. He has never seen a real farm before and cannot imagine ours spreading beyond the one walled garden. If twenty people could do what he can, then, he reasons, he wouldn't be so special any more.

We got past the jam crisis by buying in dozens of kilos of mangoes as they came in season and making a lot of jam. The absence of jars was a problem we got round by storing the jam in old instant coffee tins and, when they ran out, in glasses.

At first, Momade was very stubborn in not letting students touch our (his) *machamba*. Whenever students of agriculture were assigned a task by either Ramon or Tigo and then left to fulfil it under Momade's guidance, he would instruct everyone to down tools and sit under the big acacia tree by the entrance while he carried out whatever task the students had been assigned, jealously refusing to let them get any actual contact with the soil.

Bit by bit, we solved this problem by dividing the students into groups of three and giving each group their own vegetable bed to prepare, sow, water and tend to. Fifty per cent of all produce goes to the kitchen and 50 per cent is divided between the three students. When it comes to things to take home, the students are much more prepared to fight for their rights, even to the point of overcoming Momade's jealousy.

This method has also helped overcome the overwhelming lack of interest most of the girls and women have in anything whatsoever to do with the ground. The Cabaceiras are fishing villages; on the whole, people don't grow things here. When they do, they tend to grow manioc. Manioc is woman's work: it is a chore, almost a punishment. It is something that has to be put up with because it has always been done and the family need the money from the manioc roots. It isn't fun, it isn't interesting, it is hard work and there is very little to be gained from it.

On the other hand, it has been said that there will be money in return for farming on the college market garden, which is why the local jobless women have enrolled as students. The women want the money, but no spark of interest in the work is there naturally.

To get over the garden access impasse, I personally escorted the agricultural students in each morning and stayed with them until midday, showing them how to prepare and plant their vegetable beds and ensuring that Momade didn't shoo them away.

XXIX

Planting Dreams

AS OF OCTOBER 2005, MOMADE is prepared to believe at least some of the things I say are necessary in the *machamba*. This volte-face is thanks largely to the Italian tomato seeds I imported from Holland. Tomatoes in Mozambique are small and the plants they grow on are small. Unlike Italian tomatoes, which have to be staked, a Mozambican tomato is self-supporting.

From my return in early May 2005, I had been telling Momade to stake the tomatoes. No matter how many times I asked and then told him to do this, he refused. Even if he agreed verbally, the job just didn't get done. In the end, I hammered in bamboo canes on all the beds of tomatoes myself and personally tied each of them up. On several occasions, Momade explained to me that this was both unnecessary and wrong. Tomatoes on sticks were clearly not part of the *tradição* and he found their presence in his domain offensive.

Before going back to Europe in July 2005, I instructed Momade to stake all new tomato plants in the same way that I had staked the old ones. When I returned three weeks later, I found not only that all the new tomato plants were straggling unstaked but also that my ties had been cut and the canes had been systematically removed from the older plants.

Good as he was in his own way, I knew that if we were to make our farm commercial one day, we would have to go against some of the local taboos. To start with, we intended to grow vegetables and salads that local people didn't eat. And given our poor soil, we would have to change the local way of manuring.

Exhausted by its first crop, our walled *machamba* was in dire need of fertilizers. Momade sprinkled goat droppings onto the baking topsoil and refused either to dig it in so that the roots could get it, or to compost or mulch. His wanton destruction of the tomato stakes was a step too far in the battle of the vegetables. I took him aside and threatened to fire him unless he did what I, the Director of Agriculture for Mossuril, Ramon, Tigo and Morripa told him. Near to tears of frustration, he argued that what I was saying wouldn't work. It had never been done before and it shouldn't be done now.

I pointed out to him that from having had an abundance of salads we now had hardly any.

'Why do you think that is?' I asked him.

'*Epa!* No one has salad at this time of the year. It hasn't rained. When the rains come, everything grows.'

'But it only rains for eight weeks of the year here, and we water our plants every day, so we are not dependent on rain to make things grow.'

He shrugged and mumbled that it wouldn't work to dig the compost in.

'So if you are hungry and Sofia gives you some bread and jam, if she puts it on top of your head, have you eaten or are you still hungry?'

He thought about this and I could see he got the point, but he was not going to admit it then.

Grumpily, he and the students began to dig in the manure and, grumpily, all the vegetables were mulched with *cabí*, a local straw. Grudgingly, over the next few weeks, Momade admitted that things were doing better in the *machamba*. But it was only when the Italian tomatoes began to grow that he admitted there were things about market gardening that he didn't know and wanted to learn. One afternoon he called me into the vegetable garden and told me, '*Eeh!* Dona Lisa, you kept telling me to stake the tomatoes and I kept thinking you were wrong and I wanted to protect you from making mistakes. You told me the tomatoes would grow very tall and break under their own weight if we didn't support them. I grew up planting tomatoes. I was taught by my father and I know that they never grow past my knees. Then I saw these ones.' He pointed to a bed of plants almost two metres high and laden with fruit. 'I have never seen tomato trees before. I couldn't imagine they existed. We have taken over twenty kilos of fruit from these and they never stop flowering. I want to learn how to make more things like these grow. I want people to come from Mossuril and see what we are doing.'

Since then, we have been working together much better. In many things, Momade knows much more than I do, how to work with the relentless African sun, for example, and I am learning from him while unlearning things I too have done all my life but which just don't work here. His seedlings always do better than mine because he knows at exactly what height the palm shades need to be erected over each bed and when, to the hour, they must be thinned and then lifted. But despite having seen how much better tomatoes can grow on a support stake, Momade absolutely will not stake up the tomatoes. He *says* he will, and he will start to do it, but very early on in the process he will sabotage it by simply doing something else.

Meanwhile, away from the walled garden, paper plans were made to expand our pilot plots into several hectares of market gardens, orchards, a pineapple plantation, a poultry farm, a dairy farm, a medicinal plant farm, an ornamental nursery, and last, but not least, a new avocado plantation.

I have been told that I can bore people half to death talking about avocado pears, for which reason, I will rein in the urge to fill the next several chapters with my pet theme. It is enough to say that I set my heart on farming avocados again and decided with Morripa to plant an experimental plot in the Cabaceiras, with a larger project inland, away from the salty sea breeze.

The key to all the above projects, apart from the land, the basic materials and a workforce, is water. There were enough local people to form a workforce, if need be, several hundred strong. Farming was not natural to them, but the Faculty of Agriculture would show the way and the rapid results of the market gardening and poultry farms, for example, would be enough motivation to secure a continuous supply of willing hands. The college itself owns several hectares of land, but it wasn't enough for what was needed. When Morripa donated his own *machamba*, a nine-hectare piece of land with good soil less than a kilometre from his house in Cabaceira Grande, we had enough land to start. In the future, we would need much more terrain, but that was a bridge to be crossed later. The immediate concerns were how to get materials, livestock and water.

Unlike the College of Tourism, which can run on a shoe-string, an agricultural project needs start-up capital. Crops such as citrus fruits and avocados consume money for years before giving any back. Dairy and poultry farms require livestock, and infrastructure to be bought up-front. However, unlike the College of Tourism, which on its own could never be fully sustainable, a commercial farm could not only eventually pay its own costs, it could also help support the college and the neighbouring schools.

Despite not having the money to start up such a farm, I knew that it had to be done, and as the one member of the consortium with outside contacts, it was up to me to raise enough funds to get it going. So I went back to letter-writing, begging, urging and cajoling other organizations to join forces with the Cabaceirians so they could start and run a farm co-operative. In a classic triumph of hope over experience, my letter campaign got me nowhere further than to hone our goals into sustainable-development jargon.

We were just about to put the farm expansion on hold when we struck lucky. Mees had an old friend who was high up in Brussels in the financial world. Over dinner in the Netherlands, Mees explained that it was like getting blood from a stone to get any interest in, let alone funding for, water and energy projects in the sadly neglected area we were working in. Mikhail, his friend, took some information on various projects back with him and said he would see what he could do. The following week, he called to say that he had set up some meetings for us.

One of these was with the farmers' bank of the Netherlands, the Rabobank, which has a well-known foun-dation working world-wide. Their headquarters are in Utrecht, and we had a meeting with a lady called Anje Wind, who was Head of Africa for Rabobank Foundation. Neither of us was particularly hopeful, but it seemed worth a try and a meeting arranged via an introduction was better than the blunt 'We don't do Africa' sort of reply we had so far encountered from other Dutch banks when tentative approaches had been made to their charitable sides.

One of the biggest problems, even when meeting level is reached, is that no one has heard of the Cabaceiras, and because the main aid organizations don't help it, it lacks credentials.

'If it was really poor, it would be getting help.'

'If people were really hungry, Oxfam would be there.'

'If the malaria problem was really bad, Bill Gates or USAID would have donated.'

'If there really aren't any schools, then UNICEF would be doing something about it.'

The fact that none of these big-budget organizations extended their help that far was tantamount to discrediting the villagers' plight.

'How can so many hundreds of millions of dollars of foreign aid be pouring into Mozambique and none of it be trickling down to – where was it you said?'

At the end of a phone or across a large desk, the flicker of interest died. The Cabaceiras weren't on any development map. They weren't in the NGO guides and manuals. The people I talked to were busy people, and the implication was that I should stop wasting their time. Many were also quick to point out that they were professionals and I was an amateur. They understood and I didn't.

One thing I understood was that I had given my word to Morripa and Mestre Canira, to Ibraimo and the other Varanda workers, and to Adamji and Daniel, to Atija and Marufo, Victorino, Sergio, Amina, Sumaila, Vulai and all the other students that I would help them to help themselves. So it didn't make any difference how many people in offices in Europe and America, South Africa and Mozambique itself told me to stop, I couldn't. We'd found a spark and lit a torch, and back in the village people were running with it. I had promised to keep blowing on the flame to help keep it going. Under the circumstances, it wasn't a lot to do: I just had to keep blowing.

Back in Utrecht, Mees and I were shown into Anje

Wind's office. After initial introductions, I took a deep breath and prepared to dive into the subject while keeping a weather eye open for that by now customary moment when I might as well save my breath to cool my porridge because an unspoken 'No' was written all over whoever-I-was-pitching-to's face.

But it wasn't like that. As soon as the college brochure came out, Anje picked it up, turned to the first page and said, 'Is your Chocas, Chocas-Mar?'

I was too surprised to speak so only nodded.

'Cabaceira Grande – I've been there. I worked for some time in Nampula and I always went to Chocas at the weekends. You know the Compleixo Turístico? And Varanda: the most beautiful place in the world? How nice that you are working there because it is indeed very poor.'

At last, here was someone who knew Mossuril and had seen the Cabaceiras and who knew about Mozambique. We talked for an hour and then left. No promises had been made beyond the promise to read everything we sent her. That was actually all we needed. The rest speaks for itself, the village can speak for itself; it is just so far away and so forgotten that no one can hear its voice.

Some months later, with the utmost efficiency, Rabobank Foundation officially supported the farm project in Mossuril. The grant is much less than we need, but it is also much more than we had. It was enough to start the poultry farm and to restore four disused wells on our land, to start ordering fencing, buying seed and finding a new local partner with fertile soil inland.

In December 2005, thanks to Rabobank Foundation, the college entered into a formal merger with the *regulo* of Naguema. As the traditional leader of a large chunk of Mossuril District, with hundreds of hectares of land at his disposal and hundreds of sharecroppers to work it, he was a perfect partner. The *regulo* of Naguema is an excellent market-gardener and grain-farmer. Thanks to the swift action of Rabobank Foundation, we were able to get corn seed planted to catch the January rains. In 2006, corn for our chickens will come from that crop. The next step is to introduce soya to Naguema. Our shared dream is for a fifty-metre well.

With the farm beginning to expand, Momade feels safe from losing his job to another student. He has grasped some of the scale the college aspires to for its future farms; he too has become a dreamer. Sometimes we walk across the hectares between our current vegetable plots and the manure store and he fantasizes about how it will look in years to come when the land is covered with orchards and salads.

'One day, people will even come from Ilha to visit here and when they see all we have they will have to revise their opinion of us Cabaceirians. They might even have to stop cheating us when we go over there to buy *capulanas* and trousers.' He laughs and his small ribcage heaves.

'That will be a day to remember.'

XXX

Consider the Lilies, How They Grow

ALL OUR ATTEMPTS TO GAIN the interest of the new agricultural students failed for the first two months, with the exception of Dalaty, who took to the gardens like a natural farmer. Then, via a competition, even the doziest new students woke up and started working. At four in the morning and eleven at night, hitherto bad and uninterested students would call from the gate, 'Guarda, Adamji, Dona Lisa – we've got plants.'

When the flower-bulb campaign got going, I wished I had thought of it before. It is quite simple: I started a dune conservation project which requires thousands of bulbs. The bulbs grow wild all over the bush area and thousands of them get burnt each year to clear land for manioc or to cut down trees. I started off digging up lily bulbs and lugging them back myself but it was not easy because the biggest of them weigh over five kilograms and have long roots burrowing deep into the sandy soil. Adamji saw my spoils and asked if I wanted any more. I told him where I was getting mine from and he said he would go out after work and get some more.

I didn't actually want a few more bulbs: I wanted ten

thousand. I was touched that once again he was offering to donate some extra work and decided to put a price on the bulbs to see how many he would bring in.

Adamji then asked if he could borrow a wheelbarrow, a hoe and a couple of baskets and he jumped into action. He has a micro credit with the college with which he is now buying his own house. The house has no door and the macuti roof needs mending and one day he wants to buy a bed. No doubt spurred on by these thoughts and needs, Adamji brought in 106 giant lily bulbs and their value was duly written down in a book.

In the Western world, we laugh when we find something funny. Africans laugh when they are happy. They also laugh when they find things funny, but they laugh by themselves to themselves with sheer glee. I find this a most wonderful quality. It is how things should be. All babies do it and then lose the ability gradually as they grow up.

As the college is a harnesser and fulfiller of dreams, there is often spontaneous gleeful laughter coming from workers and students alike. During the bulb campaign, this increased to the point when anyone visiting must think ours the most hilarious place in the country.

When Adamji saw in black and white that he had just earned 40 per cent of his month's salary in one night, he laughed all the way down the steps and across the court-yard. I could hear him laughing out through the gate and past the raddled kapok tree. There was a pause as he met Daniel, his fellow guard, and shared the news of his good fortune. I could hear Daniel's disbelief and then astonishment. While Adamji started laughing again, Daniel came to me for confirmation.

'So if I go out and bring back those big bulbs, will you also pay me?'

'That's right, so long as they have roots.'

'At the same rate as Adamji?'

'That's right.'

'So let me get this clear. If I go tomorrow, on my day off, and get all the bulbs I can with roots, you will write them down as money in your book?'

'Yes, I am buying bulbs and Varanda will buy bulbs and pay your money.'

Daniel left, struggling to hold his plump face in control. He didn't make it halfway down the veranda before giving a little skip followed by a giggle. Downstairs in the garden, Adamji was waiting for him expectantly. The story was confirmed. They were going to be rich. They knew where to find the bulbs and they would work and dig, carry and count and ...

And then they stopped gabbling and swapping bulb stories to grab each other and laugh. When they finally looked up and saw I was watching them, they raised their arms and hoped I would understand: this was the first and only chance they had ever had to make some dream money. This was the first time they hadn't worked to put food on the table. Adamji saw his door, bed and bike. Daniel saw the vision of a new bicycle with a bell and a pump. And he saw a fancy knife, a bed, a mobile phone and washing-up bowls full of matapa and fried fish, goat curry and rice, potatoes and squid.

'Eeeeeee!'

For two days, they slogged to bring in giant bulbs and grow rich. Adamji paid off his micro credit and covered the cost of a new bike. Daniel covered a bike and had money over that he spent in his imagination about ten times a day doing accounts in the sand with a stick.

I hadn't expected there to be so many bulbs or for the combined staff and students to be able to bring so many in. A wild competition started up, in which each tried to break the other's record.

For the local economy, unheard-of amounts of money were being clocked up. Not since the Minister of Tourism came to visit had there been such excitement. At first, only a group of about ten students and guards were out digging. Each time they returned exhausted and dirty, little huddles of students and Varanda workers poked fun at them. It took about a week for word to spread. That Momade, Vulai, Victorino, Sumaila, Anifa, Fatima and the guards were getting rich. At first no one believed it, but once it sank in, not only did most of the students join, including the bored agricultural novices, but each developed a passion for plants. Students started coming into college with new varieties.

'I was out digging your bulbs, when I found this,' they would say, proffering some rare *Liliaceae*. 'It has medicinal properties. I haven't seen it in the college garden – perhaps you would like to plant it.'

Each new variety was gratefully received. And students who had done nothing but nod dumbly when asked anything or squeeze out a whispered 'yes' or 'no' when pressed to respond, were coming after hours to chat and help protect the bulbs while awaiting transport to the dune location.

When we first started to make a flower garden at the college, all the women and most of the men looked on it with scorn. They could see no point in helping to tend things inedible and watering them was considered a criminal waste of good water. It is still pretty much a mystery to most of the purveyors of bulbs why these bulbs have a value. With their children dying and the food not in their bowls at night – I won't say 'not on the table' because most Cabaceirians are a long way off from owning such a luxury – the idea of spending money to conserve some sand dunes is truly absurd. But bulbs have been seen to have a price. Bulbs and by association flowers have a value which they were not seen to have before. There are no nurseries here or garden shops or florists. A lot of local people will take the first leap out of the poverty pit thanks to flowers. Because of lily bulbs, several dozen people will no longer be forced to live at the very bottom of the economic pyramid.

In the third week, the Varanda workers and the team of college builders, who tend to stand aloof and guard their status as village elders and leaders, decided to join the bulb-hunters. One weekend Ibraimo went out for a day and night with his entire family and piled up 2,000, thereby beating the record to date and getting almost enough money to buy the motorbike he has coveted for the last many years.

A side effect of the bulb campaign has been to create a class of gardeners and plant-lovers. Even Momade has had to recognize the value of plants he would formerly have judged as unworthy of his attention. He has had to rethink his values as his mind was opened up, not so much via his efforts with vegetables and the many hours of explanations thereof, but by flowers.

'Consider the lilies, how they grow.'

XXXI

The Two-kilometre Sea Snake

IT IS TEN MINUTES PAST four and the sun has risen as I
follow Adamji through the salt flats to the ferry. It is a forty-
minute walk and the dhow will leave at 5am exactly. At the
various wells we pass, clusters of brightly wrapped women
carry or guard their canary-yellow jerry cans. For some it is
their second trip. When full, each heaves her 20-litre can
onto her head and sets off home as though the burden were
no heavier than a large yellow leaf.

There are fishermen heading for their boats and other
passengers for the ferry. To each one, Adamji calls out,
'*Maskamólo.*' (Good day.)

And each replies, '*Mocheleliwa.*' (And to you.)

Greetings are essential. Each and every person passed
must be acknowledged. For children, even in Macua, it is
customary to say '*Bom dia*', or the more informal joint
Macua and London cockney 'Ta ta'. But adults must be formally greeted and the greeting acknowledged. I trot behind
Adamji; we cannot slacken our pace or the boat will leave
without us. I alternate between the Portuguese '*Bom dia*' and
the local '*Maskamólo*'. The latter spoken by me, an *Akunha*,
never ceases to amuse. For instance, when I tried it at the

well, the ensuing hilarity echoed behind us for fifteen minutes.

There are clay pots again, half hidden in the roots of a baobab. Adamji watches me to see what I will say. I don't ask. I walk on as though I had not seen them. I know they contain evil spirits drawn from the sick. I don't know what else they contain except for the tips of fetishes: roots and bones and the intrinsically unmagical frayed ribbons of cloth. The *tradição* is a mystery that unfolds itself little by little and entirely in its own time. People will tell me things about it if they want to and there will be a wall of silence if they don't.

Two egrets fly low overhead and land in a fan palm tree, triggering exaggerated panic from the small yellow parrots that nest there. Not much happens at the top of their centennial home, so they wring the most out of every incident. Their basket nests shake with the excitement and the sky is momentarily golden.

We cannot stop; the other passengers move at the local pace and are already far ahead. A young mother catches us up. She has a small baby strapped to her back in a *capulana* that is starting to slip. She pauses, lowers the half-sack of manioc roots from her head and bends over, untying the offending cloth as she does so. Meanwhile, the tiny baby balances immobile on her back. Slowly, as with most things, she reties the *capulana* cloth and secures her child before moving on to catch up with the other travellers to Ilha.

Between hedges of red-fruited cactus and thorn trees, her back, swathed in green and yellow tulips, gradually disappears from sight as she twists and turns with the footpath. Her *capulana* is the same pattern as that of our agricultural students but she is not from the college.

The last stretch of land before the mangrove proper is a wide stretch of compacted sand. It is here that the local football teams play when the tide is out. Beyond it, the tepid water starts. When the tide is in, so is the ferry boat. But the tide is out and we must take off our shoes and roll or hitch up our clothes like all the other passengers and wade to it. I follow Adamji, putting my feet in his watery footsteps, as we pick our way between the pointed palisade of oxygen roots.

A woman with orange gums stained from the twigs that keep everyone's teeth a brilliant white is making rope out of coconut husks, which she buries in the sand. Without knowing this, it looks as though a senile lady is making a huge sandcastle. She smiles as we pass. We have met before in her house and at the market.

We enter the forest and the water deepens to thigh-high. It is silent and ghostly, and the red mangrove bark has ring patterns like batik round its trunk. The water is warm and clear. Adamji looks back to urge me on, we cannot linger. After ten minutes of wading through the mangrove glade, we reach shallow water again. Underfoot there are some sharp coral rocks and dozens of tiny fish. The ferry is waiting far out on the horizon and a dozen men and women are walking in the sea. As usual, I have walked too slowly and now we must run on the sandbanks to make up for it. The other passengers are already in the boat except for the mother and child, who are only a few minutes away.

We push on, paddling, wading and then gliding through waist-high water. As we board, Adamji greets the assembled passengers with the more formal, '*Assalāmo Alaiko.*'

There is a mumbled chorus of, '*Wa-Allaíko-salámo.*'

I stick to a cowardly, '*Bom dia.*'

We have between thirty minutes and three hours in this boat in which I already stick out like a sore thumb, so I decide not to stand out even further by trying to merge.

The captain waves the order to get going. We cannot set

sail yet because there are more shallows to negotiate. Two of his sons punt us out of the sands and coral rocks with long poles. There is a fair wind and everyone on board is pleased about it. Whispered conversations become debates as the captain and his sons raise the rice-bag sail and we set off across the channel.

After ten minutes, one of the captain's sons crouches on the deck and bails water out from between the dhow's rafters. He bails skilfully, proud of his cut-off 5-litre jerry can. This is a state-of-the-art boat. It is 14-feet long and has an iron anchor and a plastic bailing can. However, like all the other, poorer boats, if it were to capsize, it has no life vests or rings, no flare or other alarm, and no radio or phone. If it did have the latter, a friend or neighbour would come out to help, but they should not wait for the coast-guard on Ilha because the coastguard has no boat.

Mid-channel, where the water is thirty metres deep, I think these thoughts sometimes. Particularly as when on one occasion our dhow was becalmed for nearly two hours over the sunken VOC (Dutch East India Company) ships from the seventeenth century, and then a vicious wind blew up and whipped us into the mangrove. We arrived after dark and five minutes before a storm. On that evening, the boy-captain and his mate as sole crew were giggling nervously. Afterwards we all admitted that we had thought our hour had come.

'It was close,' the boy-captain said. 'That wind is a bad wind: it brings many complications. We are lucky to be alive. Another five minutes and ... *eeeeeeee!* ... *Epa!*'

In local terms, a 'complication' or to complicate some-thing is as dire as can be. Macua, it seems, is a language of overemphasis and understatement. It is full of grunts and exclamations. Like many other African languages, these are the non-committal sounds of the oppressed. With a grunt, no tyrant can demand, 'What did you say?' and punish you for having given a wrong answer. The range of expression in each grunt is immensely complex and still beyond my grasp.

The dhow ferry is a fine forum for grunt-learning. Communal grunts of awe, admiration, fear and surprise are all awarded to passing fish. In all the times that I have crossed from the Cabaceiras to Ilha and back, I have seen barracuda and dolphins, big beautiful fish, small ugly fish, tiny flying fish, silver leaping fish – but never a hint of the giant sea serpent.

At sea, perhaps because it is the only time we are literally in the same boat, people tell more stories. This miraculous, two-kilometre-long snake is a frequent topic and one that everyone joins in. When present, I am challenged to believe in it. I pledge my faith with an appreciative '*Eeee!*' and a timely *Epa!*' Although I am sceptical behind these grunts, I can see that in local terms it is easy to believe in. The miracles that many have witnessed with their own eyes make a mere sea serpent almost a paltry thing.

Hundreds of local people have seen a never-ending fish. Not only have they seen it, they have sailed or rowed out to it and joined in the cutting off of flesh sufficient to glut their entire families for days with still hardly any inroad made by their knives in its side. Others saw the woman-fish (the manatee). Others have seen the boys who dive stay down longer than any human can. So those who talk of the man in Naguema who transforms into a lion and the elders who can become bats at night are making lesser claims than already proven magic.

I had never seen whales here, although I knew they swim up from the Cape in October and November and have been sighted regularly off Ilha de Goa. Then in August 2006, with my friend Sofia Bianchi and her son Jacobo (who co-adopted Pacino), we all three saw a pair playing less than a hundred metres from the lighthouse shore. And they were as enormous and impressive as their myth. For a fisherman who has never seen a whale before, the abundance of flesh must seem like a miracle. I *have* seen many manatee, though not here. In some ways, I have contributed to the myths of these particular Macua by bringing magic things like a tin-opener, a digital camera, a laptop that can predict the local tides, and a LED-light torch.

I am not the first person to visit Africa and 'go native', nor, I am sure, will I be the last. If I stay long enough, maybe I *will* come to love Jolly Jus and think Nampula a beauty, and believe in a sea serpent that can feed a village from its self-renewing tail.

Without going to extremes, I am changing. I feel myself change: not into a bat or a lion, but into the person I have always wanted to be in a place that I dreamed of and always wanted to find.

AFTERWORD

FUTURE CHAPTERS OF LIFE IN the Cabaceiras must write themselves; and hopefully, like Morripa, writers will emerge to tell their own story. Meanwhile, visitors are welcome to Mossuril and the college.

It has been said that 'Africa doesn't need your money, it only needs your awareness'. I haven't the heart to tell the people here that it will all be all right because millions of people 'out there' are aware that your children are dying. The local poverty is immune even to admirable motions like Fairtrade: it drew the short straw of life so there is nothing, as yet, *to* trade. The villagers need a chance to help themselves.

They don't want a handout, they want to change their future and they believe they can do it. In the dull glaze of daily drudgery, a spark has ignited and it needs to stay alight. It is action, not talk, that will keep it burning. Concerned people often think that the problems of the Third World are too great to deal with and don't know where to start trying. Anyone who wants to can start right here.

Meanwhile, one of the things that makes Mozambique such a rewarding place to live is the fact that visible progress can be seen to be happening. It has not yet directly affected the Cabaceiras as much as it should, but there has been a start. To give credit where credit is due: to the government officials who struggle to fulfil almost impossible tasks, locally, under the leadership of the new and charismatic District Administrator, Benedito Hama Thay. In all credit to them, the following improvements have occurred in the area since I finished writing this book.

1. The cottage hospital at Mossuril received a new, state-of-the-art ambulance. There is still no doctor, but the dire transport problem was partially solved. I say 'was' because just a few months after the ambulance arrived, it broke down and there was either no budget for spare parts or no spare parts available for it. So once again, at the end of 2006, there is no ambulance and the college is often asked to make emergency ambulance runs.

2. The police force in Mossuril town received the cars they needed and they are now parked outside their still-derelict building.

3. A brand new police HQ is being built in Mossuril.

4. Dona Amana, the captain of the coastguard for Mossuril and Ilha Districts, who had no boat at all, now has three, with trained crews to patrol the coast.

5. A new secondary school has just been built for the would-be high school children in Mossuril town.

6. Cabaceira Grande, which had no drinkable water, now has a new drinking well.

7. The three graceful villas that together form the hospital on Ilha are still in a state of disgraceful ruin, but a splendid red and yellow arcade has been restored at great cost and time outside it. Delightful as this arcade looks, it begs the question why the not inconsiderable time and money spent on its restoration was not put into the hospital it mocks with its mere presence.

It will take billions of dollars to solve all of Africa's problems, but it only costs four dollars to buy a mosquito net, ten to buy a sack of rice, twenty per month to sponsor a student here, and fifty per month to pay a full-time worker or sponsor a child.

Everything helps and no amount is too small. Be aware: they need our money. For those people who want to help hands on, Morripa and Ibraimo, Atija, Momade, Marufo, Vulai, Sumaila, Anifa, Fatima, Victorino, Sergio and all the others need whatever help you can give. There is something for everyone in this beautiful place, which could live from what we throw away and which is crying out to learn what we know.

For further information, please contact us and look at our website:

www.teranfoundation.org
helping@teranfoundation.org
donations@teranfoundation.org
info@teranfoundation.org

**Colégio de Turísmo e Agricultura
Cabaceira Grande, Distrito Mossuril,
Provincia de Nampula
Mozambique**

**Caixa Postale 81
Ilha de Moçambique, Provincia de Nampula
Mozambique**

Stichting Teran Foundation is a charity registered in the Amsterdam Chamber of Commerce: registration number: KVK/ dossier number 34205610

When foreign volunteers come out here to join and help us, the list of things they must bring has been whittled down to bare essentials. The three inherent musts are: to care, to have positive energy and to have a good sense of humour. In a country as poor as Mozambique, the latter is a constant necessity. Despite all the problems here, we are surrounded by laughter. It rings out of the bush more loudly than the birdsong. It rises over the drum beats, it clusters round the well heads, and echoes over the sea.

OTTO

Lisa St Aubin de Terán

This extraordinary novel is based on a true story of
a revolutionary who was advisor to Castro, friend
of President Salvador Allende, and married to one of
the leaders of the Kurdish rebellion in Iran. Code-named
Otto, he became an enemy of both the KGB and the CIA.
Otto is a fabulous and picaresque journey of the lives
and loves (plenty of those) of an astonishing man.

'A novel about greed, lust, cruelty,
truth and poetry. Dazzling'
Guardian

**You can order other Virago titles through our website: *www.virago.co.uk*
or by using the order form below**

☐ Otto	Lisa St Aubin de Terán	£7.99
☐ Keepers of the House	Lisa St Aubin de Terán	£7.99
☐ Joanna	Lisa St Aubin de Terán	£6.99
☐ The Hacienda	Lisa St Aubin de Terán	£8.99

The prices shown above are correct at time of going to press. However, the publishers reserve the right to increase prices on covers from those previously advertised, without further notice.

———————————— 🍎 ————————————

Please allow for postage and packing: **Free UK delivery.**
Europe: add 25% of retail price; Rest of World: 45% of retail price.

To order any of the above or any other Virago titles, please call our credit card orderline or fill in this coupon and send/fax it to:

Virago, PO Box 121, Kettering, Northants NN14 4ZQ
Fax: 01832 733076   Tel: 01832 737526
Email: aspenhouse@FSBDial.co.uk

☐ I enclose a UK bank cheque made payable to Virago for £ . . . .
☐ Please charge £ . . . . . . to my Visa/Delta/Maestro

Expiry Date ☐☐☐☐   Maestro Issue No. ☐☐

NAME (BLOCK LETTERS please) . . . .

ADDRESS . . . .

. . . .

. . . .

Postcode . . . . Telephone . . . .

Signature . . . .

Please allow 28 days for delivery within the UK. Offer subject to price and availability.